ORIENTATION

TO THE

THEATER

Orientation to the *Theater*

By THEODORE W. HATLEN

Professor of Speech and Drama
UNIVERSITY OF CALIFORNIA
SANTA BARBARA

APPLETON-CENTURY-CROFTS
EDUCATIONAL DIVISION
New York MEREDITH CORPORATION

In appreciation of
Three Great Teachers
ALEXANDER DRUMMOND
THOMAS WOODS STEVENS
HUBERT C. HEFFNER

PREFACE

THE PRIMARY TASK in understanding the theater is to develop an appreciation of the drama, not merely as a way of telling a story, or as a vehicle of production, but as a special kind of artistic creation that combines its own particular methods with the universal values of all kinds of artistic creation. The basic premise of this book is that the theater is a means to an end—the appropriate and expressive interpretation of a play. Attention is placed on dramatic structure, its techniques, and the various forms and modes of dramatic composition, always in context with theatrical production.

Like all works of art, a play is caused by the conditions of creation. In part, the final product represents the personal qualities of the artist and his way of looking at life. In part, the play is symbolic of the cultural milieu in which it was created. In part, the artist's method reveals the circumstances under which he worked—the availability of materials, the technical practices of his time. This is especially true in the composite art of dramatic production where the effect of the play may depend upon the size and shape of the physical theater, the conventions of the stage, the capacities of the actors, and the tastes of the audience. The interaction of these factors is a source of constant pressure that determines the way in which the playwright will create. The effect of these influences will be examined on a number of writers whose varied structures and techniques indicate the change in dramatic composition and theatrical production from age to age.

Dramatic art, like all genuine creative expression, is a reminder that a culture is not to be judged by its material accomplishments alone, but also by the ideals and aspirations that motivate human conduct, and the faiths by which men live. In dealing with the significant actions and choices of his characters, a dramatist has at his disposal special means of delineating the human condition. Thus, a play is more than an evening's diversion in the theater, more than pages of text; it is at once a personal statement of the dramatist and a clue to the culture that produced it. The objective of this text is to provide the student with the tools of analysis which will give him insight into the total imaginative process that makes up the art of the theater.

vii

It is intended that *Orientation to the Theater* be used in connection with the reading of representative plays selected by the instructor from the great number now readily available. In my own course I have used *Antigone, Oedipus Rex, Everyman, Dr. Faustus, Hamlet, The Taming of the Shrew, Tartuffe, Phaedra, The School for Scandal, William Tell, A Doll's House, Miss Julie, Cyrano de Bergerac, Emperor Jones,* and *Death of a Salesman.*

As supplementary aids, I have found most useful commercial recordings of *Medea, Everyman, Dr. Faustus, Hamlet, The Way of the World, The School for Scandal, The Importance of Being Earnest, Juno and the Paycock, Waiting for Godot,* and *The Beggar's Opera.* FILMS: *Oedipus Rex, Hamlet, Miss Julie, Volpone,* and *All the King's Men.*

I wish to express my gratitude to Professors A. T. Weaver and John Dietrich for their helpful criticism of the manuscript; to my colleagues in the Department of Speech and Drama at the University of California, Santa Barbara—Stanley Glenn, John C. Snidecor and Upton Palmer; and to my students over the years.

I am grateful to the various persons and institutions for their cooperation in the preparation of this book: to George Freedley, Theatre Collection of the New York Public Library; Professors William Melnitz and Kenneth Macgowan of the University of California, Los Angeles; Helen D. Willard of the Harvard Theatre Collection; Professor Alois Nagler of Yale University; The Victoria and Albert Museum; the Stratford Shakespearean Festival, Ontario, Canada; Mordecai Gorelik, Jo Mielziner, Donald Oenslager, Harold Clurman, Rosamond Gilder, Margaret Gordon, Florence Sears, Felix D. Glass III, Toby Cole, and Helen Krich Chinoy.

T.W.H.

University of California
  Santa Barbara

CONTENTS

ILLUSTRATIONS

I

Ritual, Magic, and Drama

MAN TRIES TO EXTEND HIMSELF in a variety of ways. Limited by his physical attributes and circumstances, he escapes into the realm of the spirit; his imagination soars far beyond the narrow borders of his immediate surroundings. Sometimes man gives expression to his inner life by creating works of art. Sometimes he pursues adventure by making his way into the unknown—fording a strange river, crossing into undiscovered country, scaling a precipitous mountain, shooting for the moon. Sometimes man projects himself into the past by recalling his earlier experiences or by passing on the myths and legends of his ancestors. Sometimes he attempts to gain strength and perhaps immortality by linking himself with supernatural powers. Whatever conditions man has lived under, he searches for some means to extend himself.

The efforts of modern man to enlarge his scope of influence and action have led to interesting patterns of behavior. His work may confine him to a cubicle within cubicles where the scheme of organization takes its inspiration from the machine. He rides to and from work by machine, communicates with others through mechanical and electronic devices, simplifies his work through standardization of form and procedure. He may live in a mass-produced house, wear mass-produced clothing, and eat prefabricated dinners while his senses are bombarded with volleys of mass-produced words and images projected by a machine. His life is at least partially symbolized by the frustration he feels

1

in his car. Underneath the gleaming hood and chrome, several hundred units of horsepower await the touch of his foot, but he is forced to crawl along in a snarl of city traffic until he finally escapes into the open countryside, only to find his speed and direction rigidly limited by flashing lights and warning signs confining him to a narrow concrete ribbon from which he may see only an occasional glimpse of the passing landscape. The dead level of sameness in this standardized world clashes sharply with his nervous system, for beneath his sanforized, drip-dry exterior flow the same essential juices as those of Don Juan, Marco Polo and Davy Crockett. Hence, modern man, like his forebears, finds it necessary as well as desirable to break through his restricting shell to find ways of extending himself.

He may become a "joiner" and feel the warmth of good fellowship in the communal gesture of smoking the fraternal cigar and lifting the friendly cup with his fellow lodge or club members. He enjoys the feeling of belonging and being accepted. He finds satisfaction in the secret rites, the mystical symbols, the special costume. He experiences a certain amount of freedom from restraint when he shucks off his sense of responsibility and liquidates his inhibitions to become a delegate-at-large in annual conclave at Miami Beach, Las Vegas, or Atlantic City, where, for a time, he assumes another role, larger and louder than that of his ordinary work-a-day, business world.

In any case, modern man, like his ancestors, has found it necessary to extend his life beyond the stiff confines of the here and now. One of the most interesting extensions by which he has learned to share vicarious experiences and to catch a glimpse of something beyond himself has been through art and literature. Inside paper-back covers of a book he responds to the spirit of adventure that lifts him out of the regular recurrent beat of the commercial world, or huddled in a darkened theater of his own living room he gives himself up to imaginary characters whose imaginary actions are, at times, more compelling and meaningful than his own.

It is not only contemporary man who has required extension. His ancestors long ago invented patterns of conduct by which they attempted to enlarge their lives, increase their spheres of influence, and strengthen their feeble powers. The anthropologists have found the evidence in the cultures of primitive man to demonstrate this point. Consider for a moment, two examples from primitive societies.

Frazer, in *The Golden Bough*, describes the initiatory rites performed when West Ceram boys make the transition to adult life at puberty. The blindfolded initiates are taken to a special shelter deep in the forest where a high priest summons the evil spirits. The adult men set up a clamor to frighten the neophytes, who are led one at a time into the shelter. As each boy goes in, there follows an ominous chopping sound, screams of terror, and suddenly, a bloody sword pierces the roof, symbolizing that the neophyte's head has been severed, and the devils have taken him to the other world where the boy will be reborn. The adult sponsors take the initiates on a journey for a day or two, returning haggard and daubed with mud, bearing the good news that the boys have been restored to life. The initiates are so enfeebled that they are scarcely able to walk; for awhile, they cannot eat or talk. They are treated as new-born children. During the following initiatory period of three or four weeks, the boys are inducted into the mysteries of adult life and are made aware of their responsibilities to the tribe. They are taught a new language and given a new name. Finally, the ritual is completed when the high priest takes each initiate to a secret place and cuts off a lock of his hair. The boy returns to the tribe where he assumes the status of an adult and is free to marry.

A second example of man's extension of himself is found in the customs of the Iroquois Indians. At the victory ceremony following a battle, the returning warriors who have been most successful in combat are given the opportunity of recounting their exploits before the assembled tribe. Special places are set aside for the display of weapons and spoils of war.

What do we learn from these examples of the rites and customs of primitive peoples?

They are evidence of man's attempt to extend his power and experience beyond himself. In the case of the Iroquois Indian victory celebration, the initial impetus for sharing a description of a battle probably came from the sheer enjoyment of the telling and hearing, just as we find pleasure in listening to an eye-witness account of an exciting event. "What happened?" is certainly one of man's oldest questions. In describing his exploits, the Iroquois brave shared not only the factual data of his experience, but sought to recapture and communicate the emotional content as well. Since primitive man uses gesture and dance as basic means of communication, especially when he recounts a story that is full of physical action and he has his "stage props" at hand, it is an easy step from the narration to a re-enactment of the event by adding mimetic action and impersonation.

The original spontaneous, individual account becomes the property of the group as a whole and, through repetition, it is shaped into a fixed pattern. The particular exploits of an individual are joined to those of others to represent all exploits. A single combat symbolizes warfare in general. The original specific imitative gestures and movement are abstracted, set to rhythm, turned into chant and dance, and acquire the status of a tribal celebration.

The next step in development becomes a highly significant one because it marks the transition from a mere physical activity that existed for its own sake, into an established religious rite. The warrior, recalling his previous success, re-enacts his victory *before* he goes into battle, in order to invoke the aid of supernatural forces in fulfilling his wishes. Primitive man stresses the expression of his longings, rather than his satisfactions. Since he is a doer, a man of action, the primitive man demonstrates his desires. He imitates the action he wants to have happen. The ceremony assumes a functional purpose when the tribe employs *sympathetic magic* to assure it of victory in warfare. It is no longer a celebration for the joy of the activity; it becomes a serious, religious ritual expressing the deepest needs and longings of the people and associating them with the supernatural. Thus we see the progressive steps from a simple retelling of a personal experience to the establishment of a tribal ritual which is joined with religion as man seeks to extend his power.

What do we learn from the initiatory rites? The most interesting ingredient is the mimetic representation of death and rebirth, a common concept in the religion of primitive cultures, especially among agrarian peoples who see a parallel in the death of the seed in the winter and the reappearance of new growth in the spring. In his religion, man usually appeals for divine assistance in the crises of life, particularly the biological ones of birth, adulthood, and death. The West Ceram savages make use of mimetic action in their ritual *showing* the transition from puberty to adulthood, just as we have seen the Iroquois employing sympathetic magic to supplicate for supernatural assistance.

From these typical expressions of primitive activity, it is clear that man has always sought ways and means for enlarging his world. He re-enforces his own strength with a weapon—a rock, a club, a spear, a gun, a rocket, a bomb. He acts as far as he is able to insure good crops—he tills the land, plants the seed, and irrigates the soil, and then, realizing that he is subject to forces beyond his control, he invokes divine intervention to provide him with a good harvest. He links himself to the present with his mate and children and tribe; he projects himself beyond the grave with his rites of passage which will assure him of an afterlife.

These attempts of man to widen his experience and strengthen his power, result from a complex cluster of motives—his need to communicate, to survive, to understand, to secure recognition and status—these represent his basic longings to which he gives expression by means of his religious ceremonies.

It is in such rituals that we find the basic elements of drama—music, song, dance, costuming, mimetic action, and communal performance. But not all ritual becomes drama. A spark is needed to bridge the gap.

In most cultures the transition is never made. The rites continue as a functional activity, never attaining the detachment necessary to transform them into works of art which can exist for their own sake, or the ceremony remains fixed in a simple, repetitive form, never elevated to new status through creative and interpretative expression. Drama cannot begin without the disciplined construction of an orderly sequence of words and actions representing a real or imaginary experience, to which has been added impersonation. It was in Greece that this most remarkable transformation took place.

ORIGIN OF GREEK DRAMA

It would be convenient if the steps in the origin of Greek drama were clearly marked and recorded, but unfortunately, much of its background is vague and uncertain. However, certain inferences can be made from the evidence at hand.

Aristotle in his *Poetics* [1] informs us that "Tragedy . . . was at first improvisation . . . originating with the leaders of the dithyramb. It advanced by slow degrees; each new element that showed itself was in turn developed."

It is clear from this statement that the rites were at first spontaneous expressions of the participants when they summoned the gods or rhapsodized on the coming of spring. We may get some notion of the original feeling of the improvised verses by citing a passage from Pindar who wrote dithyrambs in the sixth century B.C., after they had acquired a fixed form:

Look upon the dance, Olympians
Send us the grace of victory, ye gods who come to the heart of our city
Where many feet are treading and incense steams;
In sacred Athens come to the holy center-stone.

Come hither to the god with ivy bound.
Bromios (Dionysus) we mortals name Him, and Him of the mighty voice . . .
The clear signs of his Fulfillment are not hidden,
Whensoever the chamber of the purple-robed hours is opened,
And nectarous flowers lead in the fragrant spring . . .
And voices of songs are loud amid the pipes,
The dancing floors are loud with the calling of crowned Semele (the earth,
    Mother of Dionysus).

The dithyramb seems to have been at first an improvised choral ode, a song of spring, but it becomes enriched as a part of a ceremonial rite

[1] All quotations from Aristotle are from S. H. Butcher, *Aristotle's Theory of Poetry and Fine Art* (London, Macmillan & Co., Ltd., 1907).

in honor of the god, Dionysus, with the addition of dance and written verses by such poets as Pindar and Arion. Who was Dionysus? Before answering this question specifically, it is essential to understand something of the nature of Greek religion.

Our modern concept of religious worship with its creeds, churches, and moral precepts has little in common with the Greek version of religion. Their gods were most thoroughly human, with human frailties as well as human virtues. They often impersonated forces of nature—the wind, sky and sea, and they possessed attributes such as love and wisdom. The Greeks considered their gods as their own ancestors who could intervene in human affairs. They were closely linked to the political life of the city-state. Sacred rites were under the administration of public leaders, rather than under a powerful priesthood. Out of the political-religious relationship, festivals included all kinds of competition—singing, dancing, athletic and dramatic—all expressions of religion. Tragedies were performed in the theater of Dionysus, a sacred precinct on the Acropolis. The Greek religion with its human qualities was at the very core of the social culture.

Dionysus, in whose honor drama was produced, was the god of vegetation, wine, and fertility. Although he is usually presented as a fair young man, Aristophanes delighted in ridiculing him in the *Frogs*, ignoring his divinity and portraying him as a cowardly debauchee. (See scene from the *Frogs* in chapter on Farce.) It is apparent that Dionysus because of his special qualities as the god of fertility was a particularly appropriate divinity for inspiring the spring festival, the City of Dionysia. Primitive societies invent rituals around seasonal celebrations in an effort to induce fertility, good hunting, and bountiful crops. In Greece, these objectives were centered in a single god whose relationship to fertility was not confined to vegetation, but included human fecundity as well, as is clearly evident from the phallic rites associated with Dionysus. The legend of this god tells of his rebirth as a young man— a symbolic representation of the calendrical cycle of the death of the seed as it is buried in the ground in winter, and of its rebirth with the coming of spring.

The dithyramb which Aristotle mentions as the early form of tragedy is seen, therefore, as a ceremonial rite of spring honoring the god Dionysus, the appropriate divinity for representing man's oldest needs —food and fertility.

Some scholars, in tracing the origin of drama, emphasize the seasonal celebrations of seed and harvest. Others suggest that the roots of drama are to be found in the commemorative rites honoring dead heroes, citing as a parallel the rebirth of drama in the medieval church, growing out of the Easter celebration in the spring, celebrating Christ's death and

Scene from *Oedipus Rex* with Oedipus (James Mason) surrounded by the Chorus; Jocasta (Eleanor Stuart) and Creon (Robert Goodier) in background. Stratford Shakespearean Festival, Ontario, Canada, 1954.

resurrection. In any case, the rituals from which drama emerged carried the emotional fervor of man's deepest longings and gave symbolic representation to his longest thoughts as he sought to orient himself to the universe.

In Aristotle's statement concerning the origin of Greek tragedy, he notes that "it advanced by slow degrees; each element that showed itself was in turn developed." This evolution may be traced in some detail. We know that tragedy as a specific form was first mentioned in the seventh century B.C., that a century later its improvisatory nature had given way when tragedy became more and more formalized with poets writing verses in this form, and that by 534 B.C. it had developed sufficiently in form and content so that Peisistratus inaugurated competition in tragedies in Athens as a part of the spring festivals. The transition from the improvised performance of the dithyrambs to the full flowering of Greek tragedy can be traced in the changes which took place in the structure of the plays and in the evolution of the physical theater.

The improvised dithyrambs probably were performed on threshing floors, just as today the Greeks make use of them as a place for dancing. With the altar of Dionysus in the center, the dancers moved in a circular formation setting the pattern for the orchestra circle of the later fully developed theater architecture. At first the dithyrambs were a communal activity; everyone got in on the act. When some of the worshippers broke away from the circle and became onlookers, it was possible to make the performance more specialized, with the most proficient taking part and utilizing prepared verses and passages instead of the previous improvisations.

As the spectators became more numerous, the locale of the celebration was moved to the base of an adjacent hillside so that the audience could see the action. The separation of the participants from the viewers enhanced the possibility of developing an attitude of detachment in the audience so that their enjoyment included not only *what* was done, but also the *way* in which it was performed. As writers added their imaginative contributions, the original utilitarian basis for the ritual—the invocation of the supernatural to secure growth and fertility—lost some of its validity, and the ceremony began to exist for its own sake, thus giving new freedom and sanction to the performers and poets.

An astonishing innovation now took place. Thespis appeared as the first actor. He broke away from the chorus and added the dramatic potential of impersonation. Instead of describing Dionysus, he became the god, and in antiphonal response with the chorus and leaders, he enlarged and enriched the ritual as a dramatic medium. When Aeschylus added the second actor, another new thrust forward was given to drama because the additional actor enabled the dramatist to *show in action* a dramatic conflict, rather than merely talk about it. This primacy of action became a central tenet of Aristotelian criticism. The second actor enormously increased the potentialities of theatrical tension which the playwrights were quick to exploit. Sophocles' addition of the third actor further enlarged the scope of the dramatist, providing him with the means of complicating his plot and devising more complex structural arrangements of his tragedies.

As actors were added to the performance, the emphasis of the production shifted. While at first, the chorus was the essential theatrical element, as the dramatic form evolved, the playwright focused his attention on the speech and actions of individuals, so that by the time Greek tragedy had reached its golden age, the chorus assumed a mere supporting role to the protagonists, in whom the dramatic conflict was now centered. In part this changed emphasis was due to the change in dramatists' selection of materials, as they drew heavily on Greek myth and legend for their characters and situations, which made the individual roles dominate the chorus.

The evolution of the physical theater was from the dancing circle which all of the participants occupied, to three separate entities—the orchestra circle for the chorus, the huge theatron for the audience which became quite remote from the performers, and the *skene*, where the actors carried on the essential action of the play.

We have seen then, the steps in the emergence of Greek tragedy emanating from the ritual: from improvisation to finely wrought masterpieces of drama; from a general communal activity, to participation by the proficient few; from a makeshift dance floor, to a permanent and complete theater of stone.

Questions and Exercises

1. What is needed to make the transition from ritual to drama?
2. How is sympathetic magic related to drama?
3. What contribution did Thespis make to drama? Aeschylus? Sophocles?
4. How did the addition of the second actor affect playwriting?
5. What was the relation of Greek religion to drama?
6. What effect did the increasing importance of the actor have on theater architecture? On the structure of drama?
7. Describe the role of the chorus in Greek drama.
8. What were the sources of Greek dramatic material?

Suggested Reading

FERGUSSON, Francis, *The Idea of a Theatre* (Princeton, Princeton University Press, 1949).

FREEDLEY, George and REEVES, John A., *A History of the Theatre* (New York, Crown Publishers, Inc., 1941).

HARRISON, Jane Ellen, *Ancient Art and Ritual* (New York, The Home Library of Modern Knowledge, 1913).

KITTO, H. D. F., *The Greeks* (Baltimore, Penguin Books, 1951).

NICOLL, Allardyce, *The Development of the Theatre*, new rev. ed. (New York, Harcourt, Brace & World, Inc., 1937).

PICKARD-CAMBRIDGE, A. W., *The Dramatic Festivals of Athens* (Oxford, 1953).

2

The Nature of Drama

DRAMA IS A WILY and complicated creature which may change her spots while you look at her, or vanish behind protective coloration. Penning her up behind fences of verbal definition does not really give us a notion of her true character. She may be stuffed and mounted with great skill, but the dead, inanimate form does not reveal her essential *élan vital,* so characteristic of her behavior in her natural habitat—the theater. The dead carcass in the study does not give us a complete or vivid account of the chase, and the struggle. Nor is the modern creature an accurate representative of the species as a whole. Neither does she indicate the evolutionary steps of her development, nor the forces which conditioned her past conduct. Perhaps then, we may avoid a frontal attack of definition and arrive at some sense of the nature of drama by indirection—through description, example, and an examination of various forms and styles of drama. Actually, drama is not really a creature, a thing, an object. Drama is essentially an experience—the result of combining the written words of the play with the living speech and action of the performer in the theater before an audience. Drama includes these two forces: the creative force of the dramatist and the interpretative force of the theater-worker. No theater is complete without its drama, just as no drama is complete without its theater. Thus, the forces of creation and interpretation must be examined with regard to their mutual influence on one another.

The creative process almost always takes written form (although the Italian commedia dell' arte of the sixteenth and seventeenth centuries was played from scenari, skeletal plot outlines, the dialogue and action improvised as the performance was in progress). The playwright is usually an individual, but the writing may be done by collaborators such as Beau-

11

mont and Fletcher or Kaufman and Connelly; or the play may be the joint effort of a group of writers as in Shakespeare's time when it was customary for a theater to maintain a "stable" of writers. The drama may be written in fragments, as in medieval times when the parts of a play were accumulated from a variety of hands and assembled like a cathedral, piece by piece.

The playwright's script furnishes the dialogue, stage directions for producing and acting the play, and in contemporary dramas, a description of the characters, settings, and the interpretation of many lines and actions. But the script is not the completed play. It is true that action precedes the word; gesture came before speech. Frequently this fact is lost sight of by literary critics who are preoccupied with the language. Drama is more than dialogue. Drama since its inception makes use of a means of expression which Francis Fergusson refers to as "histrionic sensibility"— the spectator's ability to perceive and discriminate actions and visual symbols, just as in music the trained ear discriminates sounds. This is a basic and primitive ability which we all acquire and employ in judging behavior. For example, although we may not hear the dialogue between an umpire and an enraged baseball player, the feelings of the two adversaries are clearly evident to us by their gestures even at a considerable distance. When we communicate with one another on important issues we prefer face-to-face contact which enables us to judge the *way* things are said, as well as the words themselves. We constantly use this sensibility in evaluating the response of others to what we say or do. "Histrionic sensibility" is a part of our basis for understanding and appreciating the full content of a play in performance. The shrug of the shoulder, the lifting of an eyebrow, the tone of the voice, the nod of the head, the atmosphere of the environment, the pace of action, constitute an eloquent vocabulary of a universal language. These forms of communication are essential to the dramatic experience, although they may be ephemeral, vanishing in the moment of creation. They are at the heart of the special resources of the theater because they stir the blood, awaken our memories, spur the imagination, set off chains of emotional reaction, engage our sympathies and help to establish the validity and meaning of the action.

Some teachers of dramatic literature contend that the sensitive reader is fully capable of imagining a better performance of a play than he can see in the theater. Certainly, no one can deny that an inept production of a play can destroy its effect and distort its meaning just as an unskilled musician can demolish a Beethoven sonata. On the other hand, a great drama given a good performance by talented interpreters may add dimensions to the production which no silent reader can create for himself.

The solitary individual cannot create the emotional climate of a responsive audience. The contagion of laughter never reaches him. He may not
visualize the atmosphere and reinforcement of the mood of the play
which the designer achieves through skillful use of stage scenery and
lighting. The reader may lack the background to sense the style of performance, the kind of theater, setting, and acting for which the play was
written. He is apt to miss the effect of tempo and pace which the actors
achieve in the playing. He will probably not be able to visualize the building of climaxes and crises as the director handles them. He may not
imagine the full effect of the lines when spoken aloud, nor be able to
create for himself the trained actor's use of movement, gesture, and facial
expression. He will not be conscious of the impact of ensemble playing,
of the effectiveness of the stage pictures, of the action and reaction of
one character upon another, the rich texture of complex emotions nor the
subliminal or barely perceptible flow of images that emanate from the
performers during the theatrical production. It is a phenomenon of the
theater that even the experienced playwright, director, and actor are un-
able fully to anticipate all of the values of a play until it is performed. A
silent reading of the play does not reveal its complete content any more
than a love letter consummates a courtship.

The dramatic experience, therefore, is an ideal union of the creative
force of the playwright and the interpretative force of the actor, director,
and scene designer. That such a combination has a wide appeal is evidenced by the virility of the theater as a social institution over most of
the recorded history of the Western World.

THE NATURE OF THE DRAMATIC APPEAL

Why do people go to the theater? Why did the citizens of Athens rise
up in the cold hours of dawn, trudge up the steep slopes of the Acropolis
to sit on hard, stone seats of the Theater of Dionysus while they watched
grim dramas of unrelieved suffering and seriousness? Why did a London
chimney-sweep find his way to the Globe Theater to stand for hours in
the pit and see and hear drama so perplexing in language and content
that scholars are still baffled by its meaning? Why did our forefathers
find the lure of the drama so entrancing that they willingly journeyed all
night and day to see a river show-boat performance? Why does contemporary man after a hectic day's grind in the office fight through the
downtown traffic of a concrete canyon, rush through dinner, and buy expensive seats to be herded into a somber, upholstered cavern where he
sits for a couple of hours participating vicariously in the actions of fictional characters? What is the secret of the appeal of a medium of entertainment and expression so compelling that we have found it necessary

to install electronic boxes in nearly every living room so that we can huddle in the dark night after night giving ourselves to make-believe characters going through make-believe actions?

The sources of the theater's appeal are manifold, and no doubt the dramatic experience is very often a blend of several satisfactions. Let us suggest four of them.

First, much of drama appeals to an audience because it tells an entertaining story. Plays and performances exist on the game level. There is nothing serious intended by the playwright. The audience finds no secondary or residual meaning, no food for thought, no universalizing experience. If the play holds the spectator's attention, arouses laughter or excitement, the play has fulfilled its purpose for him. There are many theater-goers who insist on this level of appeal. Hence most drama is journalistic rather than literary, concerned with the surface aspects of make-believe rather than with a penetration of reality. Those who support the popular theater often reject drama that deals seriously with life. Their attitude is indicated in their complaint that "there are enough troubles in this life without having to suffer in the theater. When I go to a show, I want to forget about my problems." While this point of view is not conducive to the elevation of drama as a significant form of art and communication, it represents the prevalent attitude that dominates motion picture and television fare. Although great works of drama make far more demands on an audience, no successful dramatist has been able to ignore the need to engage the theater-goer's attention. The theater must contain an element of the theatrical; drama must be dramatic, and usually this involves story appeal.

Man has always found delight in sharing tales of adventure and excitement, struggle and conflict. From his very primitive days around the fire he has enjoyed hearing what happened next. He listens with rapt attention to eye-witness accounts or to those who have a gift for recreating an experience. But even more compelling is his desire to see the events for himself. Thus the word has been joined to action, narration becomes dramatization. The spectator shares the story vicariously when he sees it re-enacted. Drama may take many forms, but the story element persists as a basic appeal. In many instances modern fiction writers have rejected the importance of the narrative. They have shifted their attention from plot to character penetration and delineation, or to the creation of atmosphere and environment. Likewise, the naturalists in drama and contemporary "absurdists" have attempted to write plays which neglect or subordinate the story element, but their efforts have not met with general acceptance. It seems likely that man's interest in a sequence of events with a beginning, a middle and an end will continue to be a primary means of attracting and holding an audience.

Second, the audience finds pleasure in witnessing an achievement, in considering the manner in which a thing is done. A spectator at the Olympic Games may marvel at a pole vaulter as he swings his body up and over a bar more than sixteen feet above the ground, or he may enjoy the precision of a high diver as he executes a complicated figure and enters the water with scarcely a splash. The theater-goer may take naïve pleasure in the illusions created by the designer and the technical crew by their skillful use of canvas, lumber, paint, and light. As a connoisseur of performances, the spectator finds pleasure in comparing Olivier's Hamlet with that of Evans or Gielgud. As a knowledgeable theater enthusiast, he notes the effectiveness of the ensemble acting, the director's adroit use of pace and rhythm, the actor's ability to react as well as to speak, the appropriateness of the scenery in reinforcing the mood of the play, the expressive use of movement and business, the psychological and emotional content implied by the groupings of characters. The enjoyment that an informed spectator feels at a fine performance of a great play stems in part from his recognition of the achievements of the interpreters in translating into theatrical terms the essential values of the play.

A third satisfaction provided by the theater has already been suggested earlier—as a means of extending ourselves beyond the narrow circle of everyday existence. Most plays elicit an empathic response from the spectator. He "feels into" the action. His sympathies are aroused as he identifies himself with the characters and action before him. He becomes emotionally involved in the outcome. He often sees in the play, universal patterns of behavior that parallel his own. In short, drama becomes a means of extending our experience, with all of the concomitant emotional overtones enhanced and augmented by theatrical production so that in the end we act out the play for ourselves.

Fourth, the dramatic experience can also be a spiritual one. As Aristotle suggested, tragedy is serious, of a certain magnitude; it is elevated in scale and it evokes a catharsis—a purging away, a cleansing of the ignoble, the mean, the base. The great works of drama depict great characters exploring the great issues of life. Greek tragedy was a declaration of faith; it exalted mankind. "Wonders are many, and none is more wonderful than man" sang Sophocles. The sufferings of Antigone, Oedipus, and Prometheus were positive statements about the Greek view of life. The medieval dramatist in composing *Everyman* had the high purpose of presenting the process of salvation to mankind. In the masterpieces of drama, good and evil are ruthlessly examined, choices are made and judgments rendered which indicate the distilled wisdom of the race. Man's loftiest ideas and aspirations have been the significant content of drama. Thus, the theater in times past has been an institution of edification and spiritual stimulation, and in our drama today we can sometimes find affirmation of the dignity of man and the greatness of his spirit.

From this brief discussion of the varied appeals of the dramatic experience it is evident that the theater has a number of ways of attracting and satisfying an audience. Harold Clurman has suggested the sources of satisfaction to be found in drama in his concept of entertainment:

I am entertained when my interest has been aroused, when my detached capacity for feeling, thought, sentiment, laughter and passion are brought into play. I am entertained when my senses are quickened, my soul touched, my mind altered. Being healthy, I cannot be fed adulterated stimulants or strong sedatives; nor am I gratified by timid stabs at my sensibilities. I want my entertainment to exercise my faculties as vigorously and as completely as possible.[1]

APPROACHES TO DRAMA

Because of the complex nature of drama and its production, there are many approaches to the study of a play. Although some of these will be developed at length in subsequent chapters, it may be helpful to describe them briefly now. Let us consider ten such approaches.

1. *Historical*

Drama may be studied historically. A thoroughly satisfying course of study may be laid out investigating the origins of drama in Egypt and Greece, the development of various modes and forms, and the influences which shaped the masterpieces of the drama from the Theater of Dionysus in Athens to the present day. A rewarding analysis can be made in tracing the influence of Greek comedy on the Romans, and in turn the effect of Plautus and Terence on the Elizabethans and Molière. The pressures which shaped Shakespeare's genius are a typical subject of investigation in this approach. To what extent was Shakespeare indebted to Seneca, Marlowe, Lyly, Kyd? What does a comparison of Kyd's *Spanish Tragedy* with *Hamlet* reveal about Shakespeare's skill as a craftsman? What Senecan devices does he employ? How did the contemporary taste for "tragedies of blood" affect Shakespeare? What aspects of *Hamlet* reflect the Renaissance culture? The medieval? These and similar questions indicate the historical approach to the art of the drama.

Drama may also be studied historically from the standpoint of theatrical production. Using this approach, the student is concerned with the physical conditions of the playhouse and their effect on playwriting and performance, the kind of audience witnessing the play, the impact of the actor on a role, and the style and conventions of the various periods

[1] From *Lies Like Truth*, by Harold Clurman. Copyright ©, 1958, by Grove Press, Inc. Reprinted by permission of the author.

of theatrical production. He asks such questions as these: How was *Hamlet* first produced in the Globe? What was Richard Burbage's original interpretation? Did Thomas Betterton carry on Burbage's interpretation in his performances in the Restoration period? How did the Globe production vary from that at Drury Lane? What are the traditions that have grown up about the playing of Hamlet? The stage history of a play is a very significant field of investigation.

2. *Structure*

A play may be studied from the standpoint of its structure, which involves an analysis of the articulation of the parts, the selection of the series of events included in the plot, the specific function of the various characters and scenes, the devices by which the playwright builds up climaxes and crises, stimulates suspense and interest and evokes an emotional response. How does the play begin and end? What are the forces which set the play in motion? How are the conflicts developed and resolved? *Hamlet,* for example, like most Elizabethan plays, has a complicated structure with a welter of overlapping relationships. To place the essential scenes before the spectator required an extremely flexible stage which Shakespeare inherited from the medieval theater. An analysis of each of the scenes in *Hamlet* reveals Shakespeare's skill in organizing an effective sequence of action. As a typical instance, Act I, Scene 1 (see pages 58-67) shows his ability in creating suspense and excitement, thrusting the action forward while he skillfully exposes the antecedent material providing the necessary orientation for the play to advance. Shakespeare's facility for creating dramatic action is shown in the play within the play, Ophelia's mad scene, the two appearances of the ghost, and the duel. These scenes with their strong visual appeal are balanced and reinforced by Shakespeare's consummate command of the language which throughout the play illuminates the action and meaning. One sees in Shakespeare, then, the complete dramatist, fully in possession of mastery of word and action, plus the ability to fashion an ordered structure of events of cumulative power.

3. *Character*

Still another method of studying a play is that of character analysis. Here we concern ourselves with the specific dramatic function of each character. We investigate the character's background and motivation in relation to the playwright's methods of character delineation. We want to know if the character is a one-dimensional, stock type or a complex individual. We search for his objectives, for the sources of his conflict. Does he succeed or fail in his efforts? Why? We look for the symbolic meaning of the character as a representative of his society. Are his actions the "necessary and probable" consequences of what he is? In many plays there is considerable latitude for interpretation. Hamlet has been endlessly probed and dissected. What was his tragic flaw? Is the basis of his inaction cowardice? guilt? love of his mother? oversensitivity? conscience? madness? the lack of opportunity? What was his relation with Ophelia? The penetration of character and the searching out of motives behind the words and behavior is certainly one of the most intriguing aspects of drama shared by the scholar, director, and actor.

4. Thought

The thought of the play is another aspect of investigation. Most drama involves characters reaching towards a goal who run into conflict with other characters. A struggle ensues. Sides are taken and the battle is joined. The motivations of both protagonists and antagonists are presented or inferred. Characters attempt to justify their choices, judgments, or courses of action. Usually, some conclusion is arrived at. In the resolution of the play, the dramatist suggests the reasons why his characters succeeded or failed. The rationale behind the action of a play provides an interesting subject of examination, especially when the characters are symbolic of a larger cultural meaning. All drama is not readily accessible to the statement of a simple thesis. *Hamlet* means many things to many people. Like life itself, drama may contain the richness and complexity of an experience which is capable of diverse interpretations. In great drama, the intriguing search for significance can be a source of profit and pleasure.

5. Language

The playwright's use of language provides another approach to drama. Since a play is set down in words, the diction may be examined like that of any other form of writing. As in fiction, the language of the writer advances the plot, accompanies and stimulates the action, characterizes the speaker, and establishes the circumstances, atmosphere and locale. But the playwright finds special restrictions in his use of language in that he is confined to dialogue which must be suitable for oral presentation to an audience in a relatively short space of time. Because of the performance factor, dramatic dialogue must be particularly economical, vivid, and expressive. Stage speech must be immediately comprehensible to the listener, and it must have the power to stir the emotions. The playwright's language may take a variety of forms—simulated conversation of everyday life, lyrical passages of verse, choric odes, messenger speeches rich in descriptive detail, soliloquies of introspective analysis, epigrams and polished witticisms, and puns, wisecracks, and insults. And all of these variations must explicitly depend upon the spoken word.

As in poetry, the language of drama may be studied for its texture and symbolic meaning. The "new criticism" has found a happy hunting-ground in the investigation of reiterative imagery—recurrent words which cluster about the root ideas of plays, arousing a "swarm of feelings." Certain key words and phrases used again and again set up imaginative reverberations beyond the level of their immediate context, and almost imperceptibly evoke and sustain emotional responses and create atmosphere. For example, Robert Heilman in his study of *King Lear*,[2] notes the repeated and varied uses of the image of sight and seeing in *Oedipus Rex*. There are many references to "thou seest not"; "thou art maimed in ear, and in wit, and in the eye"; "henceforth, ye shall be dark"; etc. In *King Lear*, Heilman traces at length the imagery patterns of disorder in nature, mental disorder, the clothes image, and madness. Such studies as these expand the already considerable area of dramatic diction, and beckon the student to an intriguing field of exploration.

6. Dramatic Symbols

Not only the language but also the events of a play may be infused with symbolic meaning. Since the drama presents characters who represent a larger humanity, their actions may be endowed with significance beyond the immediate story being played on the stage. Mr. Zero in Rice's *The Adding Machine* is more than an isolated individual; he represents the little man everywhere who is ground under by callous materialism. Pastor Manders in *Ghosts* and Torvald in *A Doll's House* are more than fictional characters in a play—they are spokesmen for the hide-bound, conventional thought of the nineteenth century. In a medieval drama like *Everyman*, it is quite apparent that the author intended for his protagonist to symbolize all of humanity. Thus characters in a play are related as representatives of the society about which the playwright is creating his play. There is another aspect of symbolism in drama. The playwright uses events as metaphors. When Hedda burns Lövborg's manuscript, she is not only destroying his life's work; she is burning his child. The hunter's wanton killing of a bird is reflected in the larger destruction of the heroine in Chekhov's *The Sea Gull*. Dr. Faustus' pact with the Devil represents the dedication of all men to the temptations of this life. The study of a play for its symbolic action adds another dimension to the meaning of a play.

[2] Robert Heilman, *This Great Stage* (Baton Rouge, Louisiana State University Press, 1948).

7. Rituals and Ceremonials

As we have seen earlier, drama originates in ritual. Although drama may have moved far from its sources of inspiration, many plays involve ceremonial situations of special significance. These are public or social occasions which transcend the personal situation to affect the larger society of which the ritual is a part. Familiar examples are a reunion, a wedding, a trial, a home-coming—nearly any festive or communal occasion with significant social implications. In *Hamlet*, there are such ceremonials as the assembly of the court, Ophelia's funeral, the duel, the play within the play. Sophocles' *Antigone* dramatizes a conflict over the rites-of-passage of a dead brother. *Agamemnon* is based on a home-coming. The significance of such rites as an expression of a given culture constitutes an interesting field of investigation.

8. Dramatic Types or Forms

Another avenue of approach is through the consideration of dramatic types or forms. Plays may be classified as comedies, tragedies, farces, melodramas, high comedies, *drames*, and many shades and combinations of these. While these categories are an arbitrary device, since many plays will not fit neatly into a single classification, nevertheless, such an arrangement provides a useful basis for the discussion of the special characteristics of each type. *Hamlet* does not fit perfectly into the Aristotelian concept of tragedy because of its mixture of serious and comic material, but critics from the Elizabethan period to the present time do not hesitate to label the play as a tragedy. But how many plays can be so classified? What are the essential elements and conditions for the genuine tragic effect? Is tragedy possible in the modern world? What is the function of comedy? What are the characteristics of melodrama? What is the nature of the comic material in *Hamlet*? What melodramatic situations does Shakespeare employ in the play? The answers to these and similar questions leads us into a consideration of the basic types and forms of drama.

9. Modes

Plays may be classified by various modes as classicism, realism, naturalism, expressionism, romanticism, etc. As in the case of the forms of drama, these categories are not rigid compartments, nevertheless, the classifications afford us a valuable way of looking at a play. Moreover, they provide an interesting frame of reference for the parallel motivations, developments, and influences of other forms of the arts. For example, the classicism of Greek drama with its emphasis on unity, balance, and proportion is also the classicism of Greek sculpture, architecture, and poetry. The realism of the nineteenth-century theater finds a parallel in the realism of the nineteenth-century novel. The distorted point of view of the expressionist of the twentieth century is echoed in nonrepresentational painting. Thus a particular art and period is recognized as one aspect of a larger expression of a culture which reflects the intellectual climate of the day. The spirit of the Renaissance which quickened the pulse of Elizabethan England, led to the exploration of the New World, and launched a wave of creative endeavor, was a part of the impetus which caused Shakespeare and his contemporaries to create such plays as *Hamlet, Romeo and Juliet, Dr. Faustus* and *Volpone.* In the nineteenth century, we shall see how the impact of science and materialism led to an intellectual revolution with the inevitable development of new modes—naturalism, realism, and expressionism.

10. *Production*

The director, actor, and scene designer investigate the play from the viewpoint of their several interests in theater production. Is the play stageworthy? How may its values be translated into theatrical terms? The director visualizes the drama taking shape as an organized entity through the use of movement, sounds, speech, color, space, tempo, rhythm, and light in relation to the living performer. The actor is apt to see the play largely in terms of his own role—weaving relationships with the other characters, visualizing the appropriate appearance, speech and behavior, and searching the script for clues to his identity. The scene designer sees the play in visual terms. He must create the special atmosphere for the action, bearing in mind the limitations of space and materials which the physical theater imposes upon him, and keeping in the forefront of his consciousness, the actor's need of a functional platform for playing. When he designs for *Hamlet,* he is not only aware of the castle of Elsinore as a cue for his image of the emotional environment, but he must also keep in mind such practical problems as that of the burial of Ophelia and the appearance and disappearance of the ghost. The actor in studying Hamlet looks for a central core of meaning that will serve as the basis for his interpretation. The director, after his investigation of the play, decides on the basic style of performance, he visualizes the areas of action and he has at least tentative ideas of what each character must contribute to the meaning of the play. The preparation of a play for production rests on a solid basis of careful research and painstaking scrutiny.

It is apparent from this brief description of various approaches to drama and its production, that it is a composite art whose understanding and appreciation must cover a wide range of study. No single work can provide all of the background for the complete understanding of drama, but it is hoped that in the ensuing chapters, keys will be found to unlock some of the significant doors. It is also apparent that full appreciation of drama is beyond the scope of book-learning. Drama in its final and most effective form must be experienced at first-hand. In addition to acquaintance with the great works of dramatic literature, satisfaction is found in becoming involved in dramatic production as a member of an audience, or perhaps, in some aspect of theatrical production.

DRAMATIC ACTION

When Aristotle defined tragedy, he made a very important point in saying that drama was "in the form of action, not of narrative." We remember that drama had its origins in actions—in rites, in *dromenon*, "the thing done." Rituals at the outset were imitations of actions which had previously occurred or which primitive man wished to happen. Action is a basic form of propitiation and communication. The language of behavior is a universal one.

Aristotle placed primary emphasis on action: "But most important of all is the structure of the incidents. For Tragedy is an imitation, not of men but of an action and of life, and life consists in action, and its end is a mode of action, not a quality. Now character determines men's qualities, but it is by their actions that they are happy or the reverse."

There are at least four applications of the term action to drama which are essential to understand:

1. In its simplest form, action refers to the movement of the players when they perform the play. Such action includes their entrances and exits, the personal business of the characters, the larger movements of the ensemble, the quarrels, love scenes, struggles—all of the overt action of the play which the dramatist, director, and actor have carefully designed and rehearsed to bring meaning to the play. Aeschylus, in his first extant work, *The Persians* (c.492 B.C.), correctly capitalized on the dramatic values inherent in action by using them as the core of his play, a strong conflict which could be *enacted* before an audience. When medieval drama grew out of the liturgy of the church, the purpose was to make the original sacred events more compelling by acting them out. A fundamental strength of the drama in showing action, is to give to the spectator the effect of an actual experience taking place before him. In a novel, the reader gains the impression of a past occurrence, but drama in the theater seems to be a process, a happening. Characters are in the act of becoming. Hence, action enhances the immediacy of the appeal in drama.

Action is not mere commotion or random activity. Dramatic action must be purposive, expressive, and significant. The quality of the action reveals the dramatic intent. While drama primarily depends upon the playwright's words, much of the significance of his language results from the actor's delivery, which includes gesture, posture, facial expression, and movement. Many of the most telling moments of the theater are those provided by the performer's actions when he gives visual expression to an idea or emotion—Hedda burning the manuscript, the abandoned servant curling up in the corner to die at the end of *The Cherry Orchard*, Claudius' guilty starting when he witnesses the re-enactment of the murder of King Hamlet. Drama is created in the performance. As an example of how much the actor contributes to the performance by his interpretation, read Rosamond Gilder's account of a scene from John Gielgud's *Hamlet*, pages 218-219.

2. Speech itself is a form of action, especially well-written speeches which cue the action and reaction, bear the freight of emotion, explain the meaning, and thrust the movement of the play forward. Implicit in most dramatic dialogue is an underlying pattern of action as the character strives toward a goal, seeks to influence the behavior of others, and searches for the meaning of his experience. Notice the full range of inferred movement in a typical passage from Shakespeare. In *Richard III*, the King is visited by the ghosts of those whom he has murdered. He awakens from his guilty nightmare and cries:

KING RICHARD:

Give me another horse: bind up my wounds.
Have mercy, Jesu!—Soft! I did but dream.
O coward conscience, how dost thou afflict me!
The light burns blue. It is now dead midnight.
Cold fearful drops stand on my trembling flesh.
What do I fear? Myself? There's none else by:
Richard loves Richard; that is, I am I.
Then fly. What, from myself? Great reason why:
Lest I revenge. What, myself upon myself?

Dramatic dialogue is dynamic—a means of exploration and examination, a way of adjustment, particularly in situations in which the interrelationship of characters is significant, and in moments of decision and change. Furthermore, the actor does not merely recite aloud; he impersonates and characterizes the speaker and creates the emotional context. His speech is a part of a process in which he is embroiled—an articulation of the emotions which surge through him. The speaking character is a character in action.

3. Dramatic action is also psychological. It involves what is happen-

ing mentally and emotionally. When the psychologist analyzes human behavior, he searches for clues to inner motivation expressed in a person's overt actions. Similarly, the playwright devises actions and speeches which give the audience insight into a character's inner life—which explain the turbulence beneath the façade of appearance. In all significant drama, there is an underlying pattern of psychological action which accompanies and supports the external speech and movement.

4. The play itself is an action, or a "system of actions"—a series of progressive incidents which require constant adjustment and revision. The scheme of construction is progressive, its drive forward and upward. The plot is a volatile selection and arrangement of a clash of wills, conflicts, choices and actions and reactions. And because drama seems to be a happening at the time of occurrence, the structure of the play possesses the quality of a living thing. Sophocles, a master craftsman, realized his drama in terms of action as Raymond Williams points out in his discussion of *Antigone:*

The more one looks at the text of the play, the more one realizes that a simple, yet radical pattern, a controlling structure of feeling, has been clearly isolated and designed in the writing. And then if one looks at the performance, one sees that this design is being continually enacted, in the parts as in the whole. For it is a design made for performance; the purpose of the play is not report, not description, not analysis, but enactment of a design. The structure of feeling is the formal written structure, and also the structure of performance. The conflict and resolution are not a story, a telling of things past, but are always present in words and movement.[3]

CONVENTIONS

Drama, like all other forms of art, is conventionalized. That is to say, there are certain common agreements between spectator and theaterworker as to the manner of creation and production—certain "ground rules" which determine how the game is to be played. In painting, there is the convention that pigment is applied to a flat surface within a regular framework. Music is a conventionalized combination of sounds and rhythms which make almost no pretense of imitating nature. The spectator, as he enters the theater becomes a partner to conventions in order that the drama can take place. He enters into the situation imaginatively by what Coleridge termed a "willing suspension of disbelief."

In our contemporary theater, the spectator of a legitimate modern play generally expects to see on stage characters and settings which resemble those of life. The speech suggests normal conversation, and the characters' behavior follows familiar patterns. Actually, much of what the play-goer

[3] Raymond Williams, *Drama in Performance* (London, F. Muller, 1954).

sees and hears is arbitrarily conventionalized even though the dramatist
has written in a realistic style. There is a tacit agreement between performer and audience that they will be separate from one another. The
audience occupies the auditorium, the actor remains on stage. The separation of these two entities is facilitated by the darkened auditorium and
the lighted stage, the architectural features of the elevated stage which
can be closed off by a curtain, and the proscenium arch itself. There is
also a psychological barrier at work, known as the "fourth wall"—a contemporary convention which developed with realism, in which the actors
pretend the audience does not exist and avoid direct communication
across the footlights. Actually, the performer employs specific techniques
to assure communication with everyone in the theater by speaking louder
and more. clearly than in normal conversation, by turning his face at
least partially toward the audience, and by exaggerating his gestures and
facial expressions. The drama itself is conventionalized. Its compressed
structure, the arrangement into scenes or acts interrupted by intermis-
sions and set changes, the climactic order of the action usually involving
only a few characters—these are arbitrary practices of the playwright.
Even scenery which gives the illusion of actuality with all the clutter and
detail of real life, is patently artificial in the arrangement of exits and
entrances, the grouping of furniture which "opens out" toward the house,
the arbitrary use of lighting, the enlarged scale of set pieces, the very use
of scenic materials—all of these are arbitrarily artificial.

Conventions are not rigid. They change from time to time and even
from one style of drama to another. In musical comedy, for example,
everyone expects scenery that is frankly theatrical, performers who break
into song and dance at the slightest provocation, accompanied by an
orchestra, a chorus of interlopers who hover in the immediate background
ready to join instantly into the action of the production. In contemporary
"arena" or center-staged productions, the audience is asked to accept
such conventions as the absence of scenery, the intimacy of the surroundings, and different kinds of movements and groupings which result from
the playing area surrounded by spectators. As modern playwrights become increasingly dissatisfied with realism, there are more and more
attempts to free the theater from restricting conventions. For example,
scenery is becoming frankly theatrical instead of representational. As an
example of this tendency a fragment of a wall picked out of the darkness
by light now serves as a setting which a generation ago would have
required a complete interior with three walls, a ceiling and practical
doors. Dramatists are using freer forms for their plays. Dialogue may be
poetic, or there may be the reintroduction of asides, soliloquies, or direct
address. Acting is oftentimes quite stylized, the separation between spectator and performer may be deliberately broken down. The point is that

theater conventions are subject to change as those who work in theater seek ways of expressing themselves more interestingly and completely, and as the established practices give way to new ones, the spectator is obliged to make a corresponding adjustment.

There have always been fashions in theatrical conventions which have differed from time to time, and in order to understand the drama of any period, it is essential to know the conventions which influenced the production. In the Greek theater for example there were such conventions as outdoor performances given in the daytime as public ceremonies. There were only three speaking characters on stage at one time, men played the female roles, there was little or no violence on-stage, actors wore masks and special footgear and headpieces, and the plays were written in verse, dramatizing ancient legends and myths, presented usually in a single permanent setting with a simple story that occurred in a short space of time. In the Elizabethan theater, like the Greek, the roles were played by male actors in an outdoor theater in the daytime with little or no use of illusionistic scenery. The plays written in verse were quite different from the Greek drama, in form and content. The play usually was a complicated one involving several plot lines, comedy matter was mixed with serious, high-born characters with low, and the playwright ransacked history and literature for material that would tell an exciting story. The plays were performed by professional actors in theaters whose dimensions and arrangement placed the actor in close proximity to the spectator so that the subtleties of the language could be exploited. The convention of the large unlocalized platform gave the dramatist a great deal of freedom in staging an animated and complicated narrative.

In each age, theater conventions have varied according to the influences of the playwrights, actors, audience and physical theaters, and in turn, the conventions have affected all elements of the drama. It is essential to recognize these conventions in evaluating any drama because of their pressure in shaping the play and its production.

Questions and Exercises

1. What is "histrionic sensibility"? How does it affect the appreciation of a play?
2. What special qualities of a theater performance of a play is the silent reader apt to miss?
3. What conventions have you observed in attending the theater? How do stage conventions differ from those of the motion picture?
4. What are the appeals of drama?
5. How may the drama and the theater be studied historically?

6. Explain the importance of the various kinds of *action* in drama.
7. How did the conventions of the Greek theater differ from those of the Elizabethan?
8. Read the first chapter of a novel and the first scene of a play. Compare the differences in structure and technique. What special advantage does the playwright have? What disadvantages?

Suggested Reading

BRICKER, Herschel, ed., *Our Theatre Today: Art, Craft, and Management* (New York, Samuel French, 1936).

DOWNER, Alan, *The Art of the Play* (New York, Holt, Rinehart and Winston, Inc., 1955).

HAMILTON, Clayton, *The Theory of the Theatre* (New York, Holt, Rinehart and Winston, Inc., 1939).

LAWSON, John Howard, *Theory and Technique of Playwriting* (New York, G. P. Putnam's Sons, 1936).

MILLETT, Fred B. and BENTLEY, G. E., *The Art of the Drama* (New York, Appleton-Century-Crofts, Inc., 1935).

NICOLL, Allardyce, *Theory of Drama* (New York, Thomas Y. Crowell Co., 1931).

ROWE, Kenneth Thorpe, *A Theatre in Your Head* (New York, Funk & Wagnalls Co., 1959).

THOMPSON, Alan Reynolds, *The Anatomy of Drama* (Berkeley, University of California Press, 1942).

WILLIAMS, Raymond, *Drama in Performance* (London, F. Muller, 1954).

3

The Elements of Drama

IN THE PREVIOUS CHAPTER we were concerned with the appeals of drama
and with the variety of approaches available for a study of its nature.
One avenue of investigation suggested earlier was that of dramatic structure. It is our purpose now to specify the particular elements of drama
which constitute its structure. In this discussion we will follow a pattern
set down by Aristotle in his *Poetics,* perhaps the most significant and influential work on dramatic criticism ever written. Aristotle categorized
drama into these six elements, which are listed in order of importance
as he viewed them:

1. PLOT
2. CHARACTER
3. THOUGHT
4. DICTION
5. MUSIC
6. SPECTACLE

We do not intend to become engaged in an argument about the relative importance of these items, but we wish to use these six elements as
a convenient frame of reference, not only in this chapter but in all considerations of dramatic literature. Hence, familiarity with Aristotle's elements and their component parts is necessary for following subsequent
discussions. These essentials must be mastered as a basic vocabulary for
analyzing dramatic structure, and as tools for taking a play apart.

1. PLOT

Aristotle's first element, *plot,* is a complex one which includes these
eleven aspects, which are involved in the construction of a play:

28

A. *Exposition*
B. *Discovery*
C. *Point of attack*
D. *Foreshadowing*
E. *Complication*
F. *Climax*
G. *Crisis*
H. *Denouement*
I. *Unity of time*
J. *Unity of place*
K. *Unity of action*

Oftentimes these parts of plot are not separate entities. For instance, the climax and crisis may occur at the same time, or exposition may be used for foreshadowing. Nevertheless, these plot materials may be identified in most plays.

Plot is the chief part of drama. Aristotle gave it primacy when he said that plot is "the life and soul of tragedy." Plot does not mean mere story. Plot is the formal aspect of the play in the sense that it gives the play its form. Plot is to the playwright what composition is to the painter and composer. It is the ordered arrangement of the parts, which are causally and logically related. A play is not a chronological series of items like a timetable or the minutes of a meeting. Just as a motion picture editor arranges a meaningful sequence of film clips by relating each frame to every other one, so, in a similar way, the playwright composes his events and builds the structure of his play. Dramatic structure is a concatenation or linking of actions into an indivisible chain.

Plots have varied from the tightly knit, simple structure of Greek tragedy, to the loose episodes of medieval drama, bound together by a theme, to the complicated action of the Elizabethans, employing several sets of characters involved in a welter of overlapping situations, to the naturalist's attempt to avoid all semblance of structure in "slice-of-life" plays, and to contemporary experiments in expressionistic, "absurd" and "epic" drama which have little regard for disciplined construction. But despite differences in composition, the underlying pattern of Western drama reflects Aristotle's concept of organic unity—a series of actions growing out of what is "necessary and probable." As a consequence, most of our plays involve human beings caught in decisive moments of struggle and conflict. Tension is increased as the drama moves toward a climax and an ultimate decision. The Greeks used such plots very early in their dramas. A typical Greek tragedy is built around a character involved in a situation that requires a choice. Antigone must decide whether or not she will bury her dead brother in defiance of the king's edict. Oedipus decides to rid his kingdom of the cause of the plague. Once the protagonist makes a decision, pressure is brought to bear on him, but the tragic hero will not be diverted from his course, and the catastrophe occurs.

A typical Greek "old comedy" likewise shows a leading character embarking on a plan of action—usually an extravagant and impracticable one. For example, in the *Acharnians,* a private citizen decides to negotiate a personal peace treaty with Sparta. Opposition is set up against his plan and the issues are contested. The idea is tried out and the results shown. The comedy ends in revelry. In both of these early forms of drama, the plot results from a character making a decision which he attempts to put into action against opposition. This essential pattern has been the characteristic dramatic structure ever since.

A play is composed of a series of units. Major divisions are the acts, which in turn may be divided into scenes, and these may be separated still further by a director into a series of "beats." "Scenes" in the French sense refers to any new grouping of characters. "Beats" are a director's device for separating small units of action for rehearsal purposes such as the appearances of the ghost in the first scene of *Hamlet,* Kate's final speech in *The Taming of the Shrew,* or Romeo's suicide in *Romeo and Juliet.* An examination of the structure of any play reveals these various units. For example, *Oedipus Rex* consists of a series of eight or nine episodes involving two or three speaking characters—Oedipus and Creon, Oedipus and Teiresias, Oedipus and the Herdsman. Between each of these episodes, which are of only a few minutes' duration, the Chorus chants lyric passages. In a contemporary three-act play, the structure of each act is composed of various groupings of characters such as Nora and Mrs. Linden, Nora and Torvald, Nora and Krogstad. Each of these scenes or groupings is designed by the playwright for specific dramatic purposes. Each scene is placed in its appropriate place in the sequence of action so that it is causally related to what happens before and after. It is this process of plot-making, of devising and arranging the incidents in a logical order that will keep the action moving toward the goal, that makes the art of playwriting a difficult one.

The plot is devised to produce a cumulative effect; it is plot which gives the play its tension and emotional momentum. In addition, the plot provides the explanation and meaning of the sum total of the parts. What are the events which cause the transition of Oedipus, the heroic king, to Oedipus, the blinded exile? What happens to Nora in between the time she makes her first gay entrance into her "doll's house," and the end of the play when she walks out on her husband and children? The plot answers these questions by providing the salient incidents which account for the changes that occur. The plot charts the course of action and carries with it the increasing burden of emotion.

In the nineteenth century Brunetière offered his celebrated "law of the drama," in which the basic tenet was that a play presents "the spectacle of the will striving toward a goal." While this concept is not valid for all kinds of drama, there is a hard core of truth in it. Most plays deal with a protagonist striving toward an objective—status, power, wealth, security, recognition, affection. The playwright selects and arranges a series of events showing the protagonist's strivings, and the effects upon him and the other characters in a series of actions and reactions. Such a series of related events constitute the plot. Although nearly every kind of plot has been used with success by some playwright, there are certain generalizations which seem warranted about dramatic structure. It is easier to describe unsatisfactory plots as follows:

Episodic plots in which characterization is weakened and action diffused by lack of consecutive progression.

Plots with obviously manipulated endings in which a solution is forced upon the action from the outside, rather than growing logically out of what the characters are and do.

Plots with extraneous scenes and digressions which are not related to the central action and have no real place in the meaning of the play.

Plots which lose compression because they attempt to encompass too much time or space.

Plots which omit scenes or action necessary for clear understanding or for the full impact of the play.

Plots which lack dramatic content.

Plots which exaggerate spectacle, and neglect characterization and sound structure.

In nearly every play, certain structural weaknesses are apparent, but in general, the plays of permanent stature support Aristotle's view of the importance of a skillfully devised dramatic structure.

A plot results from a combination of a number of structural devices which we must consider in some detail.

A. *Exposition*

When the curtain rises on a play, the dramatist faces the problem of capturing his audience's attention and providing the spectator with the necessary background so that he can understand the subsequent action. He must know who the characters are, what their relationship to one another is, what motivates them, and usually, he needs some notion of their environment. This is *exposition*. Notice how Ibsen introduces his char-

acters and their relationship to one another in the very first moments of
A Doll's House.

(NORA *enters, humming gayly. She is in outdoor dress, and carries several
parcels, which she lays on the right-hand table. She leaves the door into the
hall open, and a* PORTER *is seen outside, carrying a Christmas tree and a basket,
which he gives to the* MAIDSERVANT *who has opened the door.*)

NORA: Hide the Christmas tree carefully, Ellen; the children must on no account see it before this evening, when it's lighted up. (*to the* PORTER, *taking
out her purse*) How much?

PORTER: Fifty öre.

NORA: There is a crown. No, keep the change.

(*The* PORTER *thanks her and goes.* NORA *shuts the door. She continues
smiling in quiet glee as she takes off her outdoor things. Taking from her
pocket a bag of macaroons, she eats one or two. Then she goes on tip-toe
to her husband's door and listens.*)

Yes; he is at home.

(*She begins humming again, crossing to the table on the right*)

HELM: (*in his room*) Is that my lark twittering there?

NORA: (*busy opening some of her parcels*) Yes, it is.

HELM: Is it the squirrel frisking around?

NORA: Yes!

HELM: When did the squirrel get home?

NORA: Just this minute. (*hides the bag of macaroons in her pocket and wipes
her mouth*) Come here, Torvald, and see what I've been buying.

HELM: Don't interrupt me. (*a little later he opens the door and looks in, pen
in hand*) Buying, did you say? What! All that? Has my little spendthrift
been making the money fly again?

NORA: Why, Torvald, surely we can afford to launch out a little now. It's the
first Christmas we haven't had to pinch.

HELM: Come, come; we can't afford to squander money.

NORA: Oh, yes, Torvald, do let us squander a little, now—just the least little
bit! You know you'll soon be earning heaps of money.

HELM: Yes, from New Year's Day. But there's a whole quarter before my first
salary is due.

NORA: Never mind; we can borrow in the meantime.

HELM: Nora! (*he goes up to her and takes her playfully by the ear*)

In the scene which follows this, Ibsen uses the familiar, but legitimate,
expository device of bringing in an old acquaintance of Nora's who has
been away for a number of years. This situation seems a plausible one
for asking and answering questions which enable Ibsen to load the scene
with background information.

In addition to placing the action in its proper context by revealing
the past, the exposition also prepares the ground for future develop-

The Russian actress Nazimova as Nora in Ibsen's *A Doll's House,* 1907

ment of events and characters and establishes the appropriate atmosphere and environment. Read the first scene of *Hamlet* on pages
58-67 and notice how much skillfully contrived exposition Shakespeare
has worked into a very few lines in a rather unobtrusive fashion.

In most contemporary plays in which the dramatist is endeavoring
to create the illusion of actuality, he ordinarily introduces his exposition
into the play as an organic part of the action rather than as obvious
information. Because exposition usually bulks rather large in the first
act of a play, the writer must find ways to capture and hold the audience's interest while unobtrusively providing necessary background
material. Many playwrights find it difficult to get their action underway,
with the result that the opening scenes tend to drag. The television
producer, conscious of this tendency in the opening moments of a play,
often has resorted to the technique of beginning a production with an
excerpt of violent action from the climax of the play in order to "hook"
the spectator into the story.

Playwrights have used a variety of expository devices such as
"feather-duster scenes" of two minor characters bouncing information off
of one another to the audience, dumb-shows, confidants, narrators,
choruses, asides, soliloquies, prologues, and all kinds of visual aids including slides, charts, maps, and motion pictures. The stage setting
also serves as a means of providing background material for the audience. Notice how O'Neill's set description of *In the Zone* on page 37
provides essential information for understanding the action.

While the techniques of exposition vary from play to play, nearly
all dramatists have felt the necessity of supplying an adequate background for their present and future plot development.

B. *Discovery*

The playwright is obligated to impart a steady stream of information
to the audience. He must reveal his characters' motivations and objectives, their relationships, and their feelings. The most satisfactory kind
of *discovery* is that which comes from the characters themselves. As the
protagonist discovers the truth, the audience shares the experience of
his discovery, as in *Oedipus* and *Ghosts*. In these plays, the spectator
gains the impression of an actual happening. A skillful playwright possesses the ability to invent and organize a series of interesting and compelling discoveries. For instance, notice the number and variety of effective discoveries in *Hamlet*—the ghost's revelation of the murder, the
guilt of Claudius, the madness and death of Ophelia, the pirates' attempt to slay Hamlet, the death of Polonius, and the poisoned sword
and drink.

Discovery scenes may be those of recognition. For example, in Aeschylus' *Libation-Bearers*, Electra recognizes her brother, Orestes, by a lock of his hair and by their matching footprints. In Sophocles' *Electra*, Orestes is recognized by his father's signet ring, and in the Euripidean version, a tutor recognizes Orestes by a scar. In classic comedy, recognition scenes between long-lost relatives and lovers were effected very often by signs and symbols such as rings, lockets, and distinguishing physical markings.

Discovery is accompanied by *anagnorisis* (recognition). The truth is realized between appearance and reality, between what is expected and what actually occurs. In serious drama, this may be self-discovery, as for example, throughout *Hamlet* the protagonist submits himself to introspective analysis. And in *Oedipus Rex* the tragic hero gradually discovers the awful truth about himself. The art of playwrighting is in part the art of creating effective discoveries.

Exposition is a part of the general discovery process, but it deals primarily with antecedent or background material while discovery includes events which may happen in the course of the play on stage, as for example Nora's discovery of the true character of her husband, Jason's discovery of Medea's slaughter of their two sons, and the doctor's discovery of Lady Macbeth's madness.

C. *Point of Attack*

Once the playwright provides sufficient background to hold the audience's attention, he sets a chain of events going which constitute the main action of the play. The *point of attack* refers to that moment in the play in which the precipitating force sets the mechanism in motion—the first pitch is thrown, the football is kicked off, the first blow is landed, the battle is joined. The equilibrium that ordinarily exists at the rise of the first curtain is disturbed, turbulence results and a period of adjustment begins: Horatio meets the ghost of Hamlet's father, Othello marries Desdemona, Creon forbids the burial of Polyneices, Krogstad threatens to reveal Nora's secret, Agamemnon returns from the Trojan War, Oedipus promises to rid the kingdom of the plague. These are characteristic points of attack—when an inciting force triggers the course of action.

The location of the point of attack in the story is related directly to the physical theater and its conventions. The more flexible the stage, the freer the dramatic form and the greater the opportunity for an early attack and the presentation of a great deal of action. For example, medieval and Elizabethan playwrights exploited the freedom provided by their stages to tell complicated stories with many scenes and characters, while, in contrast, the Greek dramatists felt obliged to begin their stories as near as possible to the major crisis. If Shakespeare had dramatized *Oedipus Rex*, undoubtedly he would have presented the original warning of the oracle, perhaps show Oedipus in his clash with his father, and the marriage of his mother. In most modern plays there is a tendency to use a compact plot. As a consequence, the contemporary dramatist is apt to use a relatively late point of attack.

D. *Foreshadowing*

In the exposition, we have observed how the playwright must furnish the audience with background material. He also has the task of preparing the spectator for future developments. He does this by *foreshadowing*. He makes the subsequent action credible by supplying clues which he carefully inserts in early parts of the play. Everyone is familiar with the techniques of foreshadowing or "planting" employed by a mystery-story writer when he takes pains to drop such hints as that the butler is left-handed, that the revolver is hidden in the desk drawer, and that the chauffeur has an assumed name. The dramatist is likewise obliged to prepare for the audience's acceptance of the developments of the action by foreshadowing.

Foreshadowing has several purposes. It is used to make the events appear believable, it builds suspense, and creates tension. It may reveal character, it aids in the development of climaxes, crises, and complications. It may be used to build up an entrance, and it creates atmosphere. Within the first thirty lines of *Hamlet,* several references are made to the "dreaded sight" which has appeared twice before, as a means of preparing for the ghost's entrance, and providing the appropriate atmosphere. In *A Doll's House*, Nora's deception with the macaroons on her first appearance, prepares for the discovery of her larger deception in forging her father's signature. In *Hedda Gabler*, the pistols are involved in the stage action on two occasions before Hedda uses one to commit suicide. The dramatist's use of foreshadowing indicates his awareness of the need for an organic structure to his plot so that no turn of events will seem extraneous or incredible. The playwright values suspense more than he does surprise, and while dramas may use the unexpected, good craftsmanship requires that the chain of events has been foreshadowed.

The following excerpt from the opening of O'Neill's one-act, *In the Zone*, is an interesting one for showing all four aspects of plot which we have discussed thus far. The scene provides exposition about the characters and environment, it foreshadows future developments by raising a question about the meaning of Smitty's mysterious actions, and Davis' discovery of Smitty serves as the point of attack—the equilibrium is disturbed.

SCENE: The seamen's forecastle. On the right above the bunks three or four portholes covered with black cloth can be seen. On the floor near the doorway is a pail with a tin dipper. A lantern in the middle of the floor, turned down very low, throws a dim light around the place. Five men, Scotty, Ivan, Swanson, Smitty and Paul, are in their bunks apparently asleep. It is about ten minutes of twelve on a night in the fall of the year 1915.

Smitty turns slowly in his bunk and, leaning out over the side, looks from one to another of the men as if to assure himself that they are asleep. Then he climbs carefully out of his bunk and stands in the middle of the forecastle fully dressed, but in his stocking feet, glancing around him suspiciously. Reassured, he leans down and cautiously pulls out a suit-case from under the bunks in front of him.

Just at this moment Davis appears in the doorway, carrying a large steaming coffee-pot in his hand. He stops short when he sees Smitty. A puzzled expression comes over his face, followed by one of suspicion, and he retreats farther back in the alleyway, where he can watch Smitty without being seen.

All of the latter's movement indicates a fear of discovery. He takes out a small bunch of keys and unlocks the suit-case, making a slight noise as he does so. Scotty wakes up and peers at him over the side of the bunk. Smitty opens the suit-case and takes out a small black tin box, carefully places this under his mattress, shoves the suit-case back under the bunk, climbs into his bunk again, closes his eyes and begins to snore loudly.[1]

E. Complication

The point of attack is the first *complication*. A complication is any new force introduced into a play which affects the direction of the course of action. Once the playwright has selected his characters, determined his theme, and planned the beginning and end of the play, he constructs the plot through a series of complications. Kenneth Macgowan considers the complications so important that he says they are "the life-blood of ninety-nine and ninety-ninth hundredths per cent of a play."

Let us consider for a moment the analogy of a three-stage rocket. It is prepared for launching, its course is charted, and the destination determined. The mechanism is fired, and the rocket is projected into space, but the initial impetus is insufficient to keep it moving; additional thrusts are needed from second- and third-stage firings to send the rocket soaring on its trajectory. In a similar way, the dramatist decides on his objective, and sets his course of action. He precipitates the initial motion by means of a complication (the point of attack), but the plot,

[1] From *In the Zone*, by Eugene O'Neill. Copyright ©, 1923, 1940, by Random House, Inc. Reprinted by permission of the publishers.

like the rocket, needs additional force to keep the tension moving forward and upward. Additional complications, like the rocket's secondary and tertiary firings, accelerate and increase the action until the play reaches its highest point. The thrust of a play has a cumulative and climactic pattern from the introduction of the first complication to the major crisis when the fate of the protagonist is settled. Complications are utilized by the playwright in order to create a "straining forward of interest," to use George Pierce Baker's apt phrase. Their purpose is to intensify the emotions, arouse suspense, provide the building blocks of the play's structure and illustrate and determine what happens to the characters.

Romeo falls in love with Juliet, but the situation is complicated by the enmity between the two families. This hostility is aggravated when Romeo slays Tybalt, causing a new complication—the banishment of Romeo. Another complication is raised when Juliet's father insists that she marry Paris immediately. In order to avoid this development, a plan is devised for Juliet to feign death through the use of a magic potion. But the letter to Romeo disclosing the plan is not delivered, further complicating the action. Romeo learns of Juliet's apparent death, goes to her, and takes poison. Juliet awakens to find her lover dead—another complication. She joins him in death. Shakespeare, like most playwrights, began with a character trying to reach an objective, but complications intervene requiring a continuous readjustment of forces as the play gathers momentum and intensity. It is through complications that the playwright constructs his plot.

F. Climax

The *climax* is the culmination of a course of action, "the maximum disturbance of the equilibrium," "the moment of the most intense strain," "the crisis of maximum emotion and tension." Freytag sees the structure of the play as an isosceles triangle with five steps: (1) introduction, (2) rise, (3) climax, (4) return or fall, and (5) catastrophe. While drama does not generally conform to such a balanced and arbitrary pattern, Freytag was right in representing the climax as the apex of the triangle—as the highest point of the structure.

Actually, a play is a series of climaxes, with moments of stability and adjustment in between. The action surges forward and upward in mounting tension through minor climaxes until the major climax is reached when the emotional impact of the play reaches its strongest point. The structure, in this respect, may resemble a boxing match between two opponents of similar strength and skill. In each round, there may be moments of climactic action with first one fighter gaining the advantage and then the other. In between the peaks of action, there are relatively quiet moments and rest periods between the rounds. In the frantic last round, the major climax is reached when one boxer succeeds in knocking the other one out.

Dramatic climaxes are the result of an arrangement of a series of actions and events of increasing tension, as, for example, the climaxes of Ibsen's *A Doll's House:*

Krogstad threatens to reveal Nora's secret.

Nora pleads unsuccessfully with Helmer to retain Krogstad.

Krogstad writes his damning letter to Helmer.

Nora dances the tarantella to keep Helmer from reading the letter.

Helmer reads the letter and berates Nora.

Krogstad's second letter saves Helmer's reputation.

Nora tells Helmer of her decision to leave him.

Each of the climaxes is organically related to the central action, providing a unified effect and cumulative intensification of emotion.

G. Crisis

Although the terms *crisis* and climax are sometimes used interchangeably because they may occur at the same time, we shall consider a crisis to mean a time of decision, a turning point, a crossroads. After an accident (which may be a climax), a patient hovers between life and death. He is at a moment of crisis. A batter steps to the plate with the score tied and the bases loaded. The count reaches three balls and two strikes. The game is at a point of crisis. (It is probably at the climax too.)

A crisis involves a clash of interests. The protagonist is faced with alternatives which will determine his fate. Hamlet, sword in hand, must decide whether or not to slay the praying Claudius; Juliet must decide whether or not to take the sleeping potion; Nora must decide whether or not to leave her husband.

Sometimes a character makes his own decisions; sometimes they are thrust upon him. A crisis may lead to good fortune or catastrophe, depending upon the nature of the play and the author's intent. Plays are usually made up of a series of crises growing out of a series of complications. The major crisis toward the end of the play determines the ultimate outcome of the action.

A dramatist creates loaded situations dramatizing his characters caught in critical moments of their careers. For a while, the outcome is in doubt. The protagonist teeters on the brink of success or failure. A decisive action occurs which settles the fate of the hero. The moments of decision are the crises.

H. Denouement

The *denouement* is the end of the play, the solution to the problems which have been raised. Nora walks out the door, Hedda commits suicide, Oedipus goes into exile, Romeo and Juliet are united in death, Oswald loses his mind, Blanche du Bois is taken to the sanitarium, Willie Loman wrecks his car and takes his life. The denouement is the unravelling of the knot which the complications have formed. It indicates the ultimate disposition of the protagonist. The denouement constitutes the part of the play from the major crisis to the final curtain.

The function of the denouement is to restore order, to unify and complete the course of action, and to provide an ending that seems necessary and probable as the result of the antecedent development.

The denouement of the play is a fairly good indication of the skill and integrity of the dramatist. The inept playwright may find his characters in an inextricable situation and resort to an implausible suicide, or some other violent action with the mistaken notion that these acts in themselves are "dramatic," rather than that their legitimate use must be the credible result of the characters themselves and their previous actions. Another kind of faulty ending occurs when the playwright uses an outside force to intervene and unsnarl the entanglements. The hero is incapable of working out his own salvation, so he must be rescued by the Marines, the Coast Guard, the Air Force, the king, or a miracle from on high. Still another weak denouement occurs when the playwright suddenly changes directions for the sake of shock or surprise, which is contrary to his characters, or violates the preceding action. Another questionable, though sometimes amusing, denouement is the indeterminate ending in which the characters and the audience are left in doubt as to the outcome. Pirandello in *Right You Are If You Think You Are* makes an acceptable use of this device, but ordinarily the spectator likes to have the major questions answered before he goes home.

The denouement of comedy usually shows the protagonist successful in overcoming obstacles to reach the land of his heart's desire; the denouement of tragedy often shows disaster. The denouements of both comedy and tragedy frequently involve a complete reversal of the hero's status.

THE UNITIES

Most dramatists have sought some means of creating unity in their plays—by character, thought or mood—some way of providing a central focus. Aristotle suggested unity in an interlocking arrangement of the incidents with "a beginning, middle, and end." During the Renaissance, scholars insisted on imposing on the dramatist the alleged "classical" unities of time, place, and action. Actually, Aristotle mentions only time and action. Moreover, he does not set down rules for dramatic composition, but rather his observations record the practices of the Greek playwrights of the preceding century. Aeschylus, Sophocles, and Euripides did not write according to rules, but constructed their plays to meet the conventions of the theater and their own imaginations. They did not regard drama as a fixed and unchangeable form, but created their plays and the methods of presentation to suit themselves. The notion that playwrights must observe rules or conform to the unities has had very little acceptance in the theater except for the neoclassic drama, especially in France in the seventeenth century. In general, playwrights have written for popular approval rather than for academic acceptance.

I. *Unity of Time*

Aristotle wrote that, "Tragedy endeavors, as far as possible to confine itself to a single revolution of the sun, or but slightly to exceed this limit." The Italian scholars of the Renaissance misapplied this *unity of time,* warping it to mean a maximum of twelve hours, but preferably only as long as the action of the play itself. The Greek playwrights usually were close to Aristotle's observation, although there are several instances of plays which require a longer span of time. Greek dramatists were not concerned with strict adherence to chronology. Their interest was centered on the characters and the ideas rather than on the amount of elapsed time which the plot covered. Dramatists in other periods of theater history have felt free to use all of the time that they needed, but as a natural concomitant of the compact nature of drama, the playwright has tended to restrict his action to a relatively short space of time.

J. *Unity of Place*

Aristotle said nothing about *unity of place,* although it was customary for Greek tragic writers to use a single, or at the most two locales. Perhaps the continual presence of the chorus influenced this practice. Perhaps the fact that drama originated in a performance in a single locale set a precedent. Perhaps the outdoor performances in the daylight without the means of making rapid shifts of scenery conditioned the playwriting. But more likely, the nature of the structure of the play centering on a few characters shown in the climactic and critical stages of their careers required no change of scenic background. The Italians of the Renaissance attempted to restrict the action of a play to a single building, or at the most to a single city.

Playwrights throughout theater history have, for the most part, ignored the Renaissance scholars' dictum regarding place, moving around freely in space as their plots required, and as the physical equipment or conventions of the theater permitted. While there are numerous plays that require freedom to move from place to place, the general tendency of the dramatist is to concentrate his action in order to keep his focus clear.

K. Unity of Action

Unity of action means that the drama deals with a single course of events, involving little or no extraneous material, no mixture of comic and serious matter. Aristotle said that the plot should be simple enough so that it might be held easily in the mind of the spectator. The most important ingredient in the concept of unity is that all parts of the play should be organically related. Again quoting from Aristotle: "The structural unity of the parts is such that, if any one of them is displaced or removed, the whole will be disjointed and disturbed. For a thing whose presence or absence makes no visible difference is not an organic part of the whole." It was the practice of the Greek writers of tragedy to create simple, well-articulated plots.

The history of drama reveals that playwrights often have ignored the unity of action as Aristotle defined it, particularly in Elizabethan England where the physical theater with its unlocalized platform permitted the use of complicated stories and actions, and where the medieval tradition of mixing comedy with serious drama was an accepted practice. The Kabuki drama of Japan likewise moves around freely in time and space and makes use of complicated plots ranging from elaborately stylized battle scenes, employing the full use of the revolving stage and the flower walk, to long static scenes of domestic life in which two characters sit and talk at length over their tea or saki. But even in "panoramic drama" dramatists have been conscious of the need to find some means of unifying the effect. Marlowe achieved a kind of unity of character by focusing all of the action on a central figure. Others have sought a unity of idea by selecting only those characters and incidents which are germane to the development and projection of their theme. Still others, ignoring structural unity, have achieved a unity of atmosphere. In any case, most dramatists have been cognizant of the need for finding some means of suggesting a singleness of purpose or effect in order to clarify and organize their creative efforts.

2. CHARACTER

In placing character as his second element, Aristotle started an endless argument. Many critics and playwrights insist that character is the most important element of drama. The controversy is rather a fruitless one since there are valid arguments on both sides, but more importantly, the point needs to be made that they are not mutually exclusive. Good drama requires both good plot and good characterization; for in the last analysis Elwood is right when he says that "plot is character in action." Plot is the result of what people are. The sequence of events is rooted in the characters' wills, desires, and objectives which are revealed in effective drama by skillful selection and organization.

The nature of the dramatic method and the conditions and conventions of the physical theater have exerted important influences on characterization. Unlike the novelist who can demonstrate character by a wide range of incidents over a span of many years and under many conditions, and who has the ability to describe the character at length, and to indicate the secret thoughts coursing through his head, the playwright must select a few key incidents occurring in a short space of time and in a few locales, and he must reveal character by speech and behavior. The dramatist has no means of commenting directly on character. As a result, the characters in plays must be simplified, their qualities made clear in a few telling scenes. Because of the compression of the medium, characterization in drama often becomes one-dimensional, especially in farce, and melodrama, and in the minor roles of most plays.

As in all other aspects of drama, characterization has been exposed to a variety of fashions. In Greek, Elizabethan, and Japanese drama, the roles of women were played by men. Medieval drama often made use of allegorical figures representing single attributes of character such as Wisdom, Greed, and Gluttony. Contemporary dramatists of realistic and naturalistic persuasion, have endeavored to create the illusion of complicated character by piling up a wealth of physical details, by capitalizing on the significant trifle, and by searching for the psychological meaning beneath the act. High tragedy has dealt primarily with "men as better than they are," and low comedy with men "as worse than they are." Medieval characters ranged from God to the Devil, from purest saint to most abject sinner. Some characters have been drawn on an heroic scale, masters of their fate, working out their destinies by dint of their own resources; other characters have been treated as hapless victims of an unfortunate heredity and environment, incapable of taking action—defeated, frustrated, and resigned. The expressionists have experimented with split personalities, or effacing from characters all aspects of individuality, reducing them to X or Mr. Zero. Dramatic literature is filled with a wide variety of portraits.

During the last quarter of the nineteenth century, under the impact of the scientific method and the new developments in psychology, the playwright became concerned with delineating characters with rich inner lives and complex motivations. Ibsen, Strindberg, and Chekhov were particularly successful in creating figures with the stamp of life upon them. Ibsen's labors in this direction are indicated by his account of his method of working with character:

When I am writing I must be alone; if I have eight characters of a drama to do with I have society enough; they keep me busy; I must learn to know them. And this process of making their acquaintance is slow and painful. I make, as a rule, three casts of my dramas, which differ considerably from each other. I mean in characteristics, not in the course of treatment. When I first settle down to work out my material, I feel as if I have to get to know my characters on a railway journey; the first acquaintance is struck up, and we have chatted about this and that. When I write it down again, I already see everything much more clearly, and I know the people as if I had stayed with them for a month at a watering place. I have grasped the leading points of their characters and their little peculiarities.

Dramatists in the twentieth century have continued to strive for the creation of solid characters whose motivations conform to the findings of contemporary psychology, with the result that many of our plays give the effect of case studies. Our modern writer is also interested in the interaction of characters so that his plays exploit the tensions and turbulence which results from the impact of one upon the other.

While he is restricted in scope, the playwright's very use of selection and heightening gives clarity and directness to his figures. The fact that the dramatist is confined to a very few events places great weight on them, bringing his characters into sharp focus because all of their behavior is significant on stage. There is not the diffuseness of real life nor the looseness of many novels.

Character may be delineated in four ways. First, character is delineated by appearance. The actor's physical qualities give an immediate stimulus to the audience. Many modern playwrights have a very specific image in mind, describing the character's appearance in considerable detail. For example, Luigi Pirandello in *Six Characters in Search of an Author* describes the Father:

. . . a man of about 50: hair, reddish in color, thin at the temples; he is not bald, however; thick moustaches, falling over his still fresh mouth, which often opens in an empty and uncertain smile. He is fattish, pale; with an especially wide forehead. He has blue, oval-shaped eyes, very clear and piercing. Wears light trousers and a dark jacket. He is alternately mellifluous and violent in his manner.

The playwright frequently builds a character's entrance in order to place special attention on his initial appearance. Notice the care O'Neill has taken with the first entrance of his major character in *Anna Christie:*

There is a ring of the family entrance bell. (Larry [the bartender] comes to the door and opens it a trifle—then with a puzzled expression, pulls it wide. Anna Christopherson enters. She is a tall, blond, fully-developed girl of twenty, handsome after a large, Viking-daughter fashion but now run down in health and plainly showing all the outward evidences of belonging to the world's oldest profession. Her youthful face is already hard and cynical beneath its layers of make-up. Her clothes are the tawdry finery of peasant stock turned prostitute. She comes and sinks wearily in a chair by the table, left front.)

ANNA: Gimme a whiskey—ginger ale on the side. (*Then, as Larry turns to go, forcing a winning smile at him*) And don't be stingy, baby.[2]

Second, character is revealed by speech. The kind of language employed by the person, his manner of speaking, his voice quality, his inflection pattern, pitch, rate, and general vitality, all say something about him. The dramatist takes great care to write dialogue that makes an immediate impression about the characters. After two acts of argument over the true nature of Tartuffe, Molière brings him on stage with these lines:

> TARTUFFE: (*speaking to his valet, off the stage, as*
> *soon as he sees Dorine is there*)
> Lawrence, put up my haircloth shirt and scourge,
> And pray that Heaven may shed its light upon you.
> If any come to see me, say I'm gone
> To share my alms among the prisoners.

Up until the appearance of realism and naturalism in the late nineteenth century, the dramatist has been able to use asides and soliloquies to reveal his characters' private thoughts to the audience, but contemporary playwrights rarely employ these devices because they destroy the illusion of reality. However, some playwrights use them occasionally, and they also make use of long speeches of reminiscence as a means of conveying antecedent information or a character's state of mind so that

[2] From *Anna Christie*, by Eugene O'Neill. Copyright ©, 1922, by Random House, Inc. Reprinted by permission of the publishers.

their present condition will be understood by the audience. Many of the speeches in Chekhov's plays fulfill these functions. His characters often speak to themselves, out of context with the other characters or situations, so that the dialogue is a series of disconnected monologues. At times, playwrights give their characters long passages which virtually become arias as they express their thoughts and emotions. Conspicuous examples are found in the plays of Jean-Paul Sartre, Eugène Ionesco, Samuel Beckett, Maxim Gorki, Ugo Betti, Tennessee Williams and in almost all expressionistic plays. Whatever the form or function of the dialogue, the playwright ordinarily makes an effort to use his speeches to depict characters.

Third, character is established by action. Sometimes the playwright delineates his characters by their initial actions. For example, Ferenc Molnár in *Liliom* opens his play with a prologue in which he shows his protagonist in a characteristic action working as a barker in an amusement park:

Liliom stands at the entrance, a cigarette in his mouth, coaxing the people in. The girls regard him with idolizing glances and screech with pleasure as he playfully pushes them through the entrance. Now and then some escort resents the familiarity, whereupon Liliom's demeanor becomes ugly and menacing, and the cowed escort slinks through the entrance behind his girl or contents himself with a muttered resentful comment.

A character's external actions gives us clues to his inner motivations. His role in the root-action of the play is revealed by the final culmination of the plot, but the small detailed business of characterization helps the audience to build up a composite portrait. Sometimes, the playwright may create a misleading or ambiguous impression of a character at the beginning of the play and then gradually reveal the truth as the play progresses. In the opening scene we quoted from Ibsen's *A Doll's House*, Nora's initial appearance and actions suggest a doll-like character, but this first impression is changed by Nora's subsequent course of action. In John Osborne's *Look Back in Anger*, the audience is perplexed and even alienated by the protagonist's sadistic behavior, but as they come to know his cause for suffering, they reach an understanding of his conduct. Action is a fundamental technique for depicting character.

Fourth, character may be revealed by what others say about him, and the way in which they react to him. Sometimes the playwright uses comment about an absent character as a method of revealing the truth about him. For example, the true character behind the blustering, swaggering barker, Liliom, is indicated in Julie's line: "It is possible, dear, that some one may beat you, and beat you, and beat you—and not hurt you at all."

Willie Loman in *Death of a Salesman,* is a man who never saw himself or his motivations accurately. The truth about Willie is expressed by his son when Biff says, "He had the wrong dreams. All, all wrong . . . the man didn't know who he was."

The playwright may deliberately mislead or perplex the spectator by having characters say ambiguous or controversial things. Molière begins *Tartuffe* with a domestic quarrel in which he exposes two entirely different points of view about his leading character. Pirandello delighted in making the point time and again in his plays that it is difficult, if not impossible, to really comprehend the character of another. Hence, his plays are filled with conflicting statements about the characters in his plays. In some cases, it is the writer's purpose to leave the audience in a state of confusion. However, the more usual practice of the dramatist is to reveal the genuine nature and background of character through the speech of another.

The sharpness of a character's image is in part dependent upon the structure of the drama. Plays written for a theater which permitted most of the essential action to appear on stage, gave the playwright a greater opportunity to create a more vivid, complex character than those plays which were confined to a minimum of action. For example, one reason that Hamlet is such a rich and interesting character is because we see him through the eyes of so many other characters—Hamlet and the Ghost, Hamlet and Horatio, Hamlet and Ophelia, Hamlet and Gertrude, Hamlet and Polonius, etc. When we contrast this variety of character exposure to that of Agamemnon or Orestes or Antigone, we realize how limited the Greeks were in delineating complex characterization. Some playwrights, notably Shakespeare, possessed the ability to sketch memorable characters in a very few lines, but most dramatists have felt the need of developing their roles at length in order to achieve distinct impression.

The credibility of character is enhanced by the presence of the actor. The personal attributes of the performer add a dimension to the play which is difficult to describe and often impossible to predict in advance. In the hands of some actors, villains have become heroic, heroines insipid, comic characters dull, and minor roles have run away with the play. It is a commonplace of the theater that flat, pedestrian material has, on occasion, been made by the actor to seem rich and captivating stuff; that talented performers have taken superficially contrived parts and infused them with the warmth and glow of scintillating life. The playwright's conception of character is at the mercy of the actor. It is to the latter's credit that he very often extends and enlarges the original sketch into a fully rounded portrait.

3. THOUGHT

The third Aristotelian element, thought or *dianoia* refers to the reasoning aspect of drama. In his analysis of Aristotle's work, Bywater offers this definition of thought:

Dianoia in the sense it bears in the Poetics is, like *ethos* [character], an element in the personality of the dramatis personae. It is their intellectual capacity, as evinced in their language (or it may be in their actions), and it is to be seen whenever they argue or make an appeal to the feelings of their hearers; in other words when they reason or plead with one of the other dramatis personae in the same sort of way as a rhetor might do.[3]

Thought is more than the intellectual content, since a character's reasons for his behavior are bound up with his emotions. Plays are not objective debates, mere presentations of factual data and logical arguments leading to a clear decision. Characters in drama make subjective decisions under pressure, enmeshed in webs of conflicting emotional entanglements. In this respect, dramas are like the experiences of life with all of their complicating networks of feeling and meaning beyond the immediate moment. It is relatively easy to make a list of the arguments advanced by Nora and Helmer in *A Doll's House* leading up to her departure, but in order to grasp the significance of her decision, it was necessary for Ibsen to prepare for the scene with more than two acts of background material, thus placing the conflict between husband and wife in its appropriate emotional context. While dramatic characters often base their choices on emotion and impulse, there is usually a rational background for their actions. This constitutes the thought element of individual characters.

In presenting dramatic conflicts, the dramatist frequently presents both sides. The medieval playwright found it necessary to show the Devil as well as God, vices as well as virtues. Hence, in most plays, the dramatist presents a variety of thoughts. He shows and states the case for the antagonist as well as for the protagonist. Creon and Ismeme advance cogent arguments against Antigone, exposing the rationale for their points of view. Willie Loman's attitude toward life is contrasted with that of Biff and Charley, Marchbanks *versus* Morell, Blanche *versus* Stella and Stanley. The reasoning process, which includes the characters' motivations, constitutes one aspect of what Aristotle referred to as thought.

In addition to the rationale of individual characters, thought also concerns a play's theme—a kind of "golden text" which summarizes the moral

[3] Aristotle, *Poetics*, translated by Ingram Bywater.

and indicates the symbolic meaning of the play as a whole, such as "love conquers all," "murder will out," and "niceness pays." But drama does not always lend itself to such neat copybook maxims. A given play may convey a variety of interpretations to an audience. Most of Ibsen's contemporaries were profoundly shocked at Nora's decision to leave her husband and children, although her action is entirely credible to most of us today. Some people regard Antigone as headstrong and foolish in openly defying Creon, thus deliberately choosing to die. It is clear from Kazan's notes in directing A Streetcar Named Desire that he intended to express Williams' point of view that "if we don't watch out, the apes will take over." But in production, the impression conveyed to many spectators, as a result of the actors' performances, was that Blanche constituted a threat to the Kowalski home, and Stanley was justified in his brutal treatment of her. The ideas of great dramas have, of course, been sources of endless academic contention. What is the true interpretation of *Hamlet?* Is Shylock a comic or tragic figure? Is the tragedy of *Antigone* really that of Creon? From the varied interpretations of the meaning of the play, it is clear that the dramatist does not usually make an explicit statement of his theme, unless his purpose is didactic. The significance of the drama is subject to personal interpretations, and the individual reader and spectator is challenged to search his own mind in evaluating the action.

On the other hand it has been the express purpose of some dramatists to illustrate a theme. For example, the medieval drama, which was a sort of visual aid designed to frighten people into salvation, patently stated the point of the story. In the best known of all medieval plays, *The Moral Play of Everyman,* a Messenger prepares the audience to receive the moral in a prologue; at the end of the play a Doctor appears to re-emphasize it in these words:

> This moral men may have in mind;
> Ye hearers, take it of worth, old and young,
> And forsake Pride, for he deceiveth you in the end,
> And remember Beauty, Five-Wits, Strength and Discretion
> They all at the last do Everyman forsake,
> Save his Good-Deeds, there doth he take.
> But beware, and they be small
> Before God, he hath no help at all. (etc.)

One of the most important contributions of Ibsen, the father of modern drama, was his concern with dramatic themes which would provoke thought and discussion. His approach to the thought element of a play is clearly evident from the preliminary notes which he made when in

Rome while contemplating *A Doll's House*. These are Ibsen's "Notes for a Modern Tragedy":

There are two kinds of spiritual law, two kinds of conscience, one in man and another, altogether different, in woman. They do not understand each other; but in practical life the woman is judged by man's law, as though she were not a woman but a man.

The wife in the play ends by having no idea of what is right or wrong; natural feeling on the one hand and belief in authority on the other have bewildered her.

A woman cannot be herself in the society of the present day which is an exclusively masculine society, with laws framed by men and with a judicial system that judges feminine conduct from a masculine point of view.

She has committed forgery, and she is proud of it; for she did it out of love for her husband, to save his life. But this husband with his commonplace principles of honour is on the side of the law and regards the question with masculine eyes.

Spiritual conflicts. Oppressed and bewildered by the belief in authority, she loses faith in her moral right and ability to bring up her children. Bitterness. A mother in modern society, like certain insects who go away and die when she has done her duty in the propagation of the race. Here and there a womanly shaking-off of her thoughts. Sudden return of anxiety and terror. She must bear it all alone. The catastrophe approaches, inexorably, inevitably. Despair, conflict and destruction.

Although Ibsen in describing his method of working on a play acknowledges that he began with a clearly stated theme, he took considerable pains to present his thought by implication, indirection and innuendo, rather than by direct statement. As a consequence the spectator is not overly conscious of Ibsen's themes. Unlike the medieval writers, Ibsen did not point to a clear-cut solution to the problems which he raised. His purpose was to provoke thought rather than to persuade the audience to adopt a specific plan of action. Following Ibsen's example, many modern playwrights have found their source material in contemporary problems. The content of the plays of our day is often a direct reflection of contemporary thought as the playwright weighs the values and motives by which men live, seeks for individual fulfillment, or searches for reality.

All playwrights in representing men in action, dramatize their significant behavior and decisions, thus providing insight into the ways that men live and move and have their being. In tragedy, the dramatist is concerned with the profoundest problems and the most elevated concepts of mankind, involving the relation of his characters to their gods, the meaning of justice, and a probing into good and evil. In comedy, the playwright may exploit the ridiculous aspects of human conduct. In some forms of drama, notably farce and melodrama, the dramatist may have little or no interest in the secondary meaning of the actions of his characters. The personages of his plays are concerned only with the action itself, not with the meaning of their actions. In creating this kind of drama, the playwright has little reference to actuality, except to require the external appearance of real life. He freely manipulates his characters according to the exigencies of his plot, excusing his essential dishonesty of thought and motivation on the grounds that he is concerned only with theatrical values.

Whatever the purpose of the playwright, the action of significant drama is as meaningful as an experience of life itself. The choices which the characters make, their behavior and motivation, and the sequence of the events of the play are all rewarding subjects for investigation. The attitude of the playwright is inferred from his treatment of plot and character. He may be humane and sensible like Shakespeare and Molière; he may write with the scathing satire of Ben Jonson, the detachment of Congreve, the compassion of Chekhov and Hauptmann, the zeal of Eugène Brieux and the early Clifford Odets, the incisive and perplexing probing of Pirandello, the bleak pessimism of Sartre and Beckett, or the comic audacity of Shaw. A play, then, is more than a passing diversion unrelated to life. It is, rather, a significant revelation of the human condition.

4. DICTION

Aristotle's fourth element is diction, by which is meant the language of the play, the words which the actors speak.

The function of the diction is to provide a means for communicating the thoughts of the characters, and ultimately to convey the playwright's total meaning to the audience. As John Howard Lawson says, "Speech puts the actual impact of events into words: it dramatizes forces which are not seen." In modern drama, the dramatist has a utilitarian basis for his dialogue. His lines must, as someone has suggested, "Advance the plot, delineate character, or get a laugh." Good dialogue is a means to an end, not an end in itself, for the real merit of the drama does not reside so much in wording as in its solid structure, in the sequence of the plot, in the integrity and vividness of the characterization, and in the meaning of the action behind the façade of language.

Discourse in drama must be clear since the language must be immediately apprehended by the listener; in the theater, there is no turning back the page, no pause to weigh and consider a line before continuing to the next. The dialogue must be interesting despite the need for simplicity and economy. It should capture the spirit of life and character. As the Irish

playwright, Synge, put it: "In a good play, every speech should be as
fully flavored as a nut or an apple." The diction must be appropriate for
the character and the situation. Lines do not exist in the theater as
separate entities. They are always in context. They grow out of the emotionally charged incidents of the plot. The language of drama must be
dynamic. As we have already suggested, speech is a form of action. The
dialogue shows the character's relationship to others, reflects the progression of the action, indicates what is happening inside the characters,
reveals their suffering, growth or decline. It is a means of articulating the
clash of wills and the conflicting motivations. In high comedy, agile dialogue may be a substitute for the physical movement with characters
shooting barbed verbal shafts at one another.

The dramatist needs the poet's feeling for language—a rich imagination,
a facility for provocative imagery, an awareness of the weight, texture
and arrangement of words. Dramatic dialogue is not contemplative or
static; it is harnessed to action and change. Even in Nōh dramas, which
are often plays of reminiscence, the dialogue pulses with the life of the
remembered event and its appropriate emotional accompaniment. Finally,
good dialogue must be suited for oral expression. The lines must give the
actor a basic pattern for performance. They must reveal fully the character's emotions and motivations as the actor interprets them before the
audience.

Much of the serious drama preceding the nineteenth century was
linked to poetry. The Greek and Elizabethan masters of drama were
poets as well as playwrights. Their works, therefore, have an added
literary and linguistic dimension, and their use of verse seems particularly appropriate for their elevated tragedies of high-born characters. In
modern times, however, poetry has given way to prose when the naturalist and realist bring on stage contemporary, commonplace figures in the
everyday pursuits of life. Many have lamented the absence of poetry in
the contemporary theater; sporadic attempts have been made to recapture some of the enrichment of the poetic speech, notably in the works
of Maxwell Anderson, Christopher Fry, Bertolt Brecht, T. S. Eliot, and
Frederico García Lorca. While it is true that in general, modern drama
lacks elevated language, it would be a mistake to think that all plays
written in the poetic form were successful. Indeed, the use of verse in
the past was often puerile and ostentatious. Many poets had no sense
of dramatic form or theatrical awareness. Oftentimes, their preoccupation with the language retarded the action, filled their plays with linguistic
clutter, thus making the drama unstageworthy.

The general use of prose in the contemporary theater has resulted in
stage speech that has a tendency to become flat and pedestrian, filled
with the clichés of commonplace conversation. On the other hand, the

current emphasis on functional speech has gained in directness and clarity. In the hands of some modern playwrights, the dialogue is often vivid and evocative. The Irish drama is especially filled with the juice of life. Here is a typical fragment from Sean O'Casey's *Plough and the Stars:*

(FLUTHER *coughs.* MRS. GOGAN, *who has wandered from the chest of drawers, down L., to the fireplace, where she is fingering Peter's shirt, turns to look at* FLUTHER, *as soon as she hears the cough.*)

MRS. GOGAN: (*with an ominous note in her voice*) Oh, you've got a cold on you, Fluther.

FLUTHER: (*carelessly*) Oh, it's only a little one.

MRS. GOGAN: You'd want to be careful, all th' same. I knew a woman, a big lump of a woman, red-faced an' round-bodied, a little awkard on her feet; you'd think, to look at her, she could put out her two arms an' lift a two-storied house on th' top of her head; got a ticklin' in her throat, an' a little cough, an' th' next mornin' she had a little catchin' in her chest, an' they had just time to wet her lips with a little rum, an' off she went. (*She begins to look at and handle the shirt*)

FLUTHER: (*a little nervously*) It's only a little cold I have; there's nothing derogatory wrong with me.

MRS. GOGAN: (*warningly*) I dunno; there's many a man this minute lowerin' a pint, thinkin' of a woman, or pickin' out a winner, or doin' work as you're doin', while th' hearse dhrawn be th' horses with the black plumes is dhrivin' up to his own hall door, an' a voice that he doesn't hear is muttherin' in his ear, "Earth to earth, an' ashes t' ashes, an' dust to dust."

FLUTHER: (*faintly, affected by her talk*) A man in th' pink o' health should have a holy horror of allowin' thoughts o' death to be festherin' in his mind, for (*with a frightened cough*) be God, I think I'm afther gettin' a little catch in me chest that time—it's a creepy thing to be thinkin' about. (FLUTHER *sits weakly in chair L. of table*)

MRS. GOGAN: It is, an' it isn't; it's both bad an' good . . . It always gives me-self a kind o' thresspassin' joy to feel meself movin' along in a mournin' coach, an' me thinkin' that, maybe, th' next funeral'll be me own, an' glad, in a quiet way, that this is somebody's else's.

FLUTHER: (*very frightened*) An' a curious kind of a gaspin' for breath—I hope there's nothin' derogatory wrong with me.

MRS. GOGAN: (*examining the shirt*) Frills on it, like a woman's petticoat.

FLUTHER: (*panic-stricken*) Suddenly gettin' hot, an' then, just as suddenly, gettin' cold.

MRS. GOGAN: (*holding out the shirt towards* FLUTHER) How would you like to be wearin' this Lord Mayor's nightdress, Fluther?

FLUTHER: (*vehemently*) Blast you an' your nightshirt! Is a man fermentin' with fear to stick th' showin' off to him of a thing that looks like a shinin' shroud? [4]

[4] Sean O'Casey, *The Plough and the Stars* (New York, The Macmillan Co., 1926).

As George Bernard Shaw points out, the modern drama has gained in what he calls the "discussion" element of drama. Modern playwrights have tended to center their attention on dramatic experiences in which characters analyze and describe the forces at work on them. They do not simply pass through a series of adventures without cerebration. They talk over the issues, and expose points of view, thus adding substance to contemporary dialogue. Nora and Helmer thrash out their differences; Mrs. Alving, Manders, and Oswald articulate their attitudes; even in Chekhov, where characters often are frustrated or crushed by the forces about them, they speak their minds and discuss the circumstances which have affected their lives. Shaw, of course, was especially fond of ventilating controversial issues and his plays are full of shafts and barbs about all manner of problems.

Over the years dramatists have utilized a variety of dialogue devices. One of the most interesting which the Greeks devised is called *stichomythia,* which means lines of alternating dialogue usually of short length. The Greek dramatist employed stichomythia as a method of building tension much as a motion picture editor uses rapid intercutting of film clips to increase intensity in exciting moments of a picture.

Molière, in the seventeenth-century French theater used comic stichomythia breaking lines of dialogue into short bursts of speech by interruptions. You will find an example of this in the scene between Toinette and Argan, *La Malade Imaginaire,* pages 112-113. Stichomythia as a formal technique is not used in the modern theater, although its accelerated tempo and sharp rhythm are frequently employed.

A favorite linguistic device which Shakespeare often made use of was the soliloquy, a solo speech generally of introspective analysis or for examining and weighing a future course of action. "To be, or not to be" is, of course, the most familiar example. Playwrights, aware of the rich psychological life beneath the surface, hit upon the convention of the soliloquy as a means of revealing the workings of the mind. The neo-classicists in France often replaced this device by the use of confidants for each of the leading characters so that private thoughts could be bounced off the ears of servants, friends, and duennas to the audience. In popular melodrama, the soliloquy often was used as an expository device to reveal information directly to the audience as well as to delineate character.

The use of extended narration for recounting off-stage or antecedent action has been used from the Greeks to the present day. Effective examples are the Second Messenger's description of the death of Jocasta in *Oedipus Rex,* the Nurse's account of the burning of the magic gown in *Medea,* the sergeant's report of Macbeth's victory in battle, and Rodrigue's sixty-five line unabashed description of his valor in repulsing the

Turks in *The Cid*. Although lengthy speeches were more widely used in dramas of the past, they are still employed occasionally in contemporary drama, as for example, Blanche's extended speech in which she relates the death of her sixteen-year-old lover in *A Streetcar Named Desire* and the brutally vivid account of one of the addicts in *The Connection*, in which a single character holds the stage by himself for at least twenty minutes.

In recent times, the expressionists have revived the use of the soliloquy primarily as a means of revealing character and character relationships. In Elmer Rice's *The Adding Machine*, both Mr. and Mrs. Zero speak soliloquies of several pages in length. An ingenious adaptation of this device is used in Beckett's one-act, *Krapp's Last Tape*, in which a single character contrasts his old-age with his life some thirty years ago by listening to and commenting on a tape recording of his own voice. O'Neill and Andreyev, two twentieth-century playwrights, have used what amounts to soliloquies and asides in experimental plays to reveal a character's inner thoughts in contrast to those spoken aloud. But in general, the soliloquy and the aside are rejected as inappropriate for realistic drama.

A number of new playwrights have appeared recently who refuse to conform to the established techniques and conventions of the theater. These so-called "absurdists" are of special interest in their rejection of dramatic structure and use of dialogue. Beckett, Ionesco, and Harold Pinter, in particular, have written stage speech, which while intentionally pedestrian and hackneyed, nevertheless, is remarkably evocative. Their use of clichés in short segments of sound combined with frequent pauses is strangely expressive in performance. At times this kind of dialogue has been used to satirize the vacuity of commonplace conversation. At other times the very flatness of the language has served as a kind of desperate cover to conceal the fear of silence.

Other dialogue devices have been used from time to time in the theater such as choral speeches, antiphonal passages between a leader and a group, staccato, telegraphic fragments of speech in expressionistic plays, extensive monologues, prologues, and epilogues for exposition, foreshadowing or commenting on the action, bits of poetry and involved conceits and epigrams. But the primary form of diction in most drama is compressed dialogue, which despite its conventions, gives to the listener the impression of natural conversation.

5. MUSIC

Aristotle's fifth element is music which refers to all of the auditory material of a play, including sound effects and the tonal pattern of the spoken word. Music encompasses all aspects of sound—pitch, rate, quality, duration, volume, and rhythm. We remember that Greek drama had its origin in dithyrambs, and that music, chanting, and dancing were integral parts of the performance. The speech of the Athenian playwrights was created in rich patterns of verse in which the sound, texture, and cadence of the language were significant aspects. In the Oriental theater, music continues to play an essential part in the total effect. The language of the Elizabethans often was rich in lyricism that broke out into song. Melodrama was originally linked to music, and even though the spoken word came to dominate the genre, musical backgrounds were used to accompany exits and entrances of major characters and to reinforce the mood of emotionally-loaded scenes.

In our contemporary drama, naturalism and realism have rejected music as being an artificial intrusion, although the motion picture has always exploited the evocative power of music to heighten its effects. Even in realistic drama, occasional playwrights have made telling use of sound to enhance the mood of their plays. For example, Chekhov was very conscious of the use of sounds in *Uncle Vanya*. In the final act of the play, a melancholy atmosphere is reinforced by the click of the counting beads, the scratch of the pen, the churring of a cricket, the tapping of the night watchman's cane, the soft strumming of a guitar, and the bells of the carriage as Dr. Astrov makes his departure. Other modern dramatists with a keen ear for the expressiveness of sound are Eugene O'Neill, Tennessee Williams, Maurice Maeterlinck, Lorca, and O'Casey. The nonrealistic playwrights, particularly the expressionists, have freely introduced music into their plays.

The spoken word of all kinds of drama is allied to music in its appeal to the ear, and all successful playwrights have been mindful of the importance of rhythm and sound.

6. SPECTACLE

The sixth Aristotelian element of drama, spectacle, refers to all of the visual aspects of production—scenery, lighting, costume, make-up, and the business and movement of the actors. A glance at the openings of *A Doll's House* on page 32 and *In the Zone* on page 37 indicates the visual quality of drama. In the chapter on the Stage Designer, we will discuss at some length the nature and function of scenery, and in the chapters on forms and styles of drama, we will consider the particular contribution of spectacle to different types of plays.

The kind and amount of spectacle have varied throughout theatrical history. In the Greek, Elizabethan, and Japanese Nōh plays, virtually no representation of locale is required except that supplied by the architecture itself. Nonetheless, these plays are rich in spectacle, particularly in the use of striking costumes and in the action of the performers. The Greek chorus, the use of dance in Nōh and Kabuki drama, and the vivid use of the entire ensemble in panoramic movement in Elizabethan plays, enhanced the visual appeal of the performances. With the development of the Renaissance proscenium-arch theater, a taste was cultivated for pictorialism in the theater in which elaborate use was made of enormous and complicated settings. The realistic and naturalistic movements in the late nineteenth century gave spectacle a new importance in production because of the scientifically inspired concern with environment as a conditioning force in determining behavior. Hence spectacle came to assume an organic, psychological role in the theater, reinforcing the meaning of the play and serving as an expository device to relate character to the social milieu. This view of the function of spectacle is the current one, although there has been a tendency to temper the fashion for complete and factual representation of actuality by increasing simplicity and theatricalism.

While at times spectacle has dominated the stage, dwarfing or competing with the actor for the audience's attention, our current attitude is that the legitimate function of the visual aspects of theatrical production is to provide the appropriate psychological and physical environment for the drama, to create atmosphere, and to serve the actor's needs as he performs the play. Inasmuch as a play is intended to be acted, the action and the environment of that action contribute heavily to the impact of the play in the theater. This is spectacle.

The opening scene from *Hamlet* which follows, illustrates the work of a master playwright in full command of his materials. Notice the application of the elements which we have been discussing. There is skillful use of exposition as Shakespeare establishes the atmosphere of the scene and the relationship of the characters. He adroitly integrates the immediate situation with antecedent material in such a way as to carry the action forward.

HAMLET

Act I

SCENE I—*Elsinore. A platform before the castle.*
(FRANCISCO *at his post. Enter to him* BERNARDO.)

BERNARDO: Who's there?

FRANCISCO: Nay, answer me: stand, and unfold yourself.

BERNARDO: Long live the king!

FRANCISCO: Bernardo?

BERNARDO: He.

FRANCISCO: You come most carefully upon your hour.

BERNARDO: 'Tis now struck twelve; get thee to bed, Francisco.

FRANCISCO: For this relief much thanks: 'tis bitter cold, (1)
   And I am sick at heart. (2)

BERNARDO: Have you had quiet guard?

FRANCISCO: Not a mouse stirring.

BERNARDO: Well, good night.
   If you do meet Horatio and Marcellus,
   The rivals of my watch, bid them make haste. (3)

FRANCISCO: I think I hear them. Stand, ho! Who is there?
   (*Enter* HORATIO *and* MARCELLUS) (4)

HORATIO: Friends to this ground.

MARCELLUS: And liegemen to the Dane.

FRANCISCO: Give you good night.

MARCELLUS: O, farewell, honest soldier:
   Who hath relieved you?

FRANCISCO: Bernardo hath my place.
   Give you good night.
   (*Exit*)

MARCELLUS: Holla! Bernardo!

BERNARDO: Say,
   What, is Horatio there?

HORATIO: A piece of him.

BERNARDO: Welcome, Horatio; welcome, good Marcellus. (5)

MARCELLUS: What, has this thing appear'd again to-night? (6)

BERNARDO: I have seen nothing.

MARCELLUS: Horatio says 'tis but our fantasy,
   And will not let belief take hold of him
   Touching this dreaded sight, twice seen of us:
   Therefore I have entreated him along
   With us to watch the minutes of this night,
   That if again this apparition come,
   He may approve our eyes and speak to it. (7)

(1) Names and occupations of guards given and the time established.
(2) Question is raised by Francisco's feeling "sick at heart."

(3) Prepares for the entrance of Horatio and Marcellus.

(4) Entrance and identification of Horatio and Marcellus.

(5) Friendly character relationship indicated.
(6) Introduces the reason for the visit. Has "this thing" appeared again?

(7) Horatio's skepticism is established about the "dreaded sight" which
     guards have seen twice. Builds suspense and raises the question—will
     the ghost appear?

HORATIO: Tush, tush, 'twill not appear. (8)

BERNARDO: Sit down a while;
　And let us once again assail your ears,
　That are so fortified against our story,
　What we have two nights seen.

HORATIO: Well, sit we down,
　And let us hear Bernardo speak of this.

BERNARDO: Last night of all,
　When yond same star that's westward from the pole
　Had made his course to illume that part of heaven
　Where now it burns, Marcellus and myself,
　The bell then beating one,— (9)

　　(*Enter* GHOST) (10)

MARCELLUS: Peace, break thee off; look, where it comes again!

BERNARDO: In the same figure, like the king that's dead.

MARCELLUS: Thou art a scholar; speak to it, Horatio.

BERNARDO: Looks it not like the king? mark it, Horatio.

HORATIO: Most like it: it harrows me with fear and wonder. (11)

BERNARDO: It would be spoke to.

MARCELLUS: Question it, Horatio.

HORATIO: What art thou, that usurp'st this time of night,
　Together with that fair and warlike form
　In which the majesty of buried Denmark
　Did sometimes march? by heaven I charge thee, speak!

MARCELLUS: It is offended.

BERNARDO: See, it stalks away.

HORATIO: Stay! speak, speak! I charge thee, speak! (12)

　　(*Exit* GHOST) (13)

MARCELLUS: 'Tis gone, and will not answer.

BERNARDO: How now, Horatio! you tremble and look pale:
　Is not this something more than fantasy?
　What think you on't?

HORATIO: Before my God, I might not this believe
　Without the sensible and true avouch
　Of mine own eyes.

MARCELLUS: Is it not like the king?

HORATIO: As thou art to thyself:
　Such was the very armor he had on
　When he the ambitious Norway combated;
　So frown'd he once, when, in an angry parle,
　He smote the sledded Polacks on the ice. (14)
　'Tis strange.

MARCELLUS: Thus twice before, and jump at this dead hour,
　With martial stalk hath he gone by our watch. (15)

HORATIO: In what particular thought to work I know not;
　But, in the gross and scope of my opinion,

(8) Horatio, the scholar, voices his skepticism.

(9) Bernardo describes previous encounters. Prepares for ghost's entrance.

(10) Ghost's entrance destroys Horatio's skepticism and raises the questions—Who is the ghost? Why does it appear? First complication and point of attack.

(11) Discovery. The ghost is recognized as King Hamlet. Establishes credibility of the ghost and makes the question more specific and compelling—what is the meaning of the ghost reappearing? "Fear and wonder" emotional response.

(12) Ghost acts as if it would speak. Unsuccessful attempts to question it add suspense.

(13) Exit of ghost delays answer. Strengthens question—why does the ghost of the dead king reappear? What does it want to say?

(14) Recognition reasserted. Emotions aroused; suspense and atmosphere established.

(15) Repetition of antecedent experiences adds to anxiety.

MARCELLUS: Good now, sit down, and tell me, he that knows,
  Why this same strict and most observant watch
  So nightly toils the subject of the land,
  And why such daily cast of brazen cannon,
  And foreign mart for implements of war;
  Why such impress of shipwrights, whose sore task
  Does not divide the Sunday from the week;
  This bodes some strange eruption to our state. (16)
  What might be toward, that this sweaty haste
  Doth make the night joint-laborer with the day:
  Who is't that can inform me? (17)
HORATIO: That can I;
  At least the whisper goes so. Our last king,
  Whose image even but now appear'd to us,
  Was, as you know, by Fortinbras of Norway,
  Thereto prick'd on by a most emulate pride,
  Dared to the combat; in which our valiant Hamlet—
  For so this side of our known world esteem'd him—
  Did slay this Fortinbras; who by a seal'd compact
  Well ratified by law and heraldry,
  Did forfeit, with his life, all those his lands
  Which he stood seized of, to the conqueror:
  Against the which, a moiety competent
  Was gaged by our king; which had return'd
  To the inheritance of Fortinbras,
  Had he been vanquisher; as, by the same covenant
  And carriage of the article design'd,
  His fell to Hamlet. Now, sir, young Fortinbras,
  Of unimproved metal hot and full,
  Hath in the skirts of Norway here and there
  Shark'd up a list of lawless resolutes,
  For food and diet, to some enterprise
  That hath a stomach in't: which is no other—
  As it doth well appear unto our state—
  But to recover of us, by strong hand
  And terms compulsatory, those foresaid lands
  So by his father lost: and this, I take it,
  Is the main motive of our preparations,
  The source of this our watch and the chief head
  Of this post-haste and romage in the land. (18)
BERNARDO: I think it be no other but e'en so:
  Well may it sort, that this portentous figure
  Comes armed through our watch, so like the king
  That was and is the question of these wars. (19)
HORATIO: A mote it is to trouble the mind's eye.
  In the most high and palmy state of Rome,
  A little ere the mightiest Julius fell,

(16) Apprehension expressed for the state.

(17) Marcellus asks the meaning of the preparations for war. Are they related to the appearance of the ghost of Hamlet?

(18) Horatio provides exposition, sketching the political background. Provides the frame of reference of the social situation. Notice that Shakespeare first captures the attention, builds atmosphere and suspense, and then provides this lengthy explanation.

(19) Search for meaning of the ghost's appearance as an armed figure.

The graves stood tenantless, and the sheeted dead
Did squeak and gibber in the Roman streets:
As stars with trains of fire and dews of blood,
Disasters in the sun; and the moist star,
Upon whose influence Neptune's empire stands,
Was sick almost to doomsday with eclipse:
And even the like precurse of fierce events,
As harbingers preceding still the fates
And prologue to the omen coming on,
Have heaven and earth together demonstrated
Unto our climatures and countrymen. (20)
   (*Re-enter* GHOST) (21)
But soft, behold! lo, where it comes again!
I'll cross it, though it blast me. Stay, illusion!
If thou hast any sound, or use of voice,
Speak to me:
If there be any good thing to be done,
That may to thee do ease and grace to me,
Speak to me:
If thou art privy to thy country's fate,
Which, happily, foreknowing may avoid,
O, speak!
Or if thou hast uphoarded in thy life
Extorted treasure in the womb of earth,
For which, they say, you spirits oft walk in death,
Speak of it: stay, and speak! (22) (*The cock crows*) (23)
Stop it, Marcellus.
MARCELLUS: Shall I strike at it with my partisan?
HORATIO: Do, if it will not stand.
BERNARDO: 'Tis here!
HORATIO: 'Tis here!
   (*Exit* GHOST) (24)
MARCELLUS: 'Tis gone!
We do it wrong, being so majestical,
To offer it the show of violence;
For it is, as the air, invulnerable,
And our vain blows malicious mockery. (25)
BERNARDO: It was about to speak, when the cock crew.
HORATIO: And then it started like a guilty thing
Upon a fearful summons. I have heard,
The cock, that is the trumpet to the morn,
Doth with his lofty and shrill-sounding throat
Awake the god of day, and at his warning,
Whether in sea or fire, in earth or air,
The extravagant and erring spirit hies
To his confine: and of the truth herein
This present object made probation.

(20) Atmosphere of foreboding is reinforced by vivid imagery.
(21) Second appearance of ghost strengthens question and builds suspense
further. Will it speak? Notice that this entrance follows a static sequence
and thrusts the action forward again.

(22) Scene rises to a climax and crisis as Horatio repeatedly asks the ghost
to speak.
(23) Cock crows deferring the ghost's answers to questions.

(24) Ghost's exit adds further emphasis to suspense and purpose of the ghost.
Carries tension forward when the meaning is still in doubt.

(25) Awe and wonder at the "majestical" ghost.

MARCELLUS: It faded on the crowing of the cock.
Some say that ever 'gainst that season comes
Wherein our Saviour's birth is celebrated,
The bird of dawning singeth all night long:
And then, they say, no spirit dare stir abroad,
The nights are wholesome, then no planets strike,
No fairy takes nor witch hath power to charm,
So hallow'd and so gracious is the time.
HORATIO: So have I heard and do in part believe it.
But look, the morn, in russet mantle clad,
Walks o'er the dew of yon high eastward hill:
Break we our watch up; and by my advice,

Let us impart what we have seen to-night
Unto young Hamlet; for, upon my life,
This spirit, dumb to us, will speak to him:
Do you consent we shall acquaint him with it,
As needful in our loves, fitting our duty? (26)
MARCELLUS: Let's do't, I pray; and I this morning know
Where we shall find him most conveniently.
(*Exeunt*) (27)

(26) Guards and Horatio search for meaning. Daylight comes. They plan for future action. Will the ghost speak to Hamlet?

(27) Their exit carries the suspense and questions forward into the play. Builds up tension and anticipation for the meeting between Hamlet and his father's ghost.

Hamlet Confronts His Father's Ghost. Stage set by Donald Oenslager; Leslie Howard as Hamlet, 1936

Questions and Exercises

1. What is plot?
2. Define and give examples of the various aspects of plot.
3. By what methods does a playwright delineate character?
4. How do the so-called "classical unities" affect dramatic structure?
5. What are the special characteristics of dramatic dialogue?
6. What is meant by "thought" in a play?
7. How is spectacle important in a modern play?
8. Study a short play. Divide it into separate episodes and describe the function of each episode in the structure of the play.

Suggested Reading

BENTLEY, Eric, *The Playwright as a Thinker* (New York, Reynal and Co., 1953).

BUTCHER, S. H., *Aristotle's Theory of Poetry and Fine Art* (New York, The Macmillan Co., 1907).

HEFFNER, Hubert C., SELDEN, Samuel, and SELLMAN, Hunton D., *Modern Theatre Practice*, 4th ed. (New York, Appleton-Century-Crofts, Inc., 1959).

LAWSON, John Howard, *Theory and Technique of Playwriting* (New York, G. P. Putnam's Sons, 1936).

MILLETT, Fred B., and BENTLEY, Gerald E., *The Art of the Drama* (New York, Appleton-Century-Crofts, Inc., 1935).

THOMPSON, Alan Reynolds, *The Anatomy of Drama* (Berkeley, University of California Press, 1942).

ROWE, Kenneth Thorpe, *The Theater in Your Head* (New York, Funk and Wagnalls Co., 1959).

4

Tragedy

TRAGEDY is a strange and mysterious country despite considerable efforts to fix its boundaries, blaze its trails, and establish its configurations. Each adventurer must find his own way through an entangling jungle of conjecture and a luxuriant undergrowth of verbiage surrounding a treacherous, semantic swamp. There is no short cut, no easy known way, because tragedy is a quality of experience which each man must come to know for himself.

The first to chart his course and mark the way was Aristotle, who in his fourth-century work, the *Poetics*, sought to guide those who followed him. Although he found his original directions by the genius of his dead-reckoning from relatively limited observation, we may still trace his progress with profit, so clearly did he designate his landmarks. As a consequence, we will refer rather frequently in this chapter to Aristotle's work. It should be remembered that the *Poetics* is a short analysis of the kind of tragedy which was created a century before Aristotle in Greece. His study is an investigation of drama which preceded him rather than an attempt to frame rules for writing tragedy, although scholars of the Renaissance were to misinterpret and misapply his views as those of a law-giver. Furthermore, it must be admitted that there is considerable ground for misinterpretation in Aristotle, partially because of his language, and partially because of the examples which he cites as evidence to support his conclusions. Aristotelian doctrine, therefore, should be regarded as a lamp in the darkness, not the source of all light.

Aristotle places considerable emphasis on the structure of tragedy. Excellence of form was a source of aesthetic pleasure to the Greeks in all kinds of art. They saw things as parts of a whole. They delighted in the organization of a unified structure. Thus, while the *Poetics* is an analysis

70

of tragedy, Aristotle's discussion frequently concerns all forms of dramatic writing. It is a commentary on play-making in general.

ARISTOTLE'S DEFINITION OF TRAGEDY

Let us turn our attention to Aristotle's very significant definition of tragedy and then examine his terms: "Tragedy, then, is an imitation of an action that is serious, complete, and of a certain magnitude; in language embellished with each kind of artistic ornament, the several kinds being found in separate parts of the play; in the form of action, not of narrative; through pity and fear effecting the proper purgation of these emotions."

The origin of the word *tragedy* is a matter of conjecture. "Tragos" in Greek means goat; "oide" means song. The exact connection of goat-song to drama is not clear, although three hypotheses are advanced: (1) a goat was sacrificed as part of the original improvised ritual honoring Dionysus; (2) the chorus wore goatskins for costumes; and (3) a goat was offered as a prize in the early choral contests. In any case, tragedy was associated with goat-song or goat-singer in its early stages. The terms "tragic" and "tragedy" as we use them in everyday speech have little to do with "tragedy" as a form of drama. A person may speak of the "tragic" death of a small girl in an automobile accident. While tragedy usually involves catastrophe, it is not the calamity itself upon which attention is focused in drama. Death may even seem incidental in *Hamlet* or *Romeo and Juliet* when it occurs to such secondary characters as Polonius or Paris or Tybalt. The validity of genuine tragedy is not concerned with the act of violence, but with what that act says about life—the struggle of the protagonist, the issues at stake, the effect of his suffering.

By *imitation* is meant a made thing, as contrasted with a natural one. An imitation is not a mere copy, however, but it is a created work of art, fashioned by man. Its relation to reality is that the course of events of the drama are "necessary and probable."

An Action refers to a sequence of incidents joined together into a unified whole. *An action* is the thing done; what Professor Gerald F. Else refers to as . . . "the living out of a decisive turn of events by a significant human being." Aristotle is insistent upon the importance of action:

Now the action is represented in the play by the Fable or Plot. The Fable, in our present sense of the term, is simply this, the combination of the incidents, or things done in the story. . . . Tragedy is essentially an imitation not of persons but of action and life, of happiness and misery. All human happiness or misery takes the form of action; the end for which we live is a certain kind of activity, not a quality. Character gives us qualities, but it is in our actions —what we do—that we are happy or the reverse. In a play accordingly they do not act in order to portray the Characters; they include the Characters for the sake of the action. So that it is the action in it, i.e., its Fable or Plot, that is the end and purpose of the tragedy; and the end is everywhere the chief thing. Besides this, a tragedy is impossible without action, but there may be one without Character.

Tragedy has been called the drama of *high seriousness*. It deals with the most profound and universal problems of man—his purpose and destiny, the nature of good and evil, a man's relationship to forces greater than himself, the consequences of individual responsibility. Tragedy is never frivolous, trivial, or mean. It goes far beyond diversion or amusement to investigate spiritual values and struggles.

Tragedy attains *magnitude* in the heroic stature of its characters, through the use of poetry, and by the universality of its meaning, and the loftiness of its ideas. Tragedies are elevated; they possess scale and scope far beyond the petty vicissitudes of daily existence. Magnitude of character is realized in tragedy through the use of high-born characters, persons of nobility and prominence who occupy "exposed positions"; people who as Aristotle said, "are better than we are."

A tragedy is *complete;* it has a beginning, a middle, and an end—and each of these parts is causally related, thus creating a unified effect because the plot is a well-articulated structure with no extraneous material. The course of action is a "necessary and probable" linking of antecedents and consequents. Such unity and wholeness are fundamental to the Greek aesthetic view of life.

By *language with each kind of artistic ornament,* Aristotle explains, "I mean that with rhythm and harmony or song superadded; and by *the kinds separately,* I mean that some portions are worked out with verse only, and others in turn with song."

The chief difference between the *dramatic* and *narrative form* is a result of the manner of presentation. A narrative may be written or told; drama must be presented with impersonation and action—it is "a thing done." The dramatic form puts the creative work of the playwright before an audience in the theater by means of the actors' performance.

Pity, fear, and *catharsis* are terms which have perplexed and intrigued scholars and critics for generations. Because tragedy aims to produce this special effect, it will be discussed at length later in the chapter. For a preliminary statement let us realize that *pity* goes beyond mere pathos to include the compassion that accompanies shared grief, and that *fear* transcends sheer fright to convey a sense of anxious concern and profound reverence. Catharsis suggests purgation and purification—a release of emotional tension that results in tranquillity.

With Aristotle's definition in mind, and acknowledging its shortcomings due to his limited basis for observation, let us consider some important principles which characterize tragedy.

PLOT

Aristotle lays great stress on plot—the "soul of tragedy." He discusses at length the essentials of dramatic structure such as the necessity for a unified and complete sequence of interlocking action, the just proportions of the plot, and the proper use of such devices as reversal, discovery, and recognition. So broad is his consideration of plot, that it may be applied to all forms of drama, rather than specifically to tragedy.

Are there aspects of plot which apply exclusively to tragedy? Certainly, Aristotle's concept of unity of action—a plot simple enough to be held easily in the mind of the spectator, does not apply to Elizabethan drama. Moreover, Shakespeare and his contemporaries disregarded unity in their combination of comic and serious material, their high- and low-born characters, their mixture of verse and prose, their plots and subplots that rambled about freely on the flexible Elizabethan stage. No, the structure of tragedy does not have its own special form. The plays of the Greeks, the Elizabethans, and the Neoclassicists are too divergent in structure to fix in one pattern.

There are certain generalizations, however, that apply to the treatment of dramatic materials. Tragedy usually deals with a positive and active protagonist caught in sharp conflict with opposing forces. In the ensuing struggle, he suffers greatly, and goes to disaster. Tragic conflicts are of a particular kind. The struggle does not involve such mundane considerations as economic or sociological problems. The struggle is ethical, spiritual. Oftentimes, the tragic hero is placed in a situation in which the courses of action open to him are at war with the moral order which he has accepted. Tragic tension is built on inner conflicts which test the protagonist's integrity.

In the organization of the incidents, the playwright must solve the customary problems of plot construction; he must create climaxes, crises, reversals, discoveries, etc., but always with a view as to what the events reveal about the hero. The interest is not in the incidents themselves, but what is going on inside—the effect on the protagonist's soul. When the dramatist reverses this point of view and makes the external action his primary concern, he writes melodrama. This is precisely what happened in English drama after Shakespeare, when Beaumont and Fletcher, Ford, Massinger, and Tourneur filled the stage with grisly and violent action. The writer of genuine tragedy constructs a plot that emphasizes "inwardness."

Because tragedy is relentlessly honest, the dramatist does not contrive a denouement to save the hero from catastrophe, or to spare him from suffering. Orestes is rescued from the Eumenides by divine intervention because Aeschylus was expressing his concern about institutionalized justice. Oedipus lives on after his crimes are revealed, but not as a concession to the sentimental satisfaction of the audience. Orestes and Oedipus both undergo excruciating suffering. When Corneille worked out a happy ending for the lovers in *Le Cid*, he made his play a tragicomedy instead of a tragedy. In most tragedy, the catastrophic denouement is the "necessary and probable" outcome of the conflict.

Scenes of discovery or recognition are very important to the tragic plot. Aristotle admired discoveries which resulted in reversals, as in *Oedipus Rex*. Writers of tragedy demonstrated great skill in devising effective discoveries such as Electra's recognition of Orestes, the ghost in *Hamlet*, Creon's discovery of Antigone's burial of Polyneices, and Sophocles' consummate craftsmanship in exposing Oedipus' guilt through a gradual revelation of the past. But far more important than these plotting devices are the scenes of self-discovery, when characters examine their actions and motives against the background of their moral codes. These "moments of truth" are singularly characteristic of great tragedy. One thinks of Phaedra's and Macbeth's horror when they realize the full import of their actions; of Hamlet's agonizing self-analysis when he tries to square appearance with reality; of Creon's and Othello's bitter suffering when their worlds tumble about them; of the self-torture of Oedipus when his crimes are known. Such discoveries contribute to the feelings of pity and fear, because they cause the audience to generalize from the individual experience of the tragic hero to a universal application. As the protagonist makes his discovery, we discover something of ourselves.

TRAGEDY IS RARE

It is apparent that the special characteristics of tragedy require rather special circumstances for its creation. Tragedy is rare. Professor Alan Thompson has gone so far as to suggest that genuine high tragedy can be restricted to some twenty-odd plays. While numerous attempts have been made to write tragedy at many different times, playwrights in general have failed to ascend the heights because of deficiency of talent, shortness of vision, or prevailing circumstances that stunted their spiritual growth.

What are the conditions conducive to tragedy? Both the Golden Age of Greece and Elizabethan England were stirring periods of great intellectual stimulation. The human spirit was exalted, mankind ennobled. The world was no vale of shadows, but an exciting place full of enormous possibilities. Life was not bland or filled with despair and frustration. Man was dignified, hopeful, secure in his faith in the future and in himself. He could extend himself in many directions. The spirit of such ages was congenial to tragedy because these cultures affirmed the worth and dignity of human life. The atmosphere conformed to the three basic assumptions which Oates and O'Neill set us as necessary for the creation of tragedy: "First, the dignity of man; second, the freedom of his will and his responsibility for the use which he makes of that will; and third, the existence in the universe of a super-human factor." [1] Similarly, Joseph Wood Krutch suggested two requisites for the writing of tragedy.[2] His two assumptions are, that the soul of man is great, and the universe is concerned about his welfare.

Such assumptions are positive expressions about life and its meaning. When the philosophical climate of an age rejects these points of view, tragedy of an elevated and affirmative nature is difficult to create.

In Restoration England, attempts were made to revive the tragic spirit in heroic drama. Otway and Dryden were partially successful in *Venice Preserved* and *All for Love* but the conditions of the age undermined the foundations of tragedy. There was too much emphasis on the external aspects of life; too little regard for spiritual values. It was an artificial age whose drama reflected its pretense. The efforts to write tragedy suffered from a lack of orientation to a moral order. The superhuman heroes were too much concerned with their physical prowess and too vulnerable to the "grand passion." Their efforts to express themselves resulted in bombast and overwrought emotion. Despite their noble sentimentalizing, the essential tone was insincere and unconvincing.

Corneille and Racine made laudable attempts to create tragedies in the classic tradition in the seventeenth century but Corneille was essentially a romanticist, and the classic form and atmosphere were too austere for his tastes and talent, although in *Le Cid*, he succeeded in writing a play of intense internal suffering. Racine, imbued with the Jansenist view that human nature was corrupt, was closer to the Greeks in both technique and point of view. In his *Phaedra*, a reworking of the Hippolytus story, he presented a protagonist in a series of powerful scenes which strip bare her guilty passion. His *Bérénice* is another serious play of conspicuous merit presenting three characters torn between love and duty, although this drama lacks the stature of *Phaedra* because it is primarily a story of unrequited love without ethical complications, except as they affect Titus, in his love *versus* duty dilemma.

In seventeenth-century English drama, the tragic spirit dissolves in a wave of sentimentalism. Fear and pity are replaced by pathos. Suffering

---

[1] Whitney J. Oates and Eugene O'Neill, Jr., eds., *The Complete Greek Drama* (New York, Random House, Inc., 1938).

[2] Joseph Wood Krutch, *"Modernism" in Modern Drama* (Ithaca, Cornell University Press, 1953).

is presented for the sake of suffering rather than for what it reveals about character. The common man emerges as the new hero, with the consequent loss of elevation and magnitude. George Lillo, in *The London Merchant,* dramatizes the crime of a weak clerk. Nicholas Rowe wrote "she tragedies" in which he stressed the pathetic suffering of hapless women. The spirit of tragedy was uncongenial to the new taste for thrills and tears in the theater.

Our modern temper with its doubts and skepticism about man and supernatural forces is considered by some inhospitable ground for the nurture of the tragic spirit. The political practice of raising the proletariat to a dominant position has changed our fashion in heroes from highborn and romantic characters to common, contemporary man. The materialism résulting from the Industrial Revolution has not only worked against individualism, but also has shifted our sense of values to a high regard for products and possessions. But most importantly, the impact of science has forced modern man to reorient his thinking, to question traditional Christian morality, to look with skepticism upon the dignity of man and see him rather as a part of the animal kingdom, "red in tooth and claw." The psychologist has caused us to look at human behavior as a conditioned reflex. He studies the mechanism of conduct and explains a man's choices and decisions on the basis of his emotions and drives.

The appropriate forms of expression which resulted from these changing attitudes were realism and naturalism, which we shall discuss in subsequent chapters. The effect on drama was to drive out poetry, emphasize the conditioning of behavior from the standpoint of heredity and environment, depict contemporary characters involved in social problems in which interrelationships were extremely important, and create a new significance for accurate representation of specific locale because of its influence on the action. It is obvious that these conditions were inhospitable to the creation of high tragedy. Eugene O'Neill is a case in point. Writing both in traditional and experimental styles, he sought with moral earnestness to achieve the stature of great drama, but his efforts fell short. There was no sense of spiritual triumph because O'Neill had no position to defend. He asked important questions, but he was at a loss for answers. Among our contemporary playwrights, Arthur Miller has been most ambitious to recapture the tragic spirit although dealing with the common man. Miller's concept of tragedy is expressed in these terms: "I think the tragic feeling is evoked in us when we are in the presence of a character who is ready to lay down his life, if need be, to secure one thing—his sense of personal dignity. From Orestes to Hamlet, Medea to Macbeth, the underlying struggle is that of the individual attempting to gain his 'rightful' position in society." While Miller's plays faithfully demonstrate his philosophy of tragedy, his emphasis on environmental conditioning and the force of social pressures narrows his vision so that his protagonists remain earthbound despite their great suffering. The existentialists have written seriously about the human condition, but they have been restricted because their protagonists are cut off from outside forces—even from their contemporaries. The lack of faith and the restricted range of spiritual exploration negates the elevation of tragedy. Now the "absurdists" have taken an even more extreme position by denying even themselves in their dramatizations of life that is futile, meaningless, and grotesque.

John Mason Brown describes the difficulties of writing modern tragedy, although he sees some hope:

A period of realism and an age of prose are not the only hindrances. The lost or dwindling religious faith of many people; the encroachments of such a materialistic and earthbound theology as Marxism; an increasing uncertainty as to accepted or acceptable standards; our living with the threat of mass annihilation; great changes in the stresses and basic concepts of our economic and social life; the emergence of the "little man" as the new hero for hero worship; the shrinkage of the individual's importance under the pressures of super-states or ever-growing bureaucracies; indeed, not only the notion but the realization that the century belongs to the common rather than the exceptional man—all these factors, widening or limiting, which have altered tragedy along with everything else. Because of them, one wonders if the tragic blueprint, cherished for so long as an ideal, has not, at least in part, become a glorious anachronism.

Not that tragedy is dead or will ever die. Or that Man has lost his touch with the heroic. No one who has watched men, women, and children rise to the terrible trials of these past years can maintain that Man has become mean. The bigness of the so-called "little man" in the face of such trials and of daily living is one of the most hopeful facts of recent history. It is simply that the heroic has become different in scale and kind, and for this very reason tragedy needs to be rediscovered for our own times and in our own terms.[3]

Whether or not great tragedy can be written today is a matter of controversy. Certainly, the temper of our times seems alien to the great traditions, although in the plays of Arthur Miller, Ugo Betti, and Paul Claudel we catch glimpses of an ancient grandeur, and in biography there is considerable evidence of man's spiritual capacity which raises him toward the heights.

TRAGEDY DEALS WITH SIGNIFICANT CONTENT

Tragedy achieves significance because it is concerned with the deep and abiding questions and problems which have perplexed man through-

[3] John Mason Brown, "American Tragedy," *Saturday Review*, August 6, 1949. Reprinted by permission of the publishers.

out the ages. As Nicoll says, tragedy puts us in ". . . contact with infinity. If we are religious, we shall say it is in contact with forces divine; if we are aesthetic, we shall say it is in contact with the vast illimitable forces of the universe. Everywhere in tragedy there is this sense of being raised to loftier heights." [4]

Henry Alonzo Myers asserts that "tragedy best expresses its conceptions of the orderly and absolute nature of values"; and Francis Fergusson observes that tragedy "celebrates the mystery of human nature and destiny with the health of the soul in view." Tragedy is oriented toward man's spiritual nature. It confronts suffering and evil with relentless honesty in such a way as to reveal both the weakness and nobility of man, his strength of will, and his capacity for suffering without breaking in the face of inevitable doom. Tragedy is not the drama of small souls bedeviled by the minor irritations of humdrum life. It does not concentrate on man's physical environment or welfare, nor with his getting and spending, his thing-collecting. On the contrary, tragedy lifts our vision beyond petty cares and mundane anxieties by forcing our attention on the great issues of life which bear a relationship to our spiritual welfare. Clytemnestra is caught between avenging the death of her daughter and her duty to her husband; Antigone between her sacred obligation to the dead, and obedience to the king; Hamlet between the necessity of avenging the death of his father, and his moral sensibilities; Lear between sympathy and pride; Macbeth between ambition and conscience. Tragedy deals with matters of great consequence.

The significant content of tragedy gives this form of drama a sense of universality. The effect of the play goes beyond the particular characters and the immediate circumstances to achieve an atmosphere of broad application. If even kings may suffer, how vulnerable are we? To the Greeks and Elizabethans the fate of the ruler was connected directly with that of his subjects. There is implicit in genuine tragedy not only an elevation of life, but also an acute awareness of our common frailty and humanity. Thus the suffering and struggles of the tragic hero become a part of the universal experience of those who share the play.

In attaining magnitude and elevation, however, it must be recognized that tragedy is removed a step from life. To perceive its great scope and grandeur, a certain amount of distance and perspective is required. In high tragedy there is a sense of aloofness and detachment, which in its most severe expression, threatens to throw a chill of austerity over the drama and the characters. On the other hand, the universality of the problems and the degree of suffering draw us in to the action.

[4] Allardyce Nicoll, *The Theory of Drama* (New York, Thomas Y. Crowell Co., 1931).

TRAGEDY IS POSITIVE

Although tragedy involves suffering, evil and death, it is a positive statement about life. As Nicoll says, "Death never really matters in tragedy. . . . Tragedy assumes that death is inevitable and that its time of coming is of no importance compared with what a man does before his death." [5]

Death may overtake the protagonist, but he is spiritually victorious. He is not an abject, craven victim of fate who goes cowering to his doom. The principles for which he lived and died survive his passing. The hero dies; heroism lives on. We admire the audacity of man who, disregarding human frailty, reveals an astonishing capacity for suffering in matters of the spirit. His action is an affirmation of life. He sustains our faith in mankind.

TRAGEDY IS HONEST

The writer of tragedy is unflinchingly honest. He shows life as it is, not as one wishes it might be. He has the courage to confront the terrors and perplexities of life; he acknowledges man's frailties. His plots are not manipulated to spare the protagonist; the hero goes relentlessly to his catastrophe. Nor does tragedy demonstrate poetic justice in which the virtuous are rewarded and the wicked punished. Instead, the dramatist shows the clash between our desire for justice and what really happens. He presents the evil along with the good. In the treatment of character, the protagonist is not the white-washed, idealized hero of romanticism nor the black-hearted villain of melodrama. He is a mixture of clay and star-dust. He is an admirable character, but he usually possesses a flaw, and his imperfection links him to us. Tragedy rests on a solid basis of integrity, making no concessions to the wish-fulfillment desires of the audience. In Anouilh's modern version of *Antigone* the chorus makes this cogent statement about tragedy:

THE CHORUS:

Tragedy is clean, it is firm, it is flawless. It has nothing to do with melodrama —with wicked villains, persecuted maidens, avengers, gleams of hope and eleventh-hour repentances. Death, in melodrama, is really horrible because it is never inevitable. The dear old father might so easily have been saved; the honest young man might so easily have brought in the police five minutes earlier. In a tragedy, nothing is in doubt and everyone's destiny is known. That makes for tranquility. Tragedy is restful; and the reason is that *hope*, that

[5] Nicoll, *ibid.*

foul, deceitful thing, has no part in it. There isn't any hope. You're trapped. The whole sky has fallen on you, and all you can do about it is to shout. Now don't mistake me: I said "shout": I did not say groan, whimper, complain. *That,* you cannot do. But you can *shout* aloud; you can get all those things said that you never thought you'd be able to say—or never knew you had it in you to say. And you don't say these things because it will do any good to say them: you know better than that. You say them for their own sake; you say them because you learn a lot from them. In melodrama, you argue and struggle in the hope of escape. That is vulgar; it's practical. But in tragedy, where there is no temptation to try to escape, argument is gratuitous: it's kingly.[6]

TRAGEDY PRODUCES A CATHARSIS

The most significant element which distinguishes tragedy from other forms of drama is the tragic effect. Just what it is in tragedy that gives pleasure through pain is difficult to determine. Schlegel felt that the tragic tone was one of "irrepressible melancholy" as the audience is consoled and elevated through witnessing human weakness, exposed to the vagaries of fate and natural forces. Schopenhauer saw the meaning of tragedy as resignation and renunciation in the face of a miserable and desolate existence. On the other hand, Myers sees evidence of a just order in tragedy:

Since it is positive and affirmative, great tragic poetry satisfies our deepest rational and moral inclinations. As rational beings, we are always looking for patterns, for order, for meaning, in experience; as moral beings, we can be satisfied only by discovering in the realm of good and evil the special kind of pattern or order which we call justice. Tragedy reconciles us to evil by showing us that it is not a single, separate phenomenon but one side of change of fortune, and makes us feel that the change of fortune of a representative man is just.[7]

From these opposing statements, it is clear that what constitutes the tragic effect is capable of many interpretations. The effect is complex and highly personalized which one arrives at through his own contacts with life. In such plays as *Hamlet* and *Oedipus Rex,* we perceive values beyond the story and stage action as we seek to interpret the play with our experience and with our attitudes about life. Thus, the events of the play are raised to a universal level and move us as Professor Thompson says, ". . . to the impassioned contemplation of ultimates."

In any discussion of the tragic effect it is necessary to keep Aristotle's words "fear and pity" before us. What did he mean by them? Pity is not

[6] Jean Anouilh, *Antigone,* translated by Lewis Galantière, 1946. Reprinted with permission of Dr. Jan van Loewen, London.

[7] Henry Alonzo Myers, *Tragedy: A View of Life* (Ithaca, Cornell University Press, 1956). Reprinted with permission of the publisher.

simply pathos, a soft sentiment of sorrow for one who is weak or un-
worthy. Pity is not contemptuous or patronizing. There is implied in
tragic pity an equality, a sharing of grief. We enter into the experience
of another through our sympathy and our fellow-feeling. We feel pity for
the tragic hero as an act of compassion.

The word fear must be extended beyond sheer fright or terror to include anxious concern, solicitude, awe, reverence, and apprehension. In
tragedy, fear is not merely a hair-raising, spine-tingling reaction of the
nervous system; it is an emotion that warms the heart and illuminates the
mind. Fear carries a sense of wonder. The terms fear and pity, therefore,
must be thought of with universalizing human implications involving a
general concern for others, rather than a private and personal identification with disaster.

What kinds of events produced "fear and pity"? Aristotle is quite explicit on this point:

The tragic pleasure is that of pity and fear, and the poet has to produce it
by a work of imitation; it is clear, therefore, that the causes should be included
in the incidents of his story. Let us see, then, what kinds of incidents strike
one as horrible, or rather as piteous. In a deed of this description the parties
must necessarily be either friends, or enemies, or indifferent to one another.
Now when an enemy does it on an enemy, there is nothing to move us to pity
either in his doing or in his meditating the deed, except so far as the actual
pain of the sufferer is concerned; and the same is true when the parties are
indifferent to one another. Whenever the tragic deed, however, is done or
meditated by brother on brother, by son on father, by mother on son, or son
on mother—these are the situations that the poet should seek after. . . . The
deed of horror may be done by the doer knowingly and consciously, as in
the old poets, and in Medea's murder of her children in Euripides. Or he may
do it, but in ignorance of his relationship, and discover that afterwards, as
does Oedipus in Sophocles. Here the deed is outside the play; but it may be
within it, like the act of the Alcmeon in Astydamas, or that of Telegonus in
Ulysses Wounded. A third possibility is for one meditating some deadly injury to another, in ignorance of his relationship, to make the discovery in time
to draw back. These exhaust the possibilities, since the deed must necessarily
be either done or not done, and either knowingly or unknowingly.

The worst situation is when the personage is with full knowledge on the
point of doing the deed, and leaves it undone. It is odious and also (through
the absence of suffering) untragic; hence it is that one is made to act thus
except in some few instances, e.g. Haemon and Creon in Antigone. Next after
this comes the actual perpetration of the deed meditated. A better situation
than that, however, is for the deed to be done in ignorance, and the relationship discovered afterwards, since there is nothing odious in it, and the discovery will serve to astound us. But the best of all is the last: what we have
in Cresphontes, for example, where Merope, on the point of slaying her son,

recognizes him in time; in *Iphigenia,* where sister and brother are in a like position; and in *Helle,* where the son recognizes his mother, when on the point of giving her up to her enemy.

These are the techniques for creating incidents which will arouse fear and pity. This emotional response to tragedy is a complex one. It must be broad enough to encompass a variety of experiences—extensive enough to include shades of feeling such as the heartbreak at the end of *King Lear, Phaedra, Romeo and Juliet* and *Oedipus Rex;* the sense of triumph at the end of *Hamlet, The Crucible* and *Antigone;* and the appalling sense of waste at the end of *Macbeth, Ghosts,* and *Othello.* Aristotle obviously intended that catharsis should be a therapeutic one. The tragic effect on the spectator is to purge away his fear and pity, which results in a sense of release and tranquillity. He is cleansed and exhilarated when he is liberated from his own emotional entanglements, his disturbing passions. Fear gives way to certainty, even though that certainty is death. Pity goes beyond feeling, and becomes understanding. The spectator leaves the theater "in calm of mind, all passion spent." The end result is, as Northrop Frye suggests, that the audience experiences a "kind of buoyancy." Or again, in Edith Hamilton's words, "the great soul in pain and death transforms and exalts pain and death." Myers universalizes the meaning more explicitly:

These are the main features of the tragic spirit. It lifts us above self-pity and reconciles us to suffering by showing that evil is a necessary part of the intelligible and just order of our experience. It lifts us above the divisive spirit of melodrama by showing that men are neither naturally good nor inherently evil. It saves us all from the pitfalls of utopianism and fatalism. It teaches moderation by showing that the way of the extremist is short, but at the same time it shows the man of principle that an uncompromising stand is not without its just compensations. And most important, it teaches us that all men are united in the kinship of a common fate, that all are destined to suffer and enjoy, each according to his capacity.[8]

THE TRAGIC HERO

Another Aristotelian concept of fundamental importance to the understanding of tragedy is the nature of the tragic hero. In his analysis of suitable figures to play the heroic role, Aristotle rejects three kinds of men before arriving at his definition:

It follows, therefore, that there are three forms of Plot to be avoided. (1) A good man must not be seen passing from happiness to misery, or (2) a bad

8 Myers, *ibid.*

man from misery to happiness. The first situation is not fear-inspiring or piteous, but simply odious to us. The second is the most untragic that can be; it has no one of the requisites of Tragedy; it does not appeal either to the human feeling in us, or to our pity, or to our fears. Nor, on the other hand, should (3) an extremely bad man be seen falling from happiness into misery. Such a story may arouse the human feeling in us, but it will not move us either to pity or fear; pity is occasioned by undeserved misfortune, and fear by that of one like ourselves; so that there will be nothing either piteous or fear-inspiring in the situation. There remains, then, the intermediate kind of personage, a man not pre-eminently virtuous and just, whose misfortune, however, is brought upon him not by vice and depravity but by some error of judgment.

The tragic hero is a good man, but not free from blemish—"an intermediate kind of personage" who while not pre-eminently virtuous, is not depraved. His flaw is an error in judgment. This flaw (*hamartia*), has been the source of considerable controversy since it is not uniformly applicable to all tragedies, nor does the flaw appear consistent with the variety of characters involved in catastrophes. How does one equate the suffering of Prometheus with that of Oedipus? Antigone with that of Medea? Hamlet with that of Macbeth? The degree of guilt seems to have little or nothing to do with justice. All tragic figures suffer greatly. Frequently, their fall seems to proceed not so much from crime and punishment as it does from cause and effect. They suffer because they occupy positions of responsibility.

The tragic hero is a man of good intentions whose catastrophe may be the result of a flaw, not of guilt. He may fall because he errs, as well as sins. He often elicits our pity because of his "undeserved misfortune." In this connection, we think of the protagonists who suffer beyond all desert —Julius Caesar, Antigone, Electra, Oedipus, Othello, and Lear. Tragedy does not exist to demonstrate justice. On the contrary, it may serve to remind us of the hard fact that much of life is replete with injustice. It is a mistake, therefore, to look to tragedy for a neat apportionment of reward and punishment. Some Greek tragedies deal with protagonists whose judgment is flawed by the pressure of their emotions which causes them to lose their sense of balance and proportion. The Greek view of the good life was based on a sense of completeness and upon moderation, in which the passions were controlled and tempered by reason. The tragic flaw is in the loss of the hero's sense of perspective. Caught in a web of circumstances, he becomes an extremist; he loses sight of the golden mean, he fails to keep his balance on a high place and falls to his catastrophe.

Aristotle's view of the tragic hero and of his flaw must not be regarded as an inflexible and all-inclusive definition. It takes considerable stretching and straining to make his concepts fit the few extant Greek tragedies, not to mention the problems of the Elizabethans. Hence, it will be wise to regard Aristotle as a frame of reference for discussing tragic heroes and their qualities, rather than as a rigid measure by which plays may or may not be included in the tragic canon.

The tragic hero is a man of significance, who in representing universal human qualities, represents us. He is an active agent rather than a passive, submissive victim of accident or fate. He struggles and suffers mightily, and in his travail affirms the greatness of the human spirit.

Questions and Exercises

1. In what ways is tragedy elevated?
2. What is ·Aristotle's concept of the tragic hero?
3. Explain universality in tragedy.
4. What are the difficulties of writing a modern tragedy?
5. Evaluate the conditions which Krutch and Oates and O'Neill set up as essential for the creation of tragedy.
6. How is tragedy a spiritual affirmation of life?
7. What do you understand by Aristotle's term, catharsis?
8. How is tragedy related to good and evil?
9. What is the tragic writer's view of suffering and catastrophe?

Plays to Read

AESCHYLUS: *The Choephori*
SOPHOCLES: *Antigone, Oedipus Rex*
EURIPIDES: *Hippolytus*
SHAKESPEARE: *Hamlet, Othello, Macbeth*
MARLOWE: *Dr. Faustus*
RACINE: *Phaedra*
IBSEN, Henrik: *Ghosts*
MILLER, Arthur: *The Crucible, Death of a Salesman*
SYNGE, J. M.: *Riders to the Sea*
MACLEISH, Archibald: *J.B.*

Suggested Reading

ANDERSON, Maxwell, *The Essence of Tragedy and Other Footnotes and Papers* (Washington, D.C., Anderson House, 1937).

ELSE, Gerald Frank, *Aristotle's Poetics: The Argument* (Cambridge, Harvard University Press, 1957).

HAMILTON, Edith, *The Greek Way* (New York, W. W. Norton & Co., Inc., 1937).

KRUTCH, Joseph Wood, *"Modernism" in Modern Drama* (Ithaca, Cornell University Press, 1953).

LEVIN, Richard, *Tragedy: Plays, Theory and Criticism* (New York, Harcourt, Brace & World, Inc., 1960).

LUCAS, F. C., *Tragedy: Serious Drama in Relation to Aristotle's Poetics,* rev. ed. (New York, The Macmillan Co., 1958).

MYERS, Henry Alonzo, *Tragedy: A View of Life* (Ithaca, New York, Cornell University Press, 1956).

STUART, Donald Clive, *The Development of Dramatic Art* (New York, D. Appleton and Co., 1928).

5

Melodrama

IN THE PREVIOUS CHAPTER we considered tragedy, the loftiest and rarest form of drama. We come now to a form nearly antithetical to tragedy, because the dramatists of these two types have held two entirely different points of view. Tragedy examines values; melodrama exploits action. Tragedy confronts good and evil with unblinking honesty; melodrama escapes from life. Tragedy considers the eternal spiritual problems; melodrama deals with the transitory, the material, the physical. Tragedy evokes fear and pity; melodrama arouses suspense, pathos, terror, and sometimes, hate. However, melodrama is not mere ineffectual tragedy. As a mater of fact, a well-written melodrama may be superior to an inept tragedy. The point is that the two forms of drama are different. They are similar only in that they both *seem* serious. Like tragedy, melodrama may involve suffering and painful aspects of life—death and dishonor. But in melodrama the seriousness is a pretense because the writer is concerned only with theatrical values. Outwardly, melodrama appears to show real people in genuine jeopardy, but melodrama rigs the consequences of actuality in manipulating the plot toward escape, reprieve, or rescue, and culminates in a happy ending.

For the past two centuries, many dramatists have written for the middle-class audience which increasingly has captured the theater from the aristocracy. This new audience did not care much about tragedy or literate drama. Catering to their taste, playwrights created works of strong action and sentiment. Their plays were sometimes called tragicomedy, domestic or "bourgeoise tragedy," "tearful comedy," melodrama and *drame*. We will arbitrarily employ the last two terms in this chapter, attempting to distinguish between them, and noting their special qualities.

It is a common fallacy to associate melodrama exclusively with such nineteenth-century plays as *East Lynne, Under the Gaslight,* and *Ten Nights in a Bar Room.* While it is true that such thrillers flourished up until the end of the century, it is also true that melodrama remains today, along with farce, our most popular form of theatrical entertainment. The outward appearances of melodrama have changed throughout the years but the basic appeals which brought your great, great grandparents to the theater, are the same in kind as those which appear tonight on your television and motion picture screens.

The term melodrama combines two Greek words meaning music and drama. At one time the word was literally synonymous with opera. Melodrama was first allied with music in Italy and France. In Germany, it referred to dialogue passages spoken to orchestral accompaniment. The modern connotation of the word, however, stems from the late eighteenth-century French theater and its subsequent development, especially in England and America. Up until 1791, the Comédie Française and the Italian Comedians enjoyed monopolistic control over the legitimate theaters of Paris. Ingenious managers circumvented governmental restrictions by contriving a kind of entertainment based on pantomime accompanied by dance, song, and dialogue which elicited a popular following due to its sensational qualities. When freedom of production was granted to all theaters, the word *melodrame* was attached to the pantomime with dialogue and music. The French playwright, René Pixerécourt, achieved such great success with his melodrames because of their exciting action, that he was referred to as the "Napoleon of the Boulevard." When Thomas Holcroft adapted Pixerécourt's *A Tale of Mystery* for the English stage in 1802, the genre and the term crossed the channel. In 1804, melodrama was introduced into America in Turnbull's *Riddap; or, The Robbers of Calabria.*

Melodramatic scenes and situations were, of course, known in drama from almost the beginning of the theater. Euripides teetered precariously on the edge of melodrama in several of his plays, and Seneca fell over the brink and wallowed in sensational and horrible material. The Elizabethan "tragedies of blood" employed much of the machinery of melodrama with scenes of horror and violence. Jacobean playwrights delighted in grisly scenes of exciting action. The early eighteenth-century "she-tragedies" of Nicholas Rowe, with their sentimentalism and overwrought emotions, were in the melodramatic vein. Schiller's *The Robbers* capitalized on the fugitive situation so dear to the heart of writers of melodrama. August Kotzebue, the late eighteenth-century German playwright, enjoyed an enormous popularity and commercial success in his plays which possessed much of the flavor of melodrama, notably in *The Stranger* and *The Spaniards in Peru.* In the first half of the nineteenth

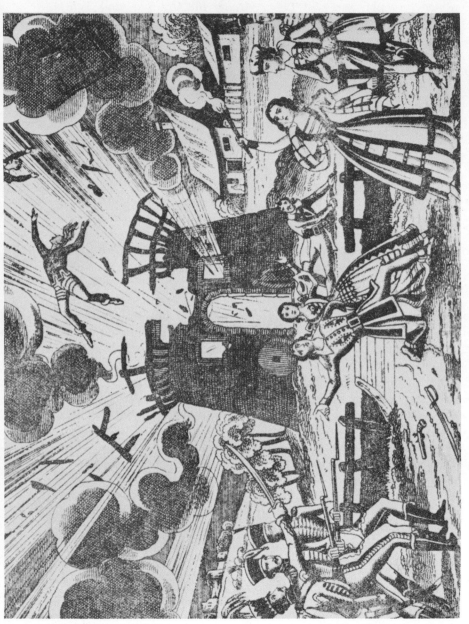

Print of a scene from an Early Nineteenth-century Melodrama, Pocock's *The Miller and His Men*

century in France, Eugène Scribe turned out superficial, but "well-made" contrivances which were skillfully constructed and theatrically exciting. In England, the way had been prepared for melodrama by the gothic novels of Mrs. Radcliffe and "Monk" Lewis. In 1829, Douglas Jerrold made a phenomenal hit in London with his *Black-Eyed Susan* which set the pattern that was endlessly copied depicting the machinations of the villain against a long-suffering heroine and a manly hero rescued at the last moment by a reprieve.

At first melodrama owed its popularity to its story appeal. Its pattern was a series of strong actions performed by clear-cut characters demonstrating the triumph of simple virtues and the ultimate defeat of villainy. Credibility was sometimes given the characters because they were performed with skill by actors who added to the original bare outline the force of their own personality. To satisfy the tremendous demand for new material, hack playwrights ground out new plays like our present television writers, and like their modern counterparts, most writers followed well-established formulae.

As the nineteenth century progressed, efforts were made to create more realistic melodramas. The easiest way to accomplish this was through the external aspects of production—especially in the stage scenery. Toward the end of the century, the theater technician ran away with the show. New and spectacular effects became a prime source of audience appeal. The stage mechanic was called upon to represent on stage not only accurate replicas of familiar landscapes, buildings, and monuments, but also he labored to reproduce all manner of sensational effects. Melodrama tended to become simply a scenario for exciting action. As a result of its elaboration of the visual aspects of production and its demand for strong stories and movement, nineteenth-century melodrama brought about its own destruction and played directly into the hands of the development of the motion-picture industry.

APPEAL OF MELODRAMA

We began Chapter 1 by saying that man extends himself in a variety of ways. Melodrama has been one of his favorite forms of extension. In Tennessee Williams' *The Glass Menagerie,* Amanda berates her son Tom, for attending too many movies, to which he replies:

Tom:

I go to the movies because I like adventure.
Adventure is something I don't have much of
at work, so I go to the movies.

Apparently, many people share Tom's need. Melodrama appeals to a wide audience which has a hunger for excitement and adventure. It awakens strong responses by its familiar black-and-white conflicts and escapades which have a basic pattern of vigorous action. Its by-products are thrills and tears. Its machinery includes chases, escapes, reprieves, conflicts, and struggles—all kinds of situations in which there is physical danger and jeopardy. Melodrama does not face problems; it avoids thought or controversy by the simple expedient of eliminating the trouble-maker. It aims at maximum identification with the audience.

Melodrama is a drama of mediocrity since it can be written and performed by mediocre people and its appeal is to a broad, undiscriminating audience which prefers its entertainment on the level of simple action with no intellectual overtones or disturbing aftermath. As Professor Thompson suggests, "the playwright's art here lies in a melodramatic golden mean between no response and painful response." Melodrama does not aspire to the austere elevation of tragedy nor does it pretend to come to grips with social problems and their conditioning effects on behavior. It is quite content to deal with effects and ignore causes.

Melodrama has strong sentimental appeals. It is concerned with what Thompson refers to as, "the pink section of the emotional spectrum." Melodrama usually deals with a story of wish-fulfillment in which dreams do come true, virtue is rewarded, evil is punished, and pure and brave hearts are united. The writer makes use of such emotionally loaded devices as a suffering heroine, a sick child, a wounded horse or dog, a tortured hero, a heartless and brutal villain, and love of motherhood, of country, and of babies. Melodrama purges the softer emotions.

The audience for melodrama must yield its critical faculties to the action. There is little solace for the skeptic. Any resemblance of the character or situations to reality is superficial. While the spectator for the duration of the play may find himself emotionally involved in the plot and identified with the hero, as Cleanth Brooks and Robert Heilman point out,[1] this kind of participation is on a game level—like an interested fan carried away momentarily by an exciting ball game. One leaves the theater with a sense of relief at the outcome and a feeling of being emotionally spent by suspense and excitement, but untroubled by the conditions which caused the suffering and conflict of the play.

While melodrama no longer occupies the same central position in the legitimate theater as it did in the nineteenth century, it continues its wide popular appeal in motion pictures and television as well as in occasional plays such as *Ladies in Retirement*, *Dead End* and *The Little Foxes*, and of course melodramatic characters and situations abound in much of our

---

[1] Cleanth Brooks and Robert Heilman, *Understanding Drama* (New York, Holt, Rinehart and Winston, Inc., 1948).

drama. Although most of the discussion which follows is concerned primarily with nineteenth-century drama, you will recognize its application to contemporary plays and the general relationship to our mass-entertainment media.

PLOT

The writers of melodrama were not men interested in the literary aspects of drama; they were men of the theater, experienced in production who knew all the tricks of the stage, and who possessed the know-how to squeeze all the excitement and suspense possible out of their scripts. They were not literary artists interested in "fine writing." They were skilled manipulators of characters and situations much like our present writers of "B" pictures and television plays whose approach to writing is grounded on the idea that anything is legitimate that works.

The plot of melodramas relied heavily on story value. The audience did not come to probe character, to listen to bright parlor talk, or to consider perplexing social problems. They came to see familiar type characters involved in stories told in scenes of clear and vigorous action. They preferred those dramatic situations which showed characters against fearful odds, trapped or marooned—holding out until help comes—the last bullet —the last drop of water—the last bite of food—the last cent. The art of playwriting, therefore, became the art of devising scenes of excitement. Melodrama exaggerated climaxes and crises so that the structure of the play is a series of peaks of action rather than a well-knit steady progression of logically related events. Stock situations were escapes, shipwrecks, murders, duels, hangings, drownings, explosions, battles, rescues, fires, avalanches, executions—all manner of cliff-hanging circumstances which placed the hero and heroine in physical jeopardy. (Their souls were never a source of contention except perhaps in the "temperance plays.") A typical scene of climax from Boucicault's great favorite, *The Colleen Bawn* (1860) illustrates not only the kind of situation, but also the major emphasis on action:

Music, low storm music. . . . Myles sings without then appears U.E.R. on rock. . . . Swings across stage by rope. Exit U.E.L.H. Music, boat floats on R.H. with Eily and Danny. Eily steps on to Rock C. (Danny) stepping onto the rock the boat floats away unseen. . . . Music. Throws her into water, L.C. She disappears for an instant then reappears clinging to Rock C. . . . Thrusts her down. She disappears. . . . Shot heard U.E.L.H. Danny falls into water behind C. Rock. Myles sings without. . . . Swings across by rope to R.H., fastens it up, then fishes up Double of Eily—lets her fall. Strips, then dives after her. Eily appears for an instant in front. Then double for Myles appears at back and dives over drum. Myles and Eily appear in front of Center Rock. Tableau. Curtain.

This kind of physical action is, of course, the standard material of melodrama, made appealing to nineteenth-century audiences by novel effects. It is interesting to note the use of character "doubles" in order to keep the scene moving. Other elements in this scene of special interest are the music for reinforcing the atmosphere and the use of the tableau at the end of the act. The writer of melodrama depended on all kinds of *coups de théâtre* for releasing strong feelings. He utilized big curtains such as in the scene above, literally as "clap traps." While he may have succeeded in jolting the audience, the use of such techniques violated the tenets of good playwriting by calling attention to the trickery of the staging rather than concentrating the audience's attention on character and the play.

The playwright, mindful of the break in the continuity of his narrative because of the multiplicity of his episodes and the emphasis on a series of climactic actions, made an attempt to bind the scenes together by a variety of techniques. Changes of scenery were covered by music or special lighting effects. Oftentimes, the scenes were changed in view of the audience. Sets were devised for the use of simultaneous or parallel action. Still another practice was that of shifting the locale from one place to another while the action continued. The following example from *A Race for Life* indicates this device, which anticipates cinematic practice:

Officers fire. Convicts rush on, struggle with officers. Shots outside; Gaspard seizes Jacques—is thrown off. Officer seizes Jacques, he throws him off when Holmes struggles off with Brady R.H. Men and officers struggle off R. and L. when all clear
   Sound Change Bell

Rocks drawn off R. and L. Prison double set center revolves to old Light House and comes down stage. Jacques and Brady come on in boat, Men work sea cloth. Patty throws rope from light house window. Brady catches it. Picture. Slow curtain.

The plot of melodrama is essentially dishonest. It is rigged like a "fixed" fight. Actually the outcome is never in doubt. This does not mean, however, that the playwright takes no pains to give the illusion of actuality. The good writer of melodrama is a skilled craftsman with a shrewd sense of pace, rhythm, and a feeling for climactic action. He is an adept story-teller and showman. He not only knows the potentialities of the stage, but he also understands the audience for whom he writes. Logic does not interest him so long as his play gives the impression of credibility which he achieves by keeping his narrative moving, and by creating the illusion of actuality through the use of realistic backgrounds, appropriate costuming, good casting and dialogue that suggests the speech of everyday life.

Realism ultimately made its impact on melodrama, although up until 1900, most American plays were written as vehicles for the exploitation of a star or for the theatrical possibilities of staging. In the early part of the twentieth century, the motion picture began to attract a popular audience. Porter's films, *The Life of an American Fireman* and *The Great Train Robbery* taught movie makers that their medium was ideally suited for narratives with bold and vigorous action. The motion picture quickly captivated the public fancy and assimilated melodrama as its staple product which has continued to find favor ever since. A glance at recent newspaper advertisements makes this evident in such blurbs as these: "Overwhelming as the elements!" "Desires at a fever pitch under a blazing sun!" "Dramatic dynamite!" "Can she pass for white? The mirror says 'yes.' What man knows the color of love?" "This is a shocker! Good for thrills and a provocative psychological premise!"

The motion pictures and television have performed a distinct service to the legitimate stage by removing a good deal of the puerile material which formerly appeared on it. But melodrama is not dead in the theater. It often changes its external appearance, takes on greater surface reality, deals more credibly with character and dialogue—but nevertheless, it is still melodrama in its exaggerated emphasis of excitement and emotion for their own sake. The characteristic appeals continue to be exploited in such plays as *Gas Light, The Bad Seed, Dial "M" for Murder, Suspect,* and *Night Must Fall.* In addition, there are any number of modern dramas which make free use of melodramatic material although they exhibit skillful craftsmanship and adroit plotting. The external action has been replaced by psychological tension, and there may be a measure of social significance in the action, but the flavor of melodrama still persists in such works as *The Children's Hour, Command Decision, Key Largo, The Traitor, Time Limit,* and *Darkness at Noon.*

CHARACTER

Myers in his book *Tragedy: A View of Life,* makes an interesting statement about character when he says: "In the black-and-white world of melodrama men are divided into two sharply opposed classes, represented by the unblemished hero and the unspeakable villain. . . . The first premise of melodrama is that there are two distinct kinds of men: the first premise of tragedy is that all men are essentially the same."[2] Nineteenth-century melodrama and our contemporary motion-picture and television plays of action testify to the validity of Myers' observation. Characters are generally stamped-out, good or bad one-dimensional figures who pursue their objectives in a straight line without thought,

[2] Henry Alonzo Myers, *Tragedy: A View of Life* (Ithaca, Cornell University Press, 1956). Reprinted with permission of the publisher.

development, or psychological complexity. They do not think, they act, and as a result of their thoughtlessness, they become involved in all sorts of absurd entanglements such as being caught on a train trestle at midnight without a lantern or match, lost in the snow barefoot, or trapped in the villain's net because they misjudge the character of their adversary. The writer of melodrama has little or no concern with delineating characters as substantial individuals conditioned by their environment and past experiences, responding to the events in which they participate as individuals. Melodramatic characters are simple in heart and mind; they are objects of desire with whom the audience can readily identify itself.

Many characters from melodrama are types, especially the comic ones, who give the illusion of being drawn from life, but who are really comic devices exploited for their eccentricities or picturesqueness, rather than substantial, fully-rounded characters. Some leading roles in melodrama provided exceptional opportunities for actors who became so identified with the characters that they gave the impression of reality. For example, James O'Neill played the *Count of Monte Cristo* 5,817 performances, and Denman Thompson appeared in *The Old Homestead* more than 7,000 times.

Nineteenth-century melodrama was the popular entertainment of the masses, and since maximum identification was the playwright's aim, he used characters from the ordinary walks of life. Heroes were not the elevated figures of the past; they were firemen, private soldiers, sailors, the farm boy, the hired hand. Very often the bad characters of the play were drawn from high society to show that hypocrisy and sham permeated the upper circle. Picturesque figures were copied from life, so that the drama in this country showed native characters as heroes and heroines, combatting the tradition of importing our dramas and characters from abroad. In all things, the common denominator prevailed.

THOUGHT

Most melodramas end with arbitrary scenes of poetic justice in which couples are paired off, and rewards and punishments are parceled out according to the actions of the characters in the play. As the final curtain descends, the audience is reassured that virtue will triumph, murder will out, and the wages of sin is death. A typical heart-throb ending occurs in the astonishingly popular *Uncle Tom's Cabin*.

(GEORGE SHELBY *enters, supporting* TOM.—*Music. They advance to front and* TOM *falls, C.*)

GEO: Oh! dear Uncle Tom! do wake—do speak once more! look up! Here's Master George—your own little Master George. Don't you know me?

Tom: (*opening his eyes and speaking in a feeble tone*) Mas'r George! Bless
de Lord! it's all I wanted! They hav'nt forgot me! It warms my soul; it does
my old heart good! Now I shall die content!

Geo: You shan't die! you mustn't die, nor think of it. I have come to buy you,
and take you home.

Tom: Oh, Mas'r George, you're too late. The Lord has bought me, and is going
to take me home.

Geo: Oh! don't die. It will kill me—it will break my heart to think what you
have suffered, poor fellow!

Tom: Don't call me, poor fellow! I *have* been poor fellow; but that's all past
and gone now. I'm right in the door, going into glory! Oh, Mas'r George!
Heaven has come! I've got the victory. The Lord has given it to me! Glory
be to his name! (*Dies.*)

(*Solemn music.*—George *covers* Uncle Tom *with his cloak and kneels
over him. Clouds work on and conceal them, and then work off.*)

Characters were motivated by conventional morality. Heroines were
long-suffering, self-sacrificing, dutiful, and pure. The home was the center
of their lives, and motherhood their crowning achievement. Heroes were
upright, manly, brave and noble who revered womanhood and their
country, and stood steadfastly for justice and honor. Villains were lustful,
greedy barbarians who chased women, preyed on widows, and searched
relentlessly and unscrupulously for dishonest gain. One could generally
spot the villain by his scarred or unshaven face, his dark looks, his foreign
dialect, or he might appear in just the opposite way as too well-dressed,
too soft-spoken, too mannerly. His smooth and suave exterior belied the
cold, hard glint in his eye, and the itching palm beneath the velvet glove.

Duty and self-sacrifice were the ennobling virtues of the lower classes.
Whatever misfortunes befell, the honorable person performed his duty,
confident that in the end, justice will be meted out, in the next world if
not here and now. Dozens of heroines declaimed such sentiments as the
following passage from Daly's highly successful hit, *Under The Gaslight*.

LAURA:

Let the woman you look upon be wise or vain, beautiful or homely, rich or
poor, she has but one thing she can really give or refuse—her heart! Her
beauty, her wit, her accomplishments, she may sell to you—but her love is
the treasure without money and without price. She only asks in return, that
when you look upon her, your eyes shall speak a mute devotion; that when
you address her, your voice shall be gentle, loving and kind. That you shall
not despise her because she cannot understand all at once, your vigorous
thoughts, and ambitious designs: for when misfortune and evil have defeated
your greatest purposes—her love remains to console you. You look to the trees
for strength and grandeur—do not despise the flowers, because their fragrance

is all they have to give. Remember—love is all a woman has to give; but it is the only earthly thing which God permits us to carry beyond the grave.

DICTION

The language of melodrama was singularly undistinguished. Since common characters carried the burden of the plot, playwrights attempted to suggest the everyday idiom on stage. This effort performed some service in undermining the bombast and extravagance of romantic diction, although the writer of melodrama was not entirely immune from flowery language. In moments of strong emotion, characters spouted such purple passages as that cited above from *Under The Gaslight*. But by and large, the playwright's emphasis on common characters, involved in scenes of violent action, led toward dialogue which suggested the texture of ordinary speech. As a result of his attempt to imitate the language of life, some playwrights endeavored to copy the dialects and provincialism of specific locales, which was a move toward increased realism.

The writer of melodrama made free use of such technical devices as asides and soliloquies, which not only aided him in the difficult problems of exposition imposed by episodic structure, but also gave him the opportunity to reveal character and motivation. In general, however, soliloquies were used for technical purposes rather than for high-sounding passages of well-worn rhetoric.

MUSIC

Melodrama, originally linked with music, continued that association. As the excerpts from *The Colleen Bawn* and *Uncle Tom's Cabin* have already indicated, music was an important accompaniment to the action. When the motion pictures took over melodrama, it was soon learned that sound was extremely useful for eliciting emotional response. Silent films were accompanied by appropriate scores for piano or pipe organ. For more ambitious productions such as *The Birth of a Nation*, a complete orchestral accompaniment was written and played for the showing of the picture. In our present motion pictures and television dramas, music continues as an indispensable element of production to establish atmosphere, bridge the action, or generate excitement.

Nineteenth-century melodrama made another interesting use of music. The entrances and exits of leading characters were accompanied by special musical themes suitable for their roles. But music in melodrama was an adjunct of production, rather than an organic part of the structure itself. Nevertheless, it was often a stronger source of emotional impact than the performance of the actors and the drama itself.

SPECTACLE

In the first half of the century, almost all theaters made use of two-dimensional stock pieces consisting of backdrops and wings, on which were painted a variety of backgrounds such as a kitchen, a palace, a prison, a grotto, a woodland glade. This system possessed two virtues—it was economic and it made shifting rapid and easy. To change to a new setting, the backdrop was raised to reveal another one behind it, while wings slid along the grooves to uncover the new ones for the following scene. Throughout the country, theaters were equipped with stock sets so that a touring company needed to bring only its special effects and costumes along. But as the taste for sensational novelties grew, productions became increasingly elaborate and expensive. Metropolitan stages became more complicated with bridges, traps, elevators, moving platforms, and all kinds of paraphernalia for producing fires, floods, explosions, and all manner of astounding displays. The two-dimensional scenery was replaced by built-up solid pieces making the sets substantial and difficult to move. Belasco actually bought pieces of buildings and moved them intact onto the stage. Playwrights were obliged to create scenes calculated to exploit visual sensations. The following scene from *Pauvrette: or, Under the Snow* shows the kind of effects required:

The summit of the Alps. Rocks and precipices occupy the stage. A rude hut on one side in front. A bridge formed by a felled tree across the chasm at the back. The stone-clad peaks stretch away in the distance. Night. . . . Storm, wind. She (Pauvrette) throws her scarf around her, and hastily ascends the rock—utters a long wailing cry—listens. . . . Descends to her hut. Maurice cries for help. Takes her alpenstock and a coil of rope, and reascends the rock. The wind increases—the snow begins to fall. She crosses the bridge and disappears off left. Bernard appears below on the rocks, L. He climbs up the path. . . . Pauvrette appears on the bridge, leading Maurice. . . . They cross the bridge. . . . They descend and enter the hut. . . . Large blocks of hardened snow and masses of rock fall, rolling into the abyss. Pauvrette falls on her knees. . . . Pauvrette enters the hut. The avalanche begins to fall—the bridge is broken and hurled into the abyss—the paths have been filled with snow—and now an immense sheet rushing down from the R. entirely buries the whole scene to the height of twelve or fifteen feet swallowing up the cabin and leaving above a clear level of snow—the storm passes away—silence and peace return—the figure of the virgin (in window) is unharmed—the light before it still burns.

It should be kept in mind that while sensational scenery called attention to itself, it was also used for more than pictorial representation. The setting was functional in that it served the actor's needs in a particular scene. A waterfall was not simply shown as an enlarged calendar picture for its visual appeal. It became a factor in the action when the hero struggled to save the heroine from plunging to her death. A railroad trestle was set on stage not merely for the novelty of showing a train, but also as a weapon of the villain who tied the hero to the tracks while the approaching light and whistle of the train were seen and heard. The setting was an essential part of the action. Hence, a considerable amount of ingenuity was required by the stage mechanic to devise effects which were not only visually credible, but also utilitarian enough to be used in chases, fights, and escapes. Incidentally, the actor had to be something of an athlete to dive from burning buildings, scale steep cliffs, and chase or be chased through a canvas jungle, and then recite lines. (It is no wonder that doubles were often used to keep the action continuous.)

One device by which melodrama sought to create the illusion of reality was through the use of actual and authentic properties on stage. Some playwrights and producers cluttered the stage with endless detail to make the stage picture seem real. Oftentimes, a real property such as a rowboat, made an incongruous contrast with the obviously painted backdrop of the sea. On the other hand, the use of genuine and homely objects on stage enhanced the realism of the acting by giving the actors an opportunity to create business and pantomime. James A. Herne, a successful writer of melodrama who attempted to emulate the new realism in his plays, was very fond of filling his scenes with the everyday objects and actions of life. In some of his plays he brought on dogs, chickens, a horse, geese, and live babies. He showed a shipyard in operation during which a boat was painted each evening. In another play, a flour mill actually worked. But perhaps his favorite device was his dinner scenes in which complete meals were eaten on stage. The following excerpt from *Sag Harbor* is typical:

Susan enters with a smoking hot clam pie in a deep dish. She is greeted with a round of applause in which everybody at the table joins with the exception of Freeman. Susan sets the pie in front of Ben, who helps himself to it. During the next scene, Susan busies herself waiting at the table, passing tea, bread and butter, and coming and going with food. Martha pours the tea, and Elizabeth helps applesauce from a dish which is placed in front of her. They all eat heartily, and there is a general atmosphere of good cheer.

As the elaboration of scenery progressed, it became increasingly difficult for a road company to tour since many of the outlying theaters could not accommodate the special scenery because of the lack of size or equipment, not to mention the increased cost of the touring production. The increasing solidity and complexity of scenery also affected playwriting.

It meant that scenes could not be shifted as rapidly as previously. The result was to reduce the number of scenes in the play so that there were fewer locales and episodes. Under these conditions, the dramatist was forced to use less physical action, the narrative lost some of its fluency, and there was a tendency toward fuller development of character and dialogue.

DRAME

Most serious modern playwrights have not aspired to scale the heights of tragedy, nor have they been content to confine themselves to sheer melodrama. They have tended to write middle-class plays for a middle-class audience dealing with contemporary man in commonplace circumstances. This vast body of dramatic literature defies definition because of its great diversity, its technical experimentation in dramaturgy and production, and because of its mixture of several forms of writing at once. Some critics simply use the general term, drama, but we prefer, as a lesser evil, the French term, *drame,* by which is meant those plays of serious intent usually dealing with contemporary life. Just as realism has been the dominant mode of modern drama, likewise, the drame has been the preponderant form used by such writers as Henrik Ibsen, Anton Chekhov, Maxim Gorki, Sean O'Casey, Eugene O'Neill, Luigi Pirandello, Jean Anouilh, Clifford Odets, Arthur Miller, and Tennessee Williams.

Drame is allied to melodrama in that the playwright often attempts to involve the spectator in the action by identification with the characters and by creating suspense and tension. Drame differs from melodrama in that it may be interested in the realm of ideas—the issues at stake may be sociological and philosophical in implication. Characters may be involved in genuinely significant action. The effect of a drame may be to provoke thought and discussion after the curtain has gone down.

Drame is allied to tragedy in its seriousness of purpose, in its relentless honesty of treatment, in its concern with the meaning of human conduct. Drame differs from tragedy in its narrowness of vision, often with its emphasis on material, temporary or local conditions which deny it universality, with its mechanistic or deterministic sense of values, and with its general lack of elevation. Frequently, the writer of drames is fascinated by the psychological complexities of character. His *dramatis personae* are not the stock characters of melodrama; they are individuals with subtle and complicated motivations. They are not the tragic heroes of great stature who fall from high places, but they are ordinary people painfully searching for meaning and security in a baffling world of shifting values.

While admittedly drame is a rather unsatisfactory term because of its omnibus qualities, it may be of some service in identifying the bulk of modern, serious dramatic literature. Much of what we will have to say about three modern modes—realism, naturalism, and expressionism, has specific application to drame.

Questions and Exercises

1. What is the effect of melodrama on an audience?
2. What are the characteristics of a melodramatic plot?
3. In what way is melodrama dishonest?
4. How does it affect character? Dialogue?
5. What situations does melodrama deal with?
6. Why is melodrama popular?
7. How important is spectacle in melodrama?
8. How does melodrama gain emphasis in production?
9. After watching an "action" play on television or motion pictures, list the melodramatic elements.
10. Distinguish between melodrama and *drame*.

Plays to Read

STOWE: *Uncle Tom's Cabin*
TAYLOR: *Ticket of Leave Man*
WOODS: *East Lynne*
STALLINGS and ANDERSON: *What Price Glory?*
WILLIAMS, Emlyn: *Night Must Fall*
COLTON and RANDOLPH: *Rain*
HELLMAN: *The Little Foxes*

Suggested Reading

HAMILTON, Clayton, *Theory of the Theatre* (New York, Holt, Rinehart and Winston, Inc., 1939).

O'HARA, F. H., and BRO, M. H., *Invitation to the Theatre* (New York, Harper and Brothers, 1939).

THOMPSON, Alan Reynolds, *The Anatomy of Drama* (Berkeley, University of California Press, 1942).

VARDAC, Nicholas A., *Stage to Screen* (Cambridge, Harvard University Press, 1949).

WHITFIELD, G. J. N., *Introduction to Drama* (New York, Oxford University Press, 1940).

6

Comedy

COMEDY wears many masks, appears in many guises, from the ill-fitting tattered rags of the drunken hobo, to the elegant evening clothes of the most sophisticated aristocrat, to the overdressed finery of the fop. Comedy makes many appeals, from the belly-laugh to the well-concealed smile. Its armor includes such a variety of weapons as the rapier, the slapstick, the barbed shaft, and the custard pie. It may invoke warm and sympathetic general laughter, or it may castigate a victim with a hard and ruthless derision. Comedy speaks many languages—epigrams, conceits, puns, obscenities, bon-mots and double-entendres. The field of comedy is broad enough to encompass many variations—romantic comedy such as Shakespeare's *As You Like It*, the brittle, high comedy of Congreve's *Way of the World*, a musical comedy like *My Fair Lady*, a bedroom farce such as Feydeau's *Keep an Eye on Emilie*, a Latin intrigue, *The Pot of Gold*, a political lampoon, *Of Thee I Sing*, a Shavian satire, *Man and Superman*, an intimate revue, *New Faces*, an Aristophanic thrust, *Lysistrata*, an historical film comedy, *The Carnival of Flanders,* a Jacques Tati pasquinade, *Mr. Hulot's Holiday.* And comedy includes the prefabricated formulae television fare of night-club monologists, and family situations built around the bewildering behavior of adolescents and the antics of their parents.

THE NATURE OF COMEDY

To define comedy is first to acknowledge the difficulties and hazards of definition. What may make one person laugh, may make another grieve. The lively oak of comedy cannot be crammed into a flower pot

101

of simple definition when one considers all of its roots and branches, its variegated fruits and foliage. We usually refer to those plays as comedy which end happily, and those with an unhappy ending as tragedy. But even this broad generalization breaks down in some instances. Euripides chose to end *Alcestis* happily, Dante calls his great work with its elevated theme and treatment the *Divine Comedy*. While classicists and neoclassicists kept tragedy and comedy separate, many playwrights, notably the English, blended comic and serious matter together as in *Hamlet, Dr. Faustus,* and *Macbeth.* Aristotle in his *Poetics* makes an important distinction in saying that in tragedy men are shown as "better than they are" and in comedy as "worse than they are." As Northrop Frye has pointed out the qualifying words which Aristotle uses for good and bad are *spoudaios* and *phaulos*, which have a figurative connotation of weighty and light. The lightness of touch is certainly one of the hallmarks of comedy.

Perhaps it is sufficient to say that comedy has as its purpose to delight, entertain, or regale an audience through the presentation of characters, situations, and ideas in the spirit of fun. As tragedy achieves its catharsis through fear and pity, so comedy aims at its special catharsis through laughter and amusement to keep man close to sanity and balance, to remind us of our human frailties, and to keep us humbly mindful of what we are rather than what we might wish ourselves to be.

KINDS OF COMEDY

The problem of classification is especially acute in comedy. Playwrights have a way of ignoring arbitrary pigeon-holes, mixing various kinds of comic matter to suit their dramatic purposes without regard to academic convenience. For example, Aristophanes frequently uses all manner of obscenities and physical humor characteristic of farce, but he blends this material with satirical thrusts at the ideas of his contemporaries, filling his comedies with political and philosophical ramifications. The perplexed scholar in an attempt to catalogue this variety has been forced to use the label of "Aristophanic" comedy. Shakespeare is similarly difficult to categorize since he writes in a variety of ways—farce, romantic, and "dark" comedies, sometimes mixing different styles in the same play.

Professor Alan Thompson, in an effort to regularize the concept of different kinds of comedy devised a comic ladder which takes this form: [1]

[1] Alan Reynolds Thompson, *The Anatomy of Drama* (Berkeley, University of California Press, 1942).

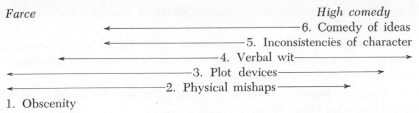

Farce   *High comedy*

←————————————————————6. Comedy of ideas

←————————————————5. Inconsistencies of character

←——————————————4. Verbal wit————————————→

←————————————3. Plot devices————————————→

←——————————2. Physical mishaps————————→

1. Obscenity

Allardyce Nicoll, in a similar effort, suggests five categories of comedy: [2]

In general, there are five main types of comic productivity which we may broadly classify. Farce stands by itself as marked out by certain definite characteristics. The comedy of humours is the second of decided qualities. Shakespeare's comedy of romance is the third, with possibly the romantic tragicomedy of his later years as a separate subdivision. The comedy of intrigue is the fourth. The comedy of manners is the fifth, again with a subdivision in the genteel comedy.

Both Thompson and Nicoll place low or physical comedy at one end of the scale and the comedy of manners or ideas at the other end—and this seems like a logical arrangement, but the problem with the gradations in between, as well as with the two extremes is, as we have already noted, that they are not mutually exclusive. Moreover, playwrights have compounded plays of all of the elements blended in various fashions which defy neat schematic compartmentalization. The juices of comedy have a way of bubbling over, penetrating all kinds of chinks and crannies. They are difficult to cork up in logic-tight containers. The safest conclusion seems to be that comedy ranges between high and low, between the physical and intellectual, and that it differs in kind according to the playwright's purposes from play to play. Perhaps the most essential ingredient for all kinds of comedy is a point of view which we shall discuss subsequently as the comic attitude.

LAUGHTER

Since the nature of comedy is linked to the sources of laughter, some measure of the complexity of the subject may be suggested by the various points of view exposed in the following observations by thinkers who have given serious thought to comedic material:

Laughter is the indication of an effort which suddenly encounters a void. (HERBERT SPENCER)

[2] Allardyce Nicoll, *The Theory of Drama* (New York, Thomas Y. Crowell Co., 1931). Reprinted by permission of the publisher.

Laughter is the result of an expectation which of a sudden ends in nothing. (IMMANUEL KANT)

. . . what either in the words or sense of an author, or in the languages or actions of men, is awry or depraved does strangely stir mean affections, and provoke for the most part to laughter. (BEN JONSON)

. . . laughter almost ever cometh of things most disproportioned to ourselves and nature. (SIR PHILIP SIDNEY)

The real cause would appear to lie in the sense of liberation which the laugh itself involves. It is the liberation of the natural man from the ties and conventions of society. In the same way, we may explain the laughter which greeted in the Middle Ages the appearance of the Devil-character of the mystery plays. (ALLARDYCE NICOLL)

The dignified, solemn and stately attributes of things require in us a certain posture of rigid constraint; and if we are suddenly relieved from this posture, the rebound of hilarity ensues, as in the case of children set free from school. (ALEXANDER BAIN)

The comic is that side of a person which reveals his likeness to a thing, that aspect of human events which, through its peculiar inelasticity, conveys the impression of pure mechanism, of automatism, of movement without life. (HENRI BERGSON)

. . . gratification of repressed tendencies. (SIGMUND FREUD)

The essence of the laughable is the incongruous, the disconnecting of one idea from another, or the jostling of one feeling against another. (WILLIAM HAZLITT)

While there is considerable structural lumber in these well-turned phrases, there is not much immediate shelter because one becomes conscious of their shortcomings when applying them to specific examples. There are, however, two points of general agreement. First, comedy implies a contrast in the juxtaposition of the normal and the abnormal, the expected and the unexpected. Second, comedy involves a sudden change. It will be helpful to keep these points in mind as we consider some of the comic theories whose root-ideas are to be found in the quotations which have just been cited. But before sketching the theories, we may gain some insight into our subject by glancing briefly at the functions of comedy.

PURPOSES OF COMEDY

Many thinkers consider comedy to have a utilitarian basis. Goldoni regarded comedy as a means to "correct faults and foibles"; Hazlitt, "To unmask ignorance and deceit"; Meredith, "to vindicate reason, common sense, rightness and justice, for no vain purpose ever"; Shaw, "for the correcting of pretensiousness, of inflation, of dullness." The French philosopher Henri Bergson in his entertaining book, *Laughter*, summarizes this function of comedy as the drama of criticism in these words: "Laughter is, above all, a corrective. Being intended to humiliate, it must make a painful impression on the person against whom it is directed. By laughter, society avenges itself for liberties taken with it." [3]

When comedy serves such a purpose, the object of laughter is usually unsociable. This has little to do with morality since we are inclined to laugh at a character's eccentricities rather than at his vices or virtues, except insofar as they make him ludicrous. A comic character's deviation from the norm in speech, manners or appearance causes us to laugh to keep him in line. This corrective use of laughter is, of course, not confined to the theater, inasmuch as the fear of ridicule is one of the primary forces in causing the members of society to conform. Hence, in comedy, the butt of the joke, by implication, suggests the sin of antisocial behavior.

But the purpose of comedy is not always critical. There is laughter which is shared in those situations when we laugh *with* a character rather than *at* him—a character, who may be fully aware of his weakness, yet is appealing because we are reminded of our common human inconsistency. As instances of this kind of comic appeal, we think of characters caught in circumstances when they are embarrassed, fearful, and confused. Our laughter often becomes a bond of sympathy, not of ridicule. We do not isolate such characters from our approval; we share with them our universal experience as human beings. While the purpose of some comedy is critical, it also exists on the level of sheer entertainment and delight, serving only secondarily as a means of releasing tensions and inhibitions, although Freud saw in this the primary reason for the phenomenon of laughter.

THE COMIC ATTITUDE

Max Eastman has devoted considerable attention to analyzing the conditions essential for the "enjoyment of laughter" in his book by the same title. He has observed that humor depends upon the existence of a favorable circumstance, and he concludes that "the condition in which joyful laughter most continually occurs is that of play." Laughter is not aroused by those situations where feelings run violent or deep. As a part of his evidence, Eastman cites the native response of a child who may welcome shock and disappointment as a pleasurable experience providing that an atmosphere of play has been established. If the child is teased, however, when he is tired or hungry, the fun is over: the atmosphere of play has been destroyed. Eastman's point of view is

[3] Henri Bergson, *Laughter,* translated by Cloudesley Brereton and Fred Rothwell (New York, The Macmillan Co., 1917).

pertinent to our understanding of the comic attitude. How much emotional involvement should the audience be made to feel during a comedy? What is the basis for the comic attitude?

In Shakespeare's romantic comedies, the sentimental plays of Sheridan and Goldsmith in the eighteenth century, and in many of our contemporary works, the spectator is invited to enter into the emotions of the characters. We become concerned about the fortunes of the protagonist, our sympathies and hostilities are aroused by the playwright's treatment of his characters, we take pleasure in seeing the hero achieve his objective, usually accompanied by the jingle of money and wedding bells. The characters may be laughable, may at times appear foolish and weak, but the playwright does not criticize them. He treats them with tolerance and indulgence. Examples of such comedies which involve our sympathies are *As You Like It, The Rivals, She Stoops to Conquer, They Knew What They Wanted, Born Yesterday, Juno and the Paycock.* We laugh with them, rather than at them; there is no malice in our laughter.

On the other hand, Bergson argues that "laughter has no greater foe than emotion. . . . Its appeal is to the intelligence, pure and simple." Myers supports Bergson in this view by saying: "Without detachment, we cannot realize the effect of comedy, which transforms the frustrations of reason into laughter." This point of view is well taken, especially at the extremes of the comic scale—low comedy and high. In most farce, our enjoyment stems from the action itself, the momentary laugh, the sudden release. We recognize that farce is a form of play; we do not take its actions seriously. These are prefabricated characters racing through the convolutions of plot; they are not real people. No one experiences any genuine pain; the feelings do not penetrate the grease paint. Thus a detachment is achieved because we consciously watch the actions of an artificial world.

High comedy has a different basis for objectivity. Its appeal is intellectual. The reaction to it arises out of perception and insight, rather than emotion. Sentiment is fatal to the aesthetic attitude required for intellectual wit and satire. Occasionally, the playwright lashes out too vigorously at his characters, stirring up an undertone of bitterness which destroys the comic effect. When Ben Jonson laid bare the human follies of his time in *Volpone* and *The Alchemist,* his unmerciful treatment of the brutality and viciousness of his characters threatened to dissipate the spirit of laughter by its savagery. The character of Shylock presents a perplexing challenge to the actor because of the wide range of emotions; he is at once an object of ridicule, and at the same time a human being whose deep suffering intrudes on the comic atmosphere. A recent example of bitterness which clashed with its intended comic tone is the bedroom scene in *The Waltz of the Toreadors* in which Anouilh depicts the wife as so spiteful and rancorous in her attack on her husband, that the attitude of detachment is undermined by pain.

The comic attitude requires a just sense of proportion so that the essential lightness of spirit is achieved, just as Eastman suggested in play with the child. The audience of comedy cannot be pushed too hard in any direction. Excessive sentimentality, bitterness, depravity, exaggeration—any conspicuous straining for effect, any flat dullness or heavy-footed plodding upsets the niceness of balance so necessary for comedy, making it the most difficult of all the forms of drama to perform. The comic attitude is described effectively by Hegel in these words: "Inseparable from the comic is an infinite geniality and confidence, capable of rising superior to its own contradiction, and experiencing therein no taint of bitterness nor sense of misfortune whatever. It is the happy frame of mind, a hale condition of the soul, which, fully aware of itself, can suffer the dissolution of its aims."

Sources of Laughter

The sources of comic effect have given scholar, critic, philosopher, and psychologist endless stimulation for speculation, and although their efforts have resulted in no uncontroversial conclusions, we may find some sustenance in their ideas. Among the various comic theories, some of which were suggested by the excerpts on pages 103-104 let us briefly examine three which Allardyce Nicoll cites as the most prominent in his *The Theory of Drama*, realizing that a good deal of their validity depends upon personal interpretation and careful selection of examples. The three theories are derision, incongruity, and automatism. You will recognize immediately the tendency of the theories to overlap because of the mercurial nature of comedy.

Derision. Aristotle's observation that comedy deals with men as "worse than they are," implies a comic theory of derision or degradation. It is ordinarily used as a form of criticism to combat pretensiousness or ignorance. Its objective is to keep man humble, balanced, and human. The legitimate targets of derision are pomposity, hypocrisy, and sanctimoniousness. As in life, laughter is used to keep people in line, to insure conformity to a socially acceptable code of behavior. Certainly Aristophanes was fully aware of the possibilities of derision as he ranged far and wide in his jibes against his contemporaries. Not even the audience was safe from his wit. For example, in *Peace*, Trygaeus after his ascent looks at the spectators and jeers at them:

> Ah! it's a rough job getting to the gods!
> My legs are as good as broken through it.

(*to the audience*) How small you were to be
sure, when seen from heaven! You all had the
appearance too of being great rascals, but
seen close, you look even worse.

Ben Jonson used his wit as an instrument of mockery against his fellow
Elizabethans as he indicated when he stated the purpose of his comedy:
"To strip the ragged follies of the time." Molière likewise brought low
those who were guilty of excess, deriding those who were too ambitious
in *Le Bourgeois Gentilhomme*, those who were too clever in *Les
Précieuses*, too exacting in *Le Misanthrope*, and too gullible in *Tartuffe*.
The satirist has always regarded comedy as a salutary scourge to cas-
tigate awkward behavior.

Greek comedy ridiculed physical deformities as well as those of
conduct. Comic characters were intentionally distorted and misshapen
in appearance through the use of masks, phallic symbols, and padded
costumes. A man's attempts to rise above himself were often counteracted by the reminder of his biological needs. Aristophanes delighted
in mocking men and gods by exhibiting them in all kinds of embarrassing
physical situations. He was ruthless in aiming his shafts of wit at all
levels of life. The pattern of derision continues throughout dramatic
literature to the present time, especially in farce, employing all manner
of physical humor, coarse gags, barbed insults, and eccentric behavior.
The satirist exploits situations in which characters are debased and reduced to objects of scorn by such formula devices as physical beatings,
bodily functions—situations in which man is caught off-balance, red-
handed, under the bed, in the closet, in his underwear—in any of the
circumstances of life in which he is exposed, his dignity punctured, his
flaw revealed, reminding everyone of his kinship with the animal world.
Even the most serious moments of life are not free from the threat of
derision. For example, the sacred liturgy of the church was burlesqued
by medieval performers in their *Feast of the Asses*. In a contemporary
film, Jacques Tati in *Mr. Hulot's Holiday,* reduces the solemnity of a
funeral to shambles when his leaking inner tube is mistaken for a wreath,
hissing and writhing during the somber ceremony.

Degradation of character often involves a reversal of status. The
deviate from normal social behavior, the inflated person is brought
down off his pedestal. Such stock offenders against common sense and
decent humanity as fools, fops, hypocrites, bumpkins, louts, misers,
philanderers, braggarts, bores, and battle-axes are ridiculed into limbo
because of their deformed behavior, their lack of wit or excess of ambition, greed, lust, or stupidity. The satirist uses barbs of derisive
laughter to prick the bubble, reputation of entrenched authority, often-

times a popular form of comic appeal since the common man finds release and enjoyment in the discomfiture of those above him.

The dialogue of degradation may be an insult calculated to reduce
the status of the recipient. The wisecrack has been a particular favorite
device in American humor as the example from *The Man Who Came to
Dinner* illustrates, see pages 137-138. An ancient example comes from
Aristophanes' *Wasps* in the scene in which three dancers enter disguised as crabs. Two characters spy them and say:

> PHILOCLEON: What's this? A shrimp or a spider?
> XANTHIAS: It's a crab—a hermit crab, the smallest
>   of its kind; it writes tragedies.

The comic theory of derision is especially effective when the dramatist
is treating ideas and characters critically. Although physical degradation, eccentric characters, and insulting language are confined mostly
to farce, the satirist bent on attacking ideas also makes use of ridicule.
Shaw's mockery of the established order of things kept an entire generation on edge; Aristophanes, Molière, and Jonson alienated many of their
contemporaries by their attacks on politicians, the clergy, the law, and
medicine. Derision is an effective weapon of criticism in the theater
and a suitable source of laughter, but because it is critical and carries
the overtones of contempt, it often ruffles those who are laughed at, and
may beget bitterness and retaliation unless it is confined to those who
have no power or status.

Incongruity. Perhaps because it is the most elastic and extensive
theory of comedy, the idea of incongruity has the widest application.
Incongruity is the result of the tension or dissonance set up by the
juxtaposition of two objects or people which expresses a risible contrast,
such as a large, fat woman matched with a small, skinny man, or a
person out of place with his surroundings—in a bathing suit at the opera
or in formal clothes at the beach. The contrast usually depends upon
the establishment of some kind of norm so that a discrepancy is emphasized. There is a gap between the expected and the unexpected, between
the intention and the realization, between the normal and the abnormal,
which results in comic discord and inconsistency.

Incongruity may take several forms—situation, character, and dialogue.
The comic situation based on incongruity presents a contrast between
the usual or accepted behavior and the unusual or unacceptable. A
typical pattern is to place a character in unfamiliar surroundings which
reveal his social incongruity, such as a country bumpkin in polite society,
the socially élite in buccolic surroundings, an intellectual among barbarians, a clown or an inebriate in a dignified gathering, a sailor in a

harem, a coed in a men's dormitory, a tramp in the mayor's bed. Some examples of incongruous situations are the mismatched sword-fight between Viola and Aguecheek in *Twelfth Night,* the two duelists striking one another with musical instruments in *Squaring the Circle,* and the English professor engaging the football star in a fist fight in *The Male Animal.* Another version of the incongruous situation occurs when carefully laid plans go awry, often having the opposite effect than that intended, such as the dinner party that turns into a fiasco in *You Can't Take It with You* and the chaotic reception of the deputation team in Chekhov's *The Anniversary.* A classic example occurs in *The Taming of the Shrew* when Petruchio destroys the dignity of the marriage ceremony with his ragged attire and his raucous behavior which culminates when:

> . . . he took the bride about the neck
> And kissed her lips with such a clamorous smack
> That at the parting all the church did echo.

Incongruity of character involves a contrast between the ideal and the real, or between appearance and actuality. This may be seen in such characters as Parolles' professed bravery and his actual cowardice when confronted with danger in *All's Well That Ends Well,* Malvolio's grotesque costuming and simpering when he attempts to create a favorable impression on Olivia in *Twelfth Night,* the depiction of Dionysus, the revered Greek god, as a cringing weakling in *The Frogs.* An aspect of incongruity of character which also fits Bergson's automatism is the inflexible character whose one-track mind separates him from the norm. We think of such examples as Molière's Alceste whose exaggerated desire for frankness makes him socially bizarre and of Jonson's Morose, whose oversensitivity to noise sets him up as the butt of an elaborate joke.

Incongruity of language occurs when the dialogue is in sharp contrast to the social context, such as the sudden interjection of vulgarity into a polite conversation, or when the language has the opposite effect of that intended by the speaker. Still another use of incongruous language is in the use of speech which is unexpected or inappropriate to the characters, such as refined epigrams spoken by rustics, or wise sayings in the mouths of babes.

Incongruity in its various forms suggests imbalance and disproportion; there is the implication of an upset equilibrium, "the disconnecting of one idea from another, or the jostling of one feeling against another."

Automatism. One of the most imaginative and provocative theories of comedy was that advanced by Bergson in his book, *Laughter,* in which he contends that the essence of the laughable is automatism—"something mechanical is encrusted on the living." Man becomes an object of laughter whenever he becomes rigid and machine-like, or whenever he loses control of himslf or breaks contact with humanity.

Automatism of character occurs when an individual loses his human flexibility, and his behavior becomes mechanical in its repetition, or when a man becomes a puppet, no longer in control of his actions. The gist of Bergson's thinking is indicated by these representative statements about comedy and character: "We laugh every time a person gives us the impression of being a thing." "Any individual is comic who automatically goes his own way without troubling himself about getting in touch with the rest of his fellow beings." "Rigidity, automatism, absent-mindedness, and unsociability are all inextricably entwined, and all serve as ingredients to the making up of the comic in character." Bergson's point of view on one-sided characters is similar to that of Ben Jonson's comedy of "humours" in which he ridiculed those characters who were guilty of some imbalance, some excess:

> As when some on peculiar quality
> Doth so possess a man, that it doth draw
> All his effects, his spirits, and his powers
> In their confluctions, all to run one way
> This may be truly said to be a humour.

In such plays as *Epicene, Volpone,* and *The Alchemist,* Jonson makes comic figures of those who have lost control and succumbed to some individual trait of character causing eccentric and antisocial behavior. Such characters fit neatly in Bergson's theory of automatism.

Automatism of situation is often based on repetition. Characters are caught in the grip of circumstances and subjected to mechanical domination. Chaplin made use of this device in his famous mechanized corn-on-the-cob eating sequence, and his hilarious shaving pantomime to the accompaniment of a Brahms' *Hungarian Dance.* Repeated patterns of behavior have been used very often as the framework for comedy as in the series of medical examinations in *Dr. Knock,* the alternating love scenes in *Squaring the Circle,* and *The Love of Four Colonels,* and the repetition of the palm tree device in *Mister Roberts.* The skillful playwright in employing repetition, adds new and unexpected twists to make the pattern more interesting. As an example of ingenious variety, refer to the scene from Aristophanes' *The Frogs* on pages 132-134. Meierhold in directing his interpretation of three Chekhov farces found thirty-eight references to fainting which the director exploited as a recurrent leitmotif in production. In musical revues, repeated variations of a comic piece of business are used in what is called a "running gag." A typical example used by Olsen and Johnson was that of an "escape artist" who,

bound hand and foot, is given half a minute to free himself, but at the
end of the allotted time he is still securely tied. Every now and then he
is shown as he continues his unsuccessful struggle. At the end of the performance, when the audience makes its exit through the lobby, the hapless escape artist is on the floor continuing his efforts.

Automatism of dialogue takes several forms. For example, Bergson
says, "Inadvertently to say or do what we have no intention of saying or
doing, as a result of inelasticity or momentum is, as we are aware, one
of the sources of the comic." Inelasticity, of course, implies repetition, a
standard form of comedy, as for example Slender's expression of his love
in *The Merry Wives of Windsor* when he sighs every now and then, "Oh,
sweet Ann Page." In a recent play to mock the monotonous dullness of
ordinary social conversation, Ionesco in *The Bald Soprano* uses the
phrases "That is curious, how bizarre, what a coincidence," in various
forms more than two dozen times in four pages of dialogue. One of the
most successful uses of automatism of language occurs in Molière's *Le
Malade Imaginaire* when Toinette, a pert maid-servant, is pretending to
be a physician examining her hypochondriac master, Argan:

TOINETTE: Let me feel your pulse. Come, come, beat properly, please. Ah!
I will soon make you beat as you should. This pulse is trifling with me. I
see that it does not know me yet. Who is your doctor?

ARGAN: Mr. Purgon.

TOINETTE: That man is not noted in my books among the great doctors. What
does he say you are ill of?

ARGAN: He says it is the liver, and others say it is the spleen.

TOINETTE: They are a pack of ignorant blockheads; you are suffering from
the lungs.

ARGAN: The lungs?

TOINETTE: Yes; what do you feel?

ARGAN: From time to time great pains in my head.

TOINETTE: Just so; the lungs.

ARGAN: At times it seems as if I had a mist before my eyes.

TOINETTE: The lungs.

ARGAN: I feel sick now and then.

TOINETTE: The lungs.

ARGAN: And I feel sometimes a weariness in all my limbs.

TOINETTE: The lungs.

ARGAN: And sometimes I have sharp pains in the stomach, as if I had the colic.

TOINETTE: The lungs. Do you eat your food with appetite?

ARGAN: Yes, Sir.

TOINETTE: The lungs. Do you like to drink a little wine?

ARGAN: Yes, Sir.

TOINETTE: The lungs. You feel sleepy after your meals, and willingly enjoy
a nap?

Molière's *Le Malade Imaginaire* performed in the gardens of Versailles during the 1670's

ARGAN: Yes, Sir.

TOINETTE: The lungs, the lungs, I tell you. What does your doctor order you for food?

ARGAN: He orders me soup.

TOINETTE: Ignoramus!

ARGAN: Fowl.

TOINETTE: Ignoramus!

ARGAN: Veal.

TOINETTE: Ignoramus!

ARGAN: Broth.

TOINETTE: Ignoramus!

ARGAN: New-laid eggs.

TOINETTE: Ignoramus!

ARGAN: And at night a few prunes to relax the bowels.

TOINETTE: Ignoramus!

ARGAN: And, above all, to drink my wine well diluted with water.

TOINETTE: *Ignorantus, ignoranta, ignorantum.*

It is apparent that Bergson's theory is an interesting extension of the idea of incongruity, the jostling together of the human and the mechanical. By his ingenuity and persuasiveness, Bergson makes quite a plausible case for automatism, especially for the comedies of Molière, but like other comic theories, automatism does not explain all of the sources of laughter, nor is it appropriate to all kinds of comic effect. Nevertheless, automatism must be recognized as one of the explanations for the phenomenon of laughter, and we are indebted to Bergson for his stimulating analysis.

From the preceding discussion of representative theories of comedy, it is apparent that a case can be made for derision, incongruity, and automatism. It should also be obvious that it is impossible to fix comedy in a single rigid mold although recurrent patterns and mechanisms show through the diverse forms. This will be increasingly evident as we consider the structure and content of comedy.

PLOT

Good comedy requires skillful plotting. A comedy is not simply a loosely knit accumulation of situations and gags. Laughs must be carefully timed and built, situations contrived and an appropriate atmosphere established. A comedy playscript is a score for playing, and just as the composer must be fully cognizant of the possibilities of his music in the hands of musicians, in a similar way, the writer of comedy must be fully aware of the techniques and resources of the actor which will animate his material. The comic writer is acutely concerned with man in his social environment. Basic patterns of comedy depict a character who deviates from the norm or who is out of place with his surroundings. The implicit contrasts and conflicts require adroit delineation of the social milieu in order to expose the laughable elements of conduct. Tragic writers may concentrate on heroic figures, isolated from other characters and unaffected by their behavior, but comedy exploits the interaction of characters, the human scene, the group situation, the juxtaposition of characters. Comedy is more involved with the particular than with the universal. Its emphasis is on the here and now, not the long perspective. The playwright frequently develops timely allusions, local references, and contemporaneous characters. His material must have a sense of crispness and spontaneity. Comedy must not smell of the museum or the dead past. Hence, it is difficult for comedy to survive its time and place of origin because many of its most telling referents are gone.

A typical Aristophanic plot shows how the leading character becomes inspired with a ridiculous idea which is vigorously opposed by others. The idea is tried out and the results are demonstrated. The play ends in revelry. In the subsequent development of comedy, the original pattern persists. A character strives for an objective but he is thwarted because his goal is an impossible one, or he misjudges his objectives and his opposition, or he fights with the wrong weapons. His problem is finally solved when misunderstandings are cleared up and the truth emerges. The play ends happily, often with the lovers united in an embrace, a vestigial reminder of the orgiastic celebrations of Greek "old comedy." In any case, the comic plot usually involves an imbalance caused by the presence of some ridiculous element through error, ignorance, or ambition. The resultant conflicts and contrasts create comic tension which is released in laughter.

The plots of most comedies are made up of sharp complications which require careful craftmanship in the use of exposition, climaxes, crises, discoveries, and the denouement. The tangled threads of action must be kept clear to the audience, which is tricky business in plays of rapid action, mixups, and misunderstandings. In previous centuries, the playwright's task was made much easier by the conventions of the aside and the soliloquy which allowed the playwright to communicate directly with the audience in informing them of the schemes and tricks of the plot and the disparity between truth and pretense. The climaxes and crises of comedy demand technical mastery because the high points of the action often involve a social situation in which a number of people are caught in the same net, obliging the playwright to deal with complex materials. Frequently, the emotional peaks are those of action and discovery, which require that the playwright have a strong sense of visual humor. Climaxes must be built and sustained without prolonging them beyond the limits of the material. The playwright's touch must be deft and sure to keep the pace rapid and to create the special climate of comedy which will insure laughter.

The materials from which comedies are made are venerable ones, as old as the theater itself. The sources of comic effect, which the classic playwrights Aristophanes, Plautus, and Terence used to delight the audiences of Athens and Rome, are still the stock in trade which you can see on your television or motion-picture screen tonight. Someone has suggested, that after all, there are only seven jokes: (1) The insult; (2) the pun; (3) sex; (4) family life; (5) reversal; (6) odd combinations; and (7) news. This may not be all-inclusive but the list is surprisingly universal. Similarly, the devices of comedy which the playwright uses are well established. Let us consider three very common devices for evoking laughter, realizing that these are representative examples and by no means an exhaustive list. Several other devices will be cited in the chapter on Farce.

COMIC DEVICES

One of the most reliable comic devices is that of teasing, which may take a variety of forms such as the delay of news which Shakespeare employs when the Nurse withholds Romeo's message from Juliet. Similarly, in the Russian comedy, *Squaring the Circle,* Emilian, the letter-bearer keeps the message from Abram's missing sweetheart until he performs a dance. Another version of the teasing device occurs in the opera, *The Night Bell,* when the elderly groom, who has married a young bride, is interrupted frequently on his wedding night by the untimely entrances of his young rival who appears in a variety of disguises. Another form of teasing occurs when characters are intentionally placed in embarrassing or awkward situations. Elmire in *Tartuffe* deliberately teases Orgon by encouraging the hypocrite's attentions while her husband observes the scene from his hiding place underneath a table. Tony Lumpkin in *She Stoops to Conquer* teases his mother by driving her around her own garden in a carriage at night pretending that they are beset by robbers. In *The Taming of the Shrew,* Petruchio exposes Katherine to a series of teasings before she is finally tamed. He tests her in the following scene when he and Kate, accompanied by Hortensio, are on the road toward home:

PETRUCHIO: Come on, i' God's name; once more toward our father's
            Good Lord, how bright and goodly shines the moon!
KATHERINE: The moon! the sun: it is not moonlight now.
PETRUCHIO: I say it is the moon that shines so bright.
KATHERINE: I know it is the sun that shines so bright.
PETRUCHIO: Now, by my mother's son, and that's myself,
            It shall be moon, or star, or what I list,

> Or ere I journey to your father's house.
> Go on, and fetch our horses back again.
> Evermore cross'd and cross'd; nothing but cross'd!

HORTENSIO: Say as he says, or we shall never go.

KATHERINE: Forward, I pray since we have come so far,
And be it moon, or sun, or what you please:
An if you please to call it a rush-candle,
Henceforth, I vow it shall be so for me.

PETRUCHIO: I say it is the moon.

KATHERINE: I know it is the moon.

PETRUCHIO: Nay, then you lie: it is the blessed sun.

KATHERINE: Then, God be blessed, it is the blessed sun:
But sun it is not, when you say it is not;
.And the moon changes even as your mind.
What you will have it named, even that it is;
And so it shall be so for Katherine.

Another familiar plot mechanism of comedy is inversion. The entire play may be based on the turnabout of a down-trodden character who ultimately achieves a dominant position as in such plays as *The Solid Gold Cadillac*, and *Born Yesterday*. The reversal may be a temporary one with the characters temporarily thrown out of their usual milieu, only to return to their customary status as in *Jeppe of the Hills*, when the drunken ne'er-do-well is placed in the mayor's bed, treated royally for a day, and then returned insensible to the gutter where he was found. Similarly, in *The Admirable Crichton*, a butler assumes control of a household when the family is marooned on an island, but at the conclusion of the play he resumes his former servile position. A very successful use of reversal occurs in *Master Pierre Pathelin*, when the trickster is himself tricked by his own device. Inversion is used when female characters assume dominant roles in *Lysistrata*, *The Warrior's Husband*, and *The Queen's Husband*.

Another well-worn comic device is the use of the unfamiliar. A character or group of characters is placed in new surroundings, or they are engaged in unaccustomed activities. One form of this device is the process of teaching an inexperienced, and oftentimes, inexpert person such as the English lesson in *Henry V*, the fencing lesson in *Everyman in His Humour* and the dancing lesson in *Le Bourgeoise Gentilhomme*. The humor may be heightened by the additional twist of having the instructor as ignorant as his pupil. The awkward, embarrassed or shy person making an adjustment to a new. experience or surroundings is used again and again for comic effect such as the love scenes in *Ah, Wilderness!*, the girls' first night in their basement apartment in *My Sister, Eileen*, and the wedding night episode in *The Fourposter*.

Perhaps these three devices are sufficient to indicate some of the mechanisms of comedy. You will notice that among these devices and those cited in the chapter on Farce, there are patterns of action which are also employed in tragedy. For example, the reversal formula of comedy is likewise utilized in tragedy: a high-born character who occupies an elevated position at the beginning of the play, falls to his catastrophe as in *Hamlet, Agamemnon,* and *Antigone.* In comedy, the reversal often goes in the other direction. The little person, ignored and beaten down, emerges at the end of the play in a dominant position as in *Three Men on a Horse* and *Beggar on Horseback.* The complications of mistaken identity used for comic purposes by Shakespeare in *A Midsummer Night's Dream, Twelfth Night,* and *Comedy of Errors* are utilized for tragic effect by Sophocles in *Oedipus Rex.* The nature of the mechanism does not determine the response, but more significant is the manner in which the playwright uses it, the spirit of the play. This point is brought forcibly home by comparing the plot mechanisms of *Romeo and Juliet* and the Pyramus and Thisbe episode in *A Midsummer Night's Dream.* The plots are strikingly similar, but one is used for comedy, the other for tragedy.

CHARACTER

Because comedy wears many guises, there is great variation in character. Not only is there a difference in kind, but there is a difference in treatment. A comic character may be the unconscious butt of the joke such as Hodge in *Poetaster* or Orgon in *Tartuffe.* Sometimes, a character may be conscious of his plight or absurdities, and shares his discomfiture with the audience as Falstaff does in *Henry IV.* Again, a comic character may through his wit and insight, direct the laughter toward an idea or situation as Mirabell does in *The Way of the World* or as many Shavian characters do in mocking contemporary ideas and institutions. Sometimes, a character may be comical because of his reversal from a downtrodden nobody to a person of status as in *The Inspector General,* and *The Doctor in Spite of Himself.* A character may arouse laughter by another kind of reversal—the pompous or inflated character who is humbled as the impostor is in *Tartuffe,* Kate in *The Taming of the Shrew,* and the Captain in *Mister Roberts.* A character may be comical because of his eccentric behavior, his lack of wit or judgment, his peculiar cast of mind, his delightful facility with language, his engaging animal spirits, his charming manner, or his buoyant attitude toward life. Character varies with the playwright's purpose.

Comic characters tend to be stock types. The playwright frequently is more concerned about developing the intricacies of plot than he is about revealing depth of character. Hence he sketches his figures lightly or else resorts to readily recognizable types. The dramatist may deliberately create one-sided roles to suit his comic purpose as a means of showing their inhumanity in their fixations and inflexibility. Again, he may purposely keep his characters in the simple mold of stock figures in order to prevent excessive emotional attachment which might destroy the light atmosphere of comedy. As character becomes more genuine and complex, drama moves away from comedy. As an example of how a type character may evolve into a sympathetic and complex human being, thus altering the flavor of the play, we may consider the case of the braggart soldier. As Lamachus in Aristophanes' *Acharnians*, Miles Gloriosus in Plautine comedy, and the Capitano in commedia dell'arte, he is an elementary source of comic effect because of the disparity between his pretended bravery and his cowardice in the face of danger. As Shakespeare's Falstaff, the character is vastly enriched as he rollicks his way through *The Merry Wives of Windsor*, and then is developed into such a complete personality in *Henry IV* that Hardin Craig referred to Falstaff as "the first great synthetic character in modern drama."

The writer of comedy is closer to surface reality than the writer of tragedy. The comic dramatist is more concerned with the immediate, the temporal, the commonplace. Hence, despite the fact that characters in comedy may be types in that they are psychologically simple, they may give a superficial effect of actuality to an audience, especially when acted by consummate comedians whose personal attributes enlarge and deepen the original image of the playwright to give the impression of credible, complex figures such as Joseph Jefferson's *Rip Van Winkle*. Furthermore, the very nature of comic material is rooted in action which gives to the actor license and latitude to transform a spare outline into a full figure.

Bergson describes the comic character as one who is "generally comic in proportion to his ignorance of himself. The comic person is unconscious." Such a character has a blind side which causes him to react in a ludicrous fashion. He is seen again and again as the victim of his ignorance: Malvolio in *Twelfth Night*, Orgon in *Tartuffe*, and Jeppe in *Jeppe of the Hills*. But Bergson's point of view is too narrow for universal application. All comic characters are not unconscious or ignorant of their shortcomings. As we have suggested earlier, there is laughter which is shared with the character when we borrow some of his humiliation as the inept lover, the raw recruit, the bashful swain, and the shy maiden. Falstaff's follies infect us all. We do not laugh at him to punish him or change him; we laugh because of the Falstaff in us. Laughter stems from sympathy as well as ridicule. It is true that numerous comic characters, especially those from classic and neoclassic comedy, fit neatly into Bergson's theory, but there are also scores of comic roles, particularly in English and American plays, which arouse our sympathy and affection such as Rosalind in *As You Like It*, Viola in *Twelfth Night*, Billie in *Born Yesterday*, Marlow in *She Stoops to Conquer*, Professor Turner in *The Male Animal*, Charles Surface in *The School for Scandal* and Tony in *They Knew What They Wanted*. The kind of response which a character elicits from an audience varies with the playwright's purpose. It may be either critical or sympathetic.

THOUGHT

Most comedy does not bear a heavy burden of thought. The playwright is much more concerned with satisfying the needs of those spectators who come to the theater for diversion—who wish to avoid facing someone else's serious problems—spectators who have no immediate interest in intellectual stimulation in the theater. They want to have a good time—to laugh and forget themselves. Because this attitude represents the dominating taste of those who come to see a comedy, the comic writer's efforts are concentrated on interesting the audience in a series of light-hearted actions and sympathetic characters whose involvements are not taken seriously. While the basis for laughter in such comedy may imply an accepted code of behavior, and a system of values, the attention is not centered on weighing the merits of conventional morality, except insofar as it serves as a frame of reference for displaying incongruity. In most comedy, the playwright is not questioning values, he is exposing ridiculous behavior. For his purposes, the comic action is important rather than the meaning of the action.

There is a particular kind of comedy, however, which reverses this point of view, and makes of it a drama of criticism in which the appeal of the play is intellectual. This is known as high comedy.

High comedy, social comedy, or the comedy of manners is a special form of drama with its own particular emphasis and techniques. It is the very antithesis of farce or low comedy in that its appeal is to a limited, cultivated audience rather than a general undiscriminating public, and its stress is on dialogue rather than on action. High and low comedy possess one similarity—they both require an attitude of detachment, a freedom from emotional involvement.

High comedy is written for an audience that is urbane, and sophisticated, with a commonly accepted code of behavior, which is a matter of manners, not morals. Indeed, the Restoration audience was notorious for its immorality and licentiousness, and yet the period is the most brilliant one of high comedy in English literature. It was the purpose of the high comedies of Congreve, Wycherly, and Vanbrugh to mock those who violated its manners. The objects of laughter were the gauche, the outsiders,

A Comedy performed at the Park Theater, New York, 1822

the pretenders whose absurd or awkward behavior caused them to lose their sense of balance. Ridicule was not a moral indictment, but a reproof for antisocial conduct. In other periods of theater history, writers of high comedy have directed their criticism at more universal targets—the foibles and follies of their age. Aristophanes scorned the militarists, Molière attacked hypocrisy and pretense, Shaw delighted in exposing the sham behind the sentimental and rigid precepts of Victorian behavior. High comedy is therefore a social weapon. Its implications extend beyond the immediate chuckle; its aim is to evoke thoughtful laughter. It is intended to have a residue of meaning. S. N. Behrman, a most successful American writer of high comedy commenting in the *New York Times,* sums up the playwright's point of view in this statement: "What makes the essence of high comedy is not the furniture of the room where the action takes place, but the articulateness of the characters, the plane on which they talk, the intellectual and moral climate in which they live. . . . One of the endless sources of high comedy is seriousness of temperament and intensity of purpose in contrast with the triviality of the occasion."

As Behrman suggests, the techniques of high comedy rely most heavily on language. Since it is addressed to an intellectual and cultivated audience, this kind of comedy employs bright repartee, conceits, epigrams, double-entendres and all of the refinements and subtleties of which the writer has command. The excerpt from Congreve's *The Way of the World* (pp. 123-125) exemplifies this style of writing. As a result of the preoccupation with dialogue, high comedy sometimes is deficient in plot and characterization as Nicoll observed: "Wit, therefore, we may say, although it is one of the highest types of comic expression, when presented in an exaggerated form, kills the play in which it appears. It carries the artificiality which is present in all high comedy to a point of absurdity, so that we can feel in no way the connection between the figures on the stage and real life." [4]

High comedy is an esoteric form of drama created for a particular kind of audience and demanding a special style of playing that is facile, suave, and artificial in keeping with the hot-house atmosphere of the play itself.

DICTION

Comedy employs a wide variety of language devices for its effect from cleverly turned conceits and bon mots to crude puns, insults, vulgarisms, and deformed words. We have already observed some of its comic uses in derision, automatism, and incongruity. Most successful comic writers have excellent ears for dialogue and they take apparent delight in their verbal

[4] Nicoll, *op. cit.*

skill. The Elizabethans were especially fond of exploiting language for comic effect. We remember the rich texture of the rustic's speech in *A Midsummer Night's Dream,* the word-play of the doorkeeper in *Macbeth* and the grave diggers in *Hamlet.* Ben Jonson similarly took pains to create earthy and lively dialogue as this excerpt from *Every Man in His Humour* illustrates:

MATTHEW: I think this be the house. What ho!

COB: Who's there? O, Master Matthew! Gi' your worship good morrow.

MATTHEW: What, Cob! How does thou, good Cob? Dost thou inhabit here, Cob?

COB: Ay, sir, I and my linage ha' kept a poor house here in our days.

MATTHEW: Thy linage, Monsieur Cob! What linage? What linage?

COBB: Why sir, an ancient linage, and a princely. Mine ance'try came from a king's belly, no worse man; and yet no man either (by you worship's leave, I did lie in that), but herring, [A cob is a young herring] the king of fish (from his belly I proceed), one o' the monarchs of the world, I assure you. The first red herring that was broiled in Adam and Eve's kitchen do I fetch my pedigree from, by my harrot's books. His cob was my great-great-mighty-great grandfather.

MATTHEW: Why mighty, why mighty, I pray thee?

COB: O, it was a mighty while ago, sir, and a mighty great cob.

MATTHEW: How knows't thou that?

COB: How know I? Why, I smell his ghost ever and anon.

MATTHEW: Smell a ghost? O unsavory jest! And the ghost of a herring cob?

COB: Ay, sir. With favor of your worship's nose, Mr. Matthew, why not the ghost of a herring cob as well as the ghost of Rasher Bacon?

MATTHEW: Roger Bacon, thou wouldst say?

COB: I say Rasher Bacon. They were both broiled o' the coals; and a man may smell broiled meat, I hope? You are a scholar; upsolve that now.

MATTHEW: O raw ignorance!

The writer of high comedy, of course, is especially concerned with dialogue since repartee becomes the drama's chief appeal, the animation of language and the nimbleness of wit replacing the physical action. The problem in writing such dialogue is to create an external sparkle and shine that masks the labor beneath it. Congreve, the Restoration playwright, was an acknowledged master of brilliant repartee as the following excerpt from the famous marriage discussion in *The Way of the World* exhibits:

MIRABELL: Do you lock yourself up from me, to make my search more curious, or is this pretty artifice contrived to signify that here the chase must end and my pursuits be crowned? For you can fly no further.

MRS. MILLAMANT: Vanity! No—I'll fly, and be followed to the last moment. Though I am upon the very verge of matrimony, I expect you should solicit me as much as if I were wavering at the grate of a monastery, with one foot over the threshold. I'll be solicited to the very last—nay, and afterwards.

MIRABELL: What, after the last?

MRS. MILLAMANT: Oh, I should think I was poor and had nothing to bestow, if I were reduced to an inglorious ease and freed from the agreeable fatigues of solicitation.

MIRABELL: But do you not know that when favors are conferred upon instant and tedious solicitation, that they diminish in their value, and that both the giver loses the grace, and the receiver lessens his pleasure?

MRS. MILLAMANT: It may be in things of common application; but never, sure, in love. Oh, I hate a lover that can dare to think he draws a moment's air, independent of the bounty of his mistress. There is not so impudent a thing in nature as the saucy look of an assured man, confident of success. The pedantic arrogance of a very husband has not so pragmatical an air. Ah! I'll never marry unless I am first made sure of my will and pleasure.

MIRABELL: Would you have 'em both before marriage? or will you be contented with the first now, and stay for the other till after grace?

MRS. MILLAMANT: Ah! don't be so impertinent.—My dear liberty, shall I leave thee? My faithful solitude, my darling contemplation, must I bid you then adieu? Ay-h adieu—my morning thoughts, agreeable wakings, indolent slumbers, all ye douceurs, ye sommeils du matin, adieu.—I can't do 't, 'tis more than impossible.—Positively, Mirabell, I'll lie abed in the mornings as long as I please.

MIRABELL: Then I'll get up in the morning as early as I please.

MRS. MILLAMANT: Ah? Idle creature, get up when you will—and d'ye hear, I won't be called names after I'm married; positively, I won't be called names.

MIRABELL: Names!

MRS. MILLAMANT: Aye, as wife, spouse, my dear, joy, jewel, love, sweetheart, and the rest of that nauseous cant, in which men and their wives are so fulsomely familiar—I shall never bear that. Good Mirabell, don't let us be familiar or fond, nor kiss before folks, like my lady Fadler and Sir Francis; nor go to Hyde Park together the first Sunday in a new chariot, to provoke eyes and whispers, and then never to be seen there together again, as if we were proud of one another the first week, and ashamed of one another ever after. Let us never visit together, nor go to a play together; but let us be very strange and well-bred. Let us be as strange as if we had been married a great while, and as well-bred as if we were not married at all.

MIRABELL: Have you any more conditions to offer? Hitherto your demands are pretty reasonable.

MRS. MILLAMANT: Trifles—as liberty to pay and receive visits to and from whom I please; to write and receive letters, without interrogatories or wry faces on your part; to wear what I please, and choose conversation with regard only to my own taste; to have no obligation upon me to converse with wits that I don't like, because they are your acquaintance: or to be intimate with fools, because they may be your relations.—Come to dinner when I please; dine in my dressing room when I'm out of humour, without giving a reason. To have my closet inviolate; to be sole empress of my teatable, which you must never presume to approach without first asking leave. And lastly, wherever I am, you shall always knock at the door before you come in. These articles subscribed, if I continue to endure you a little longer, I may by degrees dwindle into a wife.

MIRABELL: Your bill of fare is something advanced in this latter account.—Well, have I liberty to offer conditions—that when you have dwindled into a wife, I may not be beyond measure enlarged into a husband?

MRS. MILLAMANT: You have free leave. Propose your utmost; speak and spare not.

MIRABELL: I thank you.—Imprimis then, I convenant that your acquaintance be general; that you admit no sworn confidante or intimate of your own sex—no she-friend to screen her affairs under your countenance, and tempt you to make trial of mutual secrecy. No decoy-duck to wheedle you—a fop scrambling to the play in a mask—then bring you home in pretended fright, when you think you shall be found out—and rail at me for missing the play and disappointing the frolic which you had, to pick me up and prove my constancy.

MRS. MILLAMANT: Detestable imprimis! I go to the play in a mask!

COMEDY IN PERFORMANCE

More than other forms of drama, comedy depends upon performance for its full effect. The timing of the actor, his ability to play a piece of business, to project a laugh line, to bring out the risible qualities of situation and character without destroying the light atmosphere—these are special requisites for the complete realization of comedy.

One of the most puzzling aspects of the performance of comedy is in the variety of response from audience to audience. A comic line or piece of business may arouse boisterous laughter from one audience while the next performance may be greeted by a cold and stony silence. Friday and Saturday night audiences invariably outlaugh a Monday or Tuesday night one. Young spectators are more demonstrative than older ones. A scattered audience is less susceptible to laughter than a closely packed one. Within a given audience there are often individuals who are convulsed with laughter throughout, while others remain aloof and unamused.

In general, social facilitation helps create the climate for comedy. Laughter is a social gesture; it is contagious, but the audience must be in a light mood, easily susceptible to the courtship of comedy. Spectators must be wooed and won, not coerced. The comedian can lose the comic sympathy of his audience by making them conscious of his efforts to be funny. When someone says, "I am going to tell you a very funny story," he immediately doubles his difficulties in getting a laugh because the listener's critical faculties have been aroused, and he is aware of the means rather than the end. Let one performer in a comedy strain for effect by being "consciously cute," and he is likely to alienate the audience for the production as a whole.

Comedy is a framework for action. The inanimate script is brought to life by the performer, but his skill is dependent upon the craftsmanship of the playwright as Thorndike says:

Comedy finds its purpose aided by skillful use of words as well as by gesture and mimicry. It avails itself of the arts of the theatre and of literature. It delights in song as well as dance, in epigram as well as grimace, in paradox as well as slap-jack, and it can stoop to punning as readily as to buffoonery. Whatever can be used in verse or fiction to amuse and delight can be employed in the drama with the additional advantage of impersonation. It combines the humour of words and voice, of the audible and visible. Its form and movement, construction and texture, person and speeches, are all dependent on literary art. Its greatest creative triumphs are won by the pen.[5]

Questions and Exercises

1. How can comedy be called the drama of criticism?
2. What does the comedian contribute to the performance of comedy?
3. What are the sources of laughter?
4. How does topicality limit the response to comedy?
5. What conditions are necessary for high comedy?
6. Read the first act of a full-length comedy or a one-act play, and try to predict the places in the script where you would expect the audience to laugh. Justify your predictions.
7. Watch a comedy in the theater, in motion pictures. What comic devices were used? What were the sources of laughter?
8. Discuss the effect of emotion on comedy.

Comedies to Read

MOLIÈRE: *Tartuffe*
JONSON: *Volpone*
SHERIDAN: *School for Scandal*
MAUGHAM, Somerset: *The Circle*
ROMAINS, Jules: *Dr. Knock*
RIGGS, Lynn: *Green Grow the Lilacs*

[5] Ashley H. Thorndike, *English Comedy* (New York, The Macmillan Co., 1929).

O'NEILL, Eugene: *Ah, Wilderness!*
SHAW, George Bernard: *Man and Superman*
SHAKESPEARE: *A Midsummer Night's Dream*

Suggested Reading

BERGSON, Henri, *Laughter,* translated by Cloudesley Brereton and Fred Roth-well (New York, The Macmillan Co., 1917).

EASTMAN, Max, *Enjoyment of Laughter* (New York, Simon and Schuster, Inc., 1942).

ENCK, John J., FORTER, Elizabeth T., and WHITLEY, Alvin, *The Comic in Theory and Practice* (New York, Appleton-Century-Crofts, Inc., 1960).

MEREDITH, George, *Essay on the Idea of Comedy and the Uses of the Comic Spirit* (New York, Charles Scribner's Sons, 1918).

NICOLL, Allardyce, *Theory of Drama* (New York, Thomas Y. Crowell Co., 1931).

SEYLER, Athene and HAGGARD, Stephen, *The Craft of Comedy* (New York, Theatre Arts, Inc., 1946).

7

Farce

THIS CHAPTER on farce is an extension of our discussion of comedy. Just as the counterpart of tragedy is melodrama, the counterpart of high comedy is farce. As a form of drama, farce is very old, and as for its universal appeal, it has been and continues to be, along with melodrama, our most popular kind of mass media entertainment.

The purpose of farce is to entertain; the appropriate response to it is continuous and unrestrained laughter. Farce has little intellectual content or symbolic significance, is not concerned with presenting a message, makes no pretense of demanding serious consideration, has slight residue of meaning. In the journalistic fare of the theater, farce is the comic strip of the *Zam-Bang-Powie* school. Its appeal is simple, external, and spontaneous.

Farce may involve a complete play such as *Comedy of Errors* and *Charley's Aunt,* or its techniques may be injected piecemeal into other forms of drama as in *Twelfth Night* and *The Frogs.* While critics may disparage farce as a degraded form of drama that "though it make the unskillful laugh, cannot but make the judicious grieve," nevertheless, it is a matter of fact that farcical devices and characters have been employed not only by dramatic hacks, but also by some of the most pre-eminent playwrights, including Shakespeare, Molière, and Aristophanes.

The script of farce must be regarded as a scenario for action. The distinctive essence of farce can be realized only in performance by accomplished comedians before a live audience. The gags, tricks and devices which seem so absurd and flat in print may, in the hands of talented performers, move an audience to gales of laughter from which even the most sophisticated theater-goer does not remain aloof, even though, on later

128

reflection, he may wonder at his lack of judgment to have responded to such stuff.

Because the enjoyment of laughter is one of man's favorite diversions, farce is the most popular of all forms of comedy. It demands no intellectual insight, no awareness of a social norm, no linguistic sensitivity in finding nuances of meaning—all of which are necessary for understanding other forms of comedy. The response to farce is immediate and direct, offering no strain to the mind. Hence, this kind of laughing matter has a very wide appeal. The language barriers are slight because the performer in farce often expresses himself in the universal vocabulary of gesture and action. The enacted story is itself a kind of language which finds a ready audience.

PLOT

Farce is usually the comedy of situation. A good farcical plot provides a maximum opportunity for a series of complications, even though it is obvious that it has been contrived and manipulated by the playwright. The structure of farce is a framework for vigorous, rapid, and exaggerated action in which the characters move, rather than think, and where evoking laughter justifies nearly any means. Once the engine has been cranked up and set in motion, the speed is accelerated, and by unexpected blowouts, backfirings and explosions, the mechanism careens crazily through space, gathering momentum until it finally lurches to an awkward but happy ending in a cloud of steam with all of the parts still spinning; and while there has been a whirlwind of activity, the machine has not really moved an inch in any direction.

The skill of plotting farce is determined by the dramatist's ingenuity in inventing a variety of entanglements which will give the comedian a chance to play for laughs. The playwright usually exploits a basic situation which is highly improbable and atypical: a woodcutter reluctantly consents to become a court physician to cure the king's daughter of a feigned illness; two long-lost twin brothers whose servants are another pair of twins, strive for reunion; two young Communists sharing a one-room apartment fall in love with each other's newly-wed wives; a shy greeting-card verse writer becomes involved with a gang of race track touts because of his skill in predicting the winners; a young man wagers that he can tell the complete truth for twenty-four hours; a genial husband undertakes the precarious responsibility of simultaneously maintaining two separate wives and families in Wilmington, Delaware, and Philadelphia, Pennsylvania. These are characteristic plot situations employed by writers of farce. Inventing a farcical plot requires ingenuity in manipulating situations, plus a shrewd sense of the theatre. The playwright must know precisely how, when and where to tickle the audience. An example of a plot which illustrates the materials and organization that characterize this kind of comedy is the medieval farce, *Master Pierre Pathelin*.

An impoverished lawyer, Pierre Pathelin assures his wife, Guillemette, that he has a plan for procuring some cloth. He visits the draper's shop, where he flatters the shopkeeper into giving him a piece of cloth. The draper is wary about parting with the cloth on credit, but Pathelin allays his fears by inviting him to visit his house where the draper will get his money and share a roast goose dinner. The scene ends when Pathelin walks off with the cloth leaving the draper to gloat over the price.

Pathelin brings the cloth home to his delighted wife. When his dinner guest arrives, Pathelin climbs into bed, and his wife informs the hapless draper that her husband could not possibly have purchased any cloth—he has been seriously ill for some weeks. The draper goes away, but returns immediately to find Pathelin feigning a ranting fit of madness. The draper becomes convinced that the devil has hoodwinked him. Another facet of the story now develops when the draper brings a shepherd into court, accused of having eaten several sheep belonging to the draper. The shepherd engages Pathelin to defend him, who feigning a toothache, masks his face until the draper makes his accusation. When Pathelin suddenly reveals his identity, the draper loses his wits, and attacks the lawyer for stealing his cloth. The case becomes hopelessly lost in the confusing tangle of the two arguments. The bewildered judge tries to restore order by questioning the shepherd, who following Pathelin's counsel, answers all questions by bleating like a sheep. The judge abandons the trial; Pathelin has succeeded. The distraught draper dashes off saying to Pathelin: "I am going to your house to see if you are here or there." When Pathelin demands his fee from his client, the shepherd's only reply is continued bleating. The trickster is himself the victim of his own trick.

COMIC DEVICES

In the chapter on Comedy, three representative theories of comedy were cited—derision, incongruity, and automatism, and three characteristic devices were discussed—teasing, inversion and the unfamiliar. These theories and devices are also applicable to farce, although their use is generally on an elementary level. Low comedy exploits the physical aspects of man. His body, its desires and functions are a primary source for comic material. Farcical situations usually depend upon visual humor—man is shown as the victim of his biological nature, not only sex, but any drive, appetite or situation which makes him appear ridiculous, causes him to lose his balance, his control of himself or his circumstances. Farcical char-

acters move in an active physical world; they are out of place in the
rarefied atmosphere of intellectual cerebration.

With this background in mind, let us consider some characteristic forms
of farcical behavior from several entertainment media. A generation or
two ago when vaudeville was popular entertainment, comedians relied
very heavily on visual gags for their humor. George M. Cohan, one of
America's best-loved comedians and playwrights, was once asked to make
a list of his most successful pieces of comedy business. These were the
first eight items on his list in an article "The Mechanics of Emotion,"
McClure's Magazine, November, 1913.

1. Whack on the back for friendship. Repeat three times.

2. Whack woman on back absent-mindedly thinking she is a man.

3. Step on a man's sore foot.

4. Person leans on elbow for support, slips and falls.

5. Mimicing walk of another person who can't see mimic.

6. Stumble over rug. Dignified person doubles the laugh.

7. Man takes a drink in one big gulp.

8. Two argue. One leaves and anticipates kick by bending his body forward.
   No kick.

In the days of the silent motion picture, farce was exceedingly popular
in the slapstick comedies created by Mack Sennett, Charley Chaplin, and
Buster Keaton. The basic requirement for silent pictures was action—
hence, it was a medium ideally suited for farce. Comedians tumbled their
way through crazy situations at breakneck speed—wildly improbable situations, full of violence set off by the slightest provocation, and usually
ending in a chase that annihilated all the canons of time and space. Some
examples of typical farcical business were: Harold Lloyd, playing a book
salesman, approaches a tough customer and is thrown out. He returns a
dozen times accelerating the pace. On another occasion he serves as a
practice tackling dummy for a football squad. He makes a speech at a
dance with a kitten crawling inside his sweater. Buster Keaton chases
butterflies in the countryside, completely oblivious to a band of wild
Indians who pursue him. In another picture he sits on a hot stove, then
sits on a cake of ice which melts rapidly. Ben Turpin, a cross-eyed ex-
plorer, surrenders to a stuffed lion.

That these familiar farcical patterns are still in use today may be seen
by consulting the log of television programs where you will find such
comic situations as these:

Susie and Mr. Sands have dinner at the home of Vi and her spinster aunt. Thinking Mr. Sands is in love with Vi, the aunt tries to force the marriage issue.

✿   ✿   ✿

Lucy resorts to drastic measures to prevent Ricky and Fred from officiating at a Miami Beach bathing-beauty contest. She schemes to have their pleasure-boat run out of gas, but hadn't figured on everyone's being captured by a savage on a desert island.

✿   ✿   ✿

Part of Annie's payment for a towing bill is a pig named Loretta. Unknown to Annie, Loretta is the only pig in the world that can count.

✿   ✿   ✿

Three confidence men elude the police by donning ecclesiastical garb. However, they come a-cropper in the Bowery when they run into a police sergeant who believes they've come to establish a mission.

✿   ✿   ✿

The Stooges are mistaken for plumbers, and hired to fix a leak in the basement of a wealthy woman's home.

These examples from vaudeville, motion pictures, and television indicate the comedian's approach to his material when his purpose is to arouse immediate laughter from a wide and undiscriminating audience. Similarly, in the legitimate theater, the devices of farce rely on visual humor centering on physical activities and usually involve complicated misunderstandings. Let us consider two typical farcical devices. The first is physical violence.

This comic mechanism requires a playful attitude which Eastman emphasized in his analysis of laughter. The act of violence should not cause genuine suffering in either the performer or the spectator. To elicit the audience's sympathy or to give the effect of real pain, is to destroy the atmosphere for laughter. The comic possibilities of the situation are enhanced when the recipient of the violence deserves chastisement for his antisocial behavior. Thus a pompous politician or a sanctimonious puritan is much funnier falling on the ice than a kind old lady would be. Comic literature is filled with all kinds of examples of fights, duels, beatings, spankings, combats and tumbles. Standard gags are the "pratt-fall," the black-eye, the sore foot, and the custard pie in the face.

Aristophanes shows his fondness for the use of physical devices over and over in his plays, although he was also capable of lifting the level of his material to social satire and to flights of delightful poetic fantasy. A typical use of low comedy in one of Aristophanes' plays occurs in *The Frogs*, which in part is a venture into literary criticism of the tragic works of Aeschylus and Euripides. In this particular scene, the god, Dionysus, betrays his cowardice when he and his servant, Xanthias, have made their way to Hades.

(The central door opens and the porter, AEACUS comes out with three other slaves to DIONYSUS, who, fearful of his reception, pretends he is XANTHIAS.)

AEACUS: Here, seize this dog-stealer and lead him
        forth to justice, quick.
DIONYSUS: *(Imitating XANTHIAS)*
                        Here's fun for sombeody.
XANTHIAS: *(in a Heraclean attitude)*
        Stop, zounds! Not one step more!
AEACUS: You want to fight?
        Ho, Ditylas, Sceblyas, and Pardocas,
        Forward! Oblige this person with some fighting!
DIONYSUS: *(while the Scythians gradually overpower*
          XANTHIAS)
        How shocking to assault the constables—
        And stealing other people's things!
AEACUS: Unnatural,
        That's what I call it.
DIONYSUS: Quite a pain to see.
XANTHIAS: *(now overpowered and disarmed)*
        Now, by Lord Zeus, if ever I've been here
        Or stol'n from you the value of one hair
        You may take and hang me on the nearest tree!
        Now, listen; and I'll act quite fairly by you;
        (suddenly indicating DIONYSUS)
        Take this poor boy, and put him to the question!
        And if you find me guilty, hang me straight.
AEACUS: What tortures do you allow?
XANTHIAS: Use all you like.   .
        Tie him in the ladder, hang him by the feet,
        Whip off his skin with bristle-whips and rack him;
        You might well try some vinegar up his nose,
        And bricks upon his chest, and so on. Only
        No scourges made of leek or young shalott.
AEACUS: A most frank offer, most frank—If my treatment
        Disables him, the value shall be paid.
XANTHIAS: Don't mention it. Remove him and begin.
AEACUS: Thank you, we'll do it here, that you may
        Witness exactly what he says. *(To DIONYSUS)*
        Put down your bundle,
        And mind you tell the truth.
DIONYSUS: *(Who has hitherto been speechless with*
          horror, now bursting out)
                      I warn all present,
        To torture me is an illegal act,
        Being immortal! And whoever does so
        Must take the consequences.

AEACUS: Why, who are you?
DIONYSUS: The immortal DIONYSUS, son of ZEUS;
          And this is my slave.
AEACUS: (*To* XANTHIAS)
                              You hear his protest?
XANTHIAS: Yes;
          All the more reason, that, for whipping him;
          If he's a real immortal he won't feel it.
DIONYSUS: Well, but you claim to be immortal too;
          They ought to give you just the same as me.
XANTHIAS: That's fair enough. All right, whichever
          Of us you first find crying, or the least bit
          Minding your whip, you're free to say he's
          No true god.
AEACUS: Sir, you behave like a true gentlemen:
          You come to justice of yourself! —Now then,
          Strip, both.
XANTHIAS: How will you test us?
AEACUS: Easily;
          You'll each take whack and whack about.
XANTHIAS: All right.
AEACUS: (*striking* XANTHIAS)
          There.
XANTHIAS: (*controlling himself with an effort*)
              Watch now, if you see me even wince.
AEACUS: But I've already hit you!
XANTHIAS: I think not.
AEACUS: Upon my word, it looks as if I hadn't,
          Well, now I'll go and whack the other.
          (*strikes* DIONYSUS)
DIONYSUS: (*also controlling himself*)   When?
AEACUS: I've done it.
DIONYSUS: (*with an air of indifference*)
          Odd, it didn't make me sneeze!
AEACUS: It is odd!—Well, I'll try the first again.
          (*He crosses to* XANTHIAS.)
XANTHIAS: All right. Be quick. (*The blow falls*)
          Whe-ew
AEACUS: Ah, why "whe-ew"?
          It didn't hurt you?
XANTHIAS: (*recovering himself*)
                    No; I just was thinking
          When my Diomean Feast would next be due.[1]

---

[1] Aristophanes, *The Frogs*, translated by Gilbert Murray in *The Complete Greek Drama*, edited by Whitney J. Oates and Eugene O'Neill, Jr., Random House Inc., Copyright ©, 1938). Reprinted by permission of the publishers.

This scene, in addition to employing the mechanism of physical violence, also makes use of another very well-worn comic device—mistaken identity, which lends itself especially well to low comedy because it provides an easy means for complicated misunderstandings. Plautus utilized this familiar pattern when he wrote *The Menaechmi*, the story of the reunion of long-lost twins. When Shakespeare reworked this same story for his *Comedy of Errors*, he further complicated the plot by adding a set of twin servants, which multiplied the opportunities for mistaken identity. In Goldsmith's *She Stoops to Conquer*, Tony Lumpkin purposely causes mistaken identity by telling Marlow and Hastings that his home is an inn. The two visitors subsequently treat their host as the landlord and his daughter as a maid.

As a variation of the mistaken identity device, playwrights frequently have made use of disguises which have resulted in mixups and deceptions. In the *Wasps*, Aristophanes created an amusing scene in which Philocleon attempts to escape from his house by a series of outlandish efforts, the most ingenious being his disguise as smoke coming out of the chimney. In English comedy, frequent use was made of "breeches" parts in which young women disguised themselves as men, which led to all manner of involvements such as Viola's fearful duel with Aguecheek in *Twelfth Night*. *Charley's Aunt*, one of the most popular of modern farces, is based on a situation in which a young Oxford undergraduate passes himself off as an elderly aunt from South America. Molière in *Scapin* devised a scene in which the rogue hid his master, Geronte, in a bag to conceal him from imaginary danger, but once he has the old man secure, he proceeds to give him a beating, meanwhile pretending to be his enemy.

CHARACTER

Farce usually deals with simple stock characters, often from ordinary walks of life. The romantic aspects of the story are often carried by pasteboard figures who have a talent for bumbling into awkward situations. The main burden of the comedy is in the hands of two kinds of characters —crafty manipulators who keep the action going, and awkward, unlearned or unsuspecting characters who are the targets of laughter. The manipulators are often tricky servants or parasites who live by their wits; those preyed upon are rustics, foreigners, foolish old men, hypocrites and poseurs of all kinds. Low comedians may be a part of a farce or they may be introduced into other kinds of plays such as in melodrama for comic relief. In English late eighteenth- and early nineteenth-century comedy, low, farcical characters were injected into the plays in such roles as farmers, sailors and Irishmen. Their ludicrous antics met with popular favor, and frequently they ran away with the show.

The speech and behavior of farcical characters is simplified as they race through the contrived mechanism of the plot. They do not think—they scheme, manipulate and act, often in devious ways, but toward clearly defined objectives. Because farce involves so much acting out of situations, the actor is given exceptional opportunities to develop a full pattern of behavior. The playwright's original sketchy design may be filled out and enhanced by the lively performance and personality of an imaginative comedian, so that the character becomes a memorable one in the theater. Roles which are especially susceptible to such enrichment are Tony Lumpkin in *She Stoops to Conquer,* Falstaff in *The Merry Wives of Windsor,* Lady Bracknell in *The Importance of Being Earnest,* and Sgnarelle in *The Doctor in Spite of Himself.* In characterization especially, farce depends upon the doing.

THOUGHT

The writer of farce does not have a message. His aim is to divert the audience's attention by providing a pattern of comic behavior. He manipulates character and situation to serve his comic purpose. At the end of the play, questions are answered, misunderstandings cleared up, the tangled threads of the story unravelled.

Because of its gay disrespect for conventional behavior, farce is sometimes criticized for its immorality, but farce is really amoral, unconcerned with ethical implications since the actions of the characters are removed from life and exist only in the theater by tacit agreement with the audience. Eric Bentley [2] considers that farce performs a valuable function as a safety valve in releasing the pent-up frustrations imposed on man by civilization. In this respect, farce may serve a Freudian purpose in that it gratifies repressed tendencies.

Certainly in farce, there is often implicit criticism of society and its mores—for example, the attack on pretensiousness and hypocrisy in Molière, Labiche, and Feydeau, but this is a by-product of their plays, not the essential reason for their existence. Farce exists primarily as a means of entertainment.

DICTION

Diction in farce is undistinguished by any literary pretensions. Only in rare instances has a playwright like Oscar Wilde combined the framework of farce and the repartee of social comedy, because wit depends upon an intellectual frame of reference. A critical ear is incompatible with farce. The linguistic devices of low comedy are puns, repetitions, "tag

[2] Eric Bentley, *Let's Get a Divorce!* (New York, Hill and Wang, Inc., 1958).

lines," wisecracks, insults, vulgarisms, and deformed language. Although the language of farce is commonplace, it requires a special talent. The writer of farce must write dialogue that sharply distinguishes each character. The actor's speech must accompany or thrust the action forward, rather than impede it. Laugh lines demand a feeling for the flavor and cadence of language, and the ability to make dialogue crackle and snap. The playwright must have an excellent sense of theater so as to pace his dialogue, build for laughs, make effective use of repetition, and realize the comic possibilities in the juxtaposition of words and phrases—the incongruities of human speech. Writing effective farcical dialogue may seem an easy task to the reader; actually it is an exacting and rather rare skill.

Two of the most successful writers of recent farce were George Kaufman and Moss Hart whose *The Man Who Came to Dinner* provides a successful example of farcical dialogue that makes use of the American penchant for the wisecrack and insult.

Sheridan Whiteside, a celebrated critic and raconteur is visiting in a midwestern town when he falls on the ice. He decides to take advantage of the situation by feigning an injury and spending two weeks in the home of the Stanleys in Mesalia, Ohio. Seated in a wheelchair, he is pushed into the living room where he encounters the Stanleys and two of their friends who have come to admire the celebrity.

There is a hush as the wheelchair rolls into the room. Welcoming smiles break over every face. The chair comes to a halt; MR. WHITEHEAD looks slowly around, into each and every beaming face. His fingers drum for a moment on the arm of the chair. He looks slowly around once more. And then he speaks.

WHITESIDE: (*quietly to* MAGGIE). I may vomit.

MRS. STANLEY: (*with a nervous little laugh*). Good morning, Mr. Whiteside. I'm Mrs. Ernest Stanley—remember? And this is Mr. Stanley.

STANLEY: How do you do, Mr. Whiteside? I hope that you are better.

WHITESIDE: Thank you. I am suing you for a hundred and fifty thousand dollars.

STANLEY: How's that? What?

WHITESIDE: I said I am suing you for a hundred and fifty thousand dollars.

MRS. STANLEY: You mean—because you fell on our steps, Mr. Whiteside?

WHITESIDE: Samuel J. Liebowitz will explain it to you in court. . . . Who are those two harpies standing there like the kiss of death?

(MRS. McCUTCHEON, *with a little gasp, drops the calf's foot jelly. It smashes on the floor*).

MRS. McCUTCHEON: Oh, dear! My calf's-foot jelly.

WHITESIDE: Made from your own foot, I have no doubt. And now, Mrs. Stanley, I have a few small matters to take up with you. Since this corner druggist at my elbow tells me that I shall be confined in this mouldy mortuary for at least another ten days, due entirely to your stupidity and negli-

gence, I shall have to carry on my activities as best I can. I shall require
the exclusive use of this room, as well as that drafty sewer which you call
the library. I want no one to come in or out while I am in this room.

STANLEY: What do you mean, sir?

MRS. STANLEY: (*stunned*) But we have to go up the stairs to get to our rooms,
Mr. Whiteside.

WHITESIDE: Isn't there a back staircase?

MRS. STANLEY: Why—yes.

WHITESIDE: Then use that. I shall also require a room for my secretary, Miss
Cutler. I shall have a great many incoming and outgoing calls, so please
do not use the telephone. I sleep until noon and require quiet through the
house until that hour. There will be five for lunch today. Where is the cook?

STANLEY: Mr. Whiteside, if I may interrupt for a moment—

WHITESIDE: You may not, sir. . . . Will you take your clammy hand off my
chair? (*This last to the nurse*) . . . And now will you all leave quietly or
must I ask Miss Cutler to pass among you with a baseball bat? [3]

SPECTACLE

Farce makes little demands of stage scenery, except in occasional plays
when the locale is an important aspect of the comic situation as in *George
Washington Slept Here, My Sister Eileen,* and *You Can't Take It With
You.* In general, the main interest is in the actions of the character. The
set designs should not impede the actor, but should give him ample space
and opportunity for vigorous and rapid movement. The visual aspects of
costume may be important in some instances and in nearly all cases the
playing of farce will appeal to the eye in the use of pantomime and business.

FARCE IN PERFORMANCE

Because the performer contributes so much to the final effect of farce,
a good deal depends on his sense of timing, his skillful use of movement,
gesture, and posture, and his manner of playing and inventiveness in
comedic creativity. One of the characteristics of talented performers of
farce, is in their ingenuity in devising comic business. W. C. Fields and
Charley Chaplin were past masters in their pantomimic ability. Chaplin
was especially gifted with a fertile comic imagination. Here, for example,
is Gilbert Seldes' description of a sequence from one of Chaplin's early
short silent film comedies, *The Pawnshop,* which reveals what the actor
may contribute to the performance.

Charlie enters the pawnshop; it is evident that he is late. He compares his
watch with the calendar pad hanging on the wall, and hastily begins to make

[3] *The Man Who Came to Dinner* by Moss Hart and George S. Kaufman. Copyright
©, 1939, by Random House, Inc. Reprinted by permission of the publishers.

up for lost time by entering the back room and going busily to work. He takes
a duster out of a valise and meticulously dusts his walking-stick. Then proceed-
ing to other objects, he fills the room with clouds of dust, and when he begins
to dust the electric fan, looking at something else, the feathers are blown all
over the room. He turns and sees the plucked butt of the duster—and carefully puts it away for tomorrow.

With the other assistant he takes a ladder and a bucket of water and goes
out to polish the three balls and the shop sign. After some horseplay he rises
to the top of the ladder and reaches over to polish the sign; the ladder sways,
teeters, with Charlie on top of it. A policeman down the street looks aghast,
and sways sympathetically with the ladder. Yet struggling to keep his balance, Charlie is intent on his work, and every time the ladder brings him near
the sign he dabs frantically at it until he falls.

A quarrel with his fellow-worker follows. The man is caught between the
rungs of the ladder, his arms imprisoned. Charlie calls a boy over to hold the
other end of the ladder and begins a boxing match. Although his adversary
is incapable of moving his arms, Charlie sidesteps, feints, and guards, leap-
ing nimbly away from imaginary blows. The policeman interferes and both
assistants run into the shop. By a toss of a coin Charlie is compelled to go
back to fetch the bucket. He tiptoes behind the policeman, snatches the bucket,
and with a wide swing and a swirling motion evades the policeman and returns. He is then caught by the boss in another fight and is discharged.

He makes a tragic appeal to be reinstated. He says he has eleven children,
so high, and so high, and so high—until the fourth one is about a foot taller
than himself. The boss relents only as Charlie's stricken figure is at the door.
As he is pardoned, Charlie leaps upon the old boss, twining his legs around
his abdomen; he is thrown off and surreptitiously kisses the old man's hand.
He goes into the kitchen to help the daughter and passes dishes through the
clothes wringer to dry them—passes a cup twice, as it seems not to be dry
the first time. Then his hands. The jealous assistant provokes a fight; Charlie
has a handful of dough and is about to throw it when the boss appears. With
the same motion Charlie flings the dough into the wringer, passes it through
as a pie crust, seizes a pie plate, trims the crust over it, and goes out to work.

At the pawnshop counter pass a variety of human beings. Charlie is taken
in by a sob-story about a wedding ring; he tries to test the genuineness of
goldfish by dropping acid on them. Sent to the back room, he takes his lunch
out of the safe, gets into another fight, in which he is almost beating the
rival to death when the girl enters. Charlie falls whimpering to the floor and
is made much of. He returns to the counter and the episode of the clock begins.

A sinister figure enters, offering a clock in pawn. Charlie looks at it; then
takes an auscultator and listens to its heart-beat; then taps it over crossed
fingers for its pulmonary action; then raps it with a little hammer to see the
quality, as with porcelain; then snaps his thumb on the bell. He takes an
augur and bores a hole in it; then a can-opener, and when he has pried the
lid off he smells the contents and with a disparaging gesture makes the owner
smell them, too. He then does dentistry on it, with forceps; then plumbing.

Finally he screws a jeweler's magnifying glass into his eye and hammers what is left in the clock, shakes out the contents, measures the mainspring from the tip of his nose to arm's length, like cloth, squirts oil on the debris to keep it quiet, and, lifting the man's hat from his head, sweeps the whole mess into it and returns it with a sad shake of the head.

A pearl-buyer has meanwhile come in and Charlie retraces his steps to the back room (carefully stepping over the buyer's hat) and begins to sweep. His broom becomes entangled with a piece of tape, which fights back and gets longer and longer. Suddenly Charlie begins to tight-rope upon it, balancing with the broom, and making a quick turn, coming forward for applause. A final quarrel with the other assistant ensues. As they are swarming around the legs of the kitchen table, the boss comes in and Charlie flees, leaps into a trunk, and is hidden. As the others enter the room, the pearl-buyer, who has stolen all the valuables, holds them up with a revolver. Charlie leaps from the trunk, fells the robber, and embraces the lovely maiden for a fade-out.[4]

Questions and Exercises

1. Contrast farce and high comedy.
2. What are the basic ingredients of a farcical plot?
3. What are the characteristics of farcical dialogue?
4. What does the performer contribute to farce?
5. Discuss the use of physical humor in farce.
6. What kinds of characters are used in farce?
7. Read a short farce. Identify the comic devices used.
8. What is the purpose of farce?
9. What comic devices can you recall having seen on stage or in the motion-picture theater or on TV?
10. What skills are required to write farce?

Farces

CHEKHOV: *The Marriage Proposal, The Boor, The Anniversary*
GOLDSMITH: *She Stops to Conquer*
MOLIÈRE: *The Doctor in Spite of Himself*
WILDE: *The Importance of Being Earnest*
SHAKESPEARE: *The Merry Wives of Windsor*

[4] From *The Seven Lively Arts* (1924), by Gilbert Seldes. Reprinted by permission of Harper & Brothers.

Suggested Reading

BENTLEY, Eric R., *Let's Get a Divorce! and Other Plays* (New York, Hill and Wang, Inc., 1958).

ENCK, John J., FORTER, Elizabeth T., and WHITLEY, Alvin, *The Comic in Theory and Practice* (New York, Appleton-Century-Crofts, Inc., 1960).

HEWITT, Barnard, *Art and Craft of Play Production* (Philadelphia, J. B. Lippincott Co., 1940).

NICOLL, Allardyce, *History of Early 18th Century Drama, 1700-1750* (New York, The Macmillan Co., 1925).

O'HARA, F. H. and BRO, M. H., *Invitation to the Theatre* (New York, Harper and Brothers, 1938).

8

Realism

IN THE previous four chapters we have been considering *types* or *forms* of drama. Now we turn our attention to dramatic *modes*—realism and two of its derivatives, naturalism and expressionism. Type or form refers to a particular kind of dramatic composition just as in painting we speak of still-life or portrait painting, and in music we talk about a sonata or fugue. By mode we mean the temper or spirit that affects the creator's point of view. The mode reflects the cultural climate in which a work of art was created. The classicism of the Greeks grew out of their ideal of the golden mean and of the emphasis on reason, while the romanticism of the eighteenth century was a response to the new emphasis placed on man as a child of nature, a creature of strong feelings and vivid imagination. In the past century, enormous changes took place in our intellectual outlook, with concomitant results in artistic expression. As a generalization, we may say that modern dramatic literature has centered around the form of drame and the mode of realism. Let us now examine the attributes of this mode.

To set down a clear-cut definition of realism is a precarious task since realism varies with the attitudes of writers, critics, and literary historians. Furthermore, the writer has very little interest in setting as his objective the creation of a work which will neatly dovetail into a pigeon-hole. The problem of definition is further complicated by the fact that realism has been used to refer both to a literary technique and a literary theory. In spite of the divergent meanings, there is fairly common agreement that realism relies upon sense impressions; that it deals with the here and now; that it is "concerned essentially with detail"; it is a "copying of actual facts"; it is a "deliberate choice of the commonplace"; it is a "factual interpretation of life"; it is in short, "Truth." Since man expresses himself in

142

art forms which by their very nature are conventionalized and artificial, complete reality is impossible in art. The term "illusion of reality" is in itself an anachronism. What the realistic dramatist and actor strive to achieve, is to "suggest actuality," and to give "the impression of truth" by employing symbols which communicate the effect of reality to an audience.

Any method of communication must necessarily rely on a set of symbols which have mutual acceptance and meaning to the artist and the person for whom the work is intended. The function of the artist is to create symbols and organize them in such a fashion as to elicit a desired, appropriate response. In the theater, the playwright uses all aspects of production as symbols—characters, setting, dialogue, light, sound, movement, and properties, which are arranged into a unified projection of the play, which is itself a symbol. The realist uses symbols which have a direct and immediate reference to life.

Symbols are dynamic. They vary as the artist responds to the environment and influences which press in upon him. Thus, every work of art is an expression not only of the individual who created it, but it is also an expression of the social forces which shaped the artist and his attitudes toward life. A Raphael Madonna, a Bach Chorale, a Louis Sullivan skyscraper, a Restoration comedy are more than works of individual men; they are also social documents of the age which produced them. The dynamic nature of symbolic expression is due not only to the artist's personality, but also to his philosophic outlook which he shares with his contemporaries. A society which has a philosophic outlook in which reality is considered to have an existence and validity independent of the psychic processes, does not demand of its artists the representation of actuality of objects and actions. Conversely, when a society becomes concerned primarily with the physical and material aspects of living based on sense knowledge, then the artist looks to real life for his means of expression. Throughout the history of Western civilization, there has been an ebb and flow of philosophic thought, now emphasizing a metaphysical view of life, now stressing materialism. In those periods when a materialistic attitude prevails, expression in the theater employs the techniques of realism. A complete aesthetic theory of realism could not evolve until the intellectual revolution of the nineteenth century, when the advance of science, materialism, and industrialism made such a theory not only possible, but inevitable.

THE REALISTIC MOVEMENT

From the change in speculative thought arising from the works of such men as Darwin, Freud, and Marx, three implications are of particular significance to drama and the theater. The first of these was the dynamic notion of change. In place of the older, static concept of a perfect creation a few thousand years ago, the scientist presented the idea that all life is in a constant process of alteration, and as a creature of nature, man too, is subject to change.

A second implication was that man is a "biochemical entity." Said the biologist: there seems to be nothing about human life or behavior that is not susceptible to explanation according to naturalistic laws and principles. Man is a product of a callous nature, rather than a child of special providence whose life is subject to divine intervention and revelation. Man acts mechanistically. His physiology is as important as his intellect in determining his conduct. Man is merely the leading member of the simian group, and for the time being, the dominant species of the animal kingdom on this planet.

A third implication of the new thought was that man is subject to scientific study. He is a case study, capable of being examined and investigated.

These changes in speculative thought were variously interpreted. At one extreme, Zola, and his fellow naturalists, saw in the teachings of science, license to emphasize the sordid and mechanistic aspects of life to the exclusion of all else. Their thinking was shadowed by a somber view of life which threw a blighting chill of determinism on all human conduct. At the opposite extreme, realists of the Spencer-Fiske persuasion saw in science a buoyantly optimistic assurance of the ultimate perfectability of mankind. They extended the doctrine of evolution to include the entire universe finding the promise of one glorious purpose—the elevation of mankind. Clarence Darrow reveals this interpretation in his article, "Realism in Literature and Art," in the *Arena*, IX, (1893):

Realism worships at the shrine of nature. It does not say that there may not be spheres in which beings higher than man can live or that some time an eye may not rest upon a fairer sunset than was ever born behind the clouds and sea; but it knows that through the countless ages nature has slowly fitted the brain and eye of man to the earth on which we live and the objects which we see, and the perfectly earthly eye must harmonize with the perfect earthly scene. To say that realism is coarse and vulgar is to declare against nature and her work.

In between the optimistic realist and the pessimistic naturalist was a variety of interpretations, but all found common agreement in stressing the importance of the individual and the significance of the environment as a formative influence on behavior. In addition, most realists were conscious of the humanitarian implications of the new way of looking at life. The artist plays a part in the elevation of mankind by insisting on the necessity of a congenial social atmosphere. The realist deals with the ugly and untrue because they are forces inimical to personal fulfillment. This point of view did not cause the realist to become a professed propagandist; his desire to be objective ruled against this. Nevertheless, humanitarian concern colors the selection of material, the delineation and motivation of character, and the nature of the dramatic conflicts.

The realistic movement had its origin in French fiction. Balzac, Flaubert, and the brothers Goncourt created conspicuous examples of the new attitude at work. The nature of that realism and its guiding principles is summed up in these words of Bernard Weinberg:

Realism stating its case in "las bataille realiste," states it in approximately these terms: Romanticism and classicism, striving for an ideal beauty and seeking it mainly in the historical subjects, arrives only at affectation and falseness. Realism, on the contrary, aims to attain truth. Now truth is attainable only by the observation (scientific and impersonal) of reality—and hence of contemporary life—and by the unadulterated representation of that reality in the work of art. Therefore, in his observations, the artist must be sincere, unprejudiced, encyclopedic. Whatever is real, whatever exists is a proper subject for art; this means that the beautiful and ugly, the physical and spiritual, are susceptible of artistic treatment; it does not imply that the artist refrains from choosing his subject and his detail, for choice is fundamental in art. The principal object of imitation is always man; description of the material world, construction of plot, are thus subsidiary and contributory to character portrayal. In setting down his observations, the artist must of course arrange and dispose his materials; but he avoids all possible falsification of them by practicing the utmost simplicity of style and form. The product of this method is moral in the highest sense—truth being the highest morality—and is eminently adapted to the needs of a materialistic, "realistic" society.[1]

In French drama, the theory of realism was rooted in the teachings of Didcrot, who in the eighteenth century, called for "middle-class tragedy." In the early nineteenth century when Pixerécourt popularized romantic melodrama, he required realistic scenery employing practical steps, bridges, and boats for the exciting action of his bourgeois plays. When Scribe came to the theater, his technical dexterity in manipulating plots and his portrayal of types found in contemporary society gave to his plays an air of superficial probability. His skill as a craftsman resulted in the writing of what became known as "well-made plays," whose techniques were so popular in the theater that his structural pattern was widely imitated. Scribe was followed by Augier, an enormously successful playwright whose impartiality of treatment, careful depiction of background through minute observation of objects and incidents, and his

[1] Bernard Weinberg, *French Realism: The Critical Reaction, 1830-1870* (New York, Oxford University Press, 1937). Reprinted by permission of the author.

competence in characterization took drama a step nearer to realism. Dumas *fils,* continued the advance by his concern with the decadence of the social scene in such plays as *Le Demi-Monde* (1855) and *La Question D'Argent* (1857). His treatment of men and women who were not heroic, but weak, sensuous, and selfish added a new role to the theater. Elsewhere in Europe, the intellectual revolution taking place found expression in the new playwrights—Henrik Ibsen, Leo Tolstoy, Anton Chekhov, August Strindberg, and Gerhart Hauptmann. These men were interested in telling the truth about the common man in everyday circumstances, but because their dramas were so outspoken and their subject matter was so bold, they found it difficult to get a hearing until the Independent Theater movement, a group of subscription theaters, was organized for the specific purpose of opening the doors of the theater to the new drama. This movement under the leadership of André Antoine in Paris, Otto Brahm in Berlin, Constantin Stanislavski in Moscow, and John Grein in London, broke the shackles of tradition and introduced a new exuberant spirit into the drama, linking the stage once more with literature and life. Ibsen's *Ghosts* was an especially important play because of its sensational impact wherever it was produced. In America, in the last decade of the nineteenth century, James A. Herne, and a number of disciples of the new realism in fiction, attempted to introduce the new spirit into the drama through a production of Herne's *Margaret Fleming,* and the sponsorship of performances of the continental playwrights, but the audiences were not hospitable to the shocking *drame.*

In addition to the development of realism as literary theory, during the latter part of the nineteenth century, there was also considerable change taking place in the techniques of writing and producing farces and melodramas which made up most of the popular stage fare. Characters of humble origin became more and more prominent; local color was exploited; native speech and costuming was more accurately reproduced; and the stage scenery and effects became increasingly substantial and convincing. Although much of the plot material and character motivation was patently artificial, realism made its influence felt, especially in the external aspects of production, even in those plays which were written primarily for entertainment.

The ultimate result of the revolution which took place in the late nineteenth-century theater was to win the twentieth century over to realism. While realism as a complete aesthetic theory soon lost its impetus, nevertheless, the techniques and attitudes of the realist have continued to dominate our modern stage, even in the face of a great deal of experimentation with new forms, and despite a rather general dissatisfaction with its restrictive outlook.

OBSERVATION AND OBJECTIVITY

Having received his inspiration from the scientist, the realist turned to him for his techniques, attempting to follow the basic concepts drawn from the scientific method. The first of these was dependence on observation. If the artist is to select symbols which will approximate a one-to-one relationship between symbol and referent, it is imperative that the object be known as completely as possible. The realist, therefore, came to rely on meticulous and precise observation, analysis and recording of specific details. The minutae which previous writers passed by, were accumulated a bit at a time to build up character or locale in much the same manner that Seurat used to apply his paint in tiny spots of broken color. And like Courbet and Manet, who took their easels out of their studios to paint commonplace subject matter from direct observation, rather than saints and miracles from their inspiration and imagination, the realistic writer looked hard at life at first hand, jotted down in his notebook the texture of his response. The realist was devoted to the sanctity of facts and the deduction of truth based on the evidence of collected data. It was his mission to see, hear, and report everything. Such an emphasis on observation not only affected the realists' choice of subject matter, but it also affected his method of handling it. He must allow the plot to develop where an honest treatment of his characters takes it; he must depict the environment and its atmosphere with scrupulous fidelity; he must concern himself with people rather than plot; he must employ emotion without artificiality or sentimentalism; he must be faithful to the facts as he observed them.

A second technique of the realist was to maintain an attitude of objectivity toward his work, just like the scientist conducts his experiments, examines his data and draws impersonal conclusions. As the realist avoids idealism and romanticism, he is equally opposed to cynicism and pessimism. As an impartial observer he attempts to escape personal bias and reports accurately on life as it is.

With this general background in mind, of a literary theory stemming from the intellectual revolution of the nineteenth century and noting especially the impact of science, let us now consider the application of realism to specific dramatic problems.

PLOT

The dramatic structure of the realist resembles classic drama in its unity of action, time, and place, and in its concentration on characters caught in moments of crisis. Thus, the realist generally uses a late point of attack, employs a few incidents, and ordinarily deals with a small group of characters over a short space of time. The result of this dramaturgy is a gain in intensity and dramatic tension because the action is continuous and concentrated, free from the extraneous diversions of constantly changing locales and complicated plots and subplots. The writer of popular nineteenth-century melodrama dramatized simple people in a complicated plot based on a pattern of physical conflicts. The realist reversed this approach by showing complex characters in a simple plot involving psychological action. The result was realistic *drame*.

Realistic plays are not full of arbitrary climaxes, built-up "big scenes" of violent action. Even in moments of great stress, the emotional expression is often deliberately restrained, underplayed, suggested rather than exploited: The playwright learned that the most telling moments of his plays might be the quiet closing of a door, the distant sound of an axe on a tree. There is an absence of sensational and "stagey" devices, but not an absence of emotional effect. There is more genuine horror in the last scene in *Ghosts* when Mrs. Alving holds the morphia powders in her hand staring at her deranged son, than there is in a wide screen filled with the slaughtered bodies of an Indian massacre filmed in Technicolor.

To secure the semblance of reality, the realist was obligated to make his work seem logical and plausible, with no clanking machinery or whirr of motors. He avoided all manner of contrivances that might destroy illusion. He did not interrupt the action to make explanations, preferring to integrate his exposition of antecedent action by gradual revelation throughout the course of the play.

The realist's method of handling plot was responsible for clearing away much of the manipulated and "hopped-up" trickery of popular drama. Plays became much more credible, closer to actual experience, and the observed facts of life. Because he based his dramas on ideas, rather than on external action, and because he was concerned with character revelation, the realist achieved an intensity of effect. On the other hand, his method of working narrowed the scope of action, slowed down the pace, and sometimes became downright sedentary. Critics were quick to point out, that in his attempt to condense the action and frame it in a solid mold amid a welter of concrete details, the realist sacrificed his chance to stimulate the imagination, and to give free play to his fancy. He had trapped himself in the stuffy atmosphere of a middle-class living room. As realism has developed in the past half century, the validity of this criticism has been acknowledged, and the contemporary playwright increasingly seeks ways to break through the confining walls to find a more poetic, a more theatrical realism.

CHARACTER

The realists' interest in characterization was centered in problems of motivation. He discarded the stock silhouette figures of the popular theater so obviously manipulated by the playwright to suit the needs of the plot—figures which reacted from conscious intent based on contemporary morality. Such flimsy characterization did not jibe with the realist's concept of behavior rooted in the pressures of environment, the dynamics of childhood, and the interaction of desires and inhibitions. The new dramatist was primarily concerned with the analysis and interpretation of character in the light of these forces which conditioned him. As Taine, the nineteenth-century French critic and historian, had observed:

Whether phenomena are physical or moral does not matter; they can always be traced back to causes. There are causes for ambition, for courage, or for truthfulness as there are for muscular contraction and for bodily temperature. Vice and virtue are products just as are vitriol and sugar. . . . Let us then seek out the simpler data of moral qualities as scientists those of physical properties.

The realist's attempt to achieve objectivity and his reliance on observation lead him to bring into the theater an entirely new gallery of characters which were delineated in a new way. In the past, playwrights had used people of the lower classes—servants, domestic figures, and tradesmen, and in the hands of skillful performers, some of these types created the effect of life-sized portraits, but they were only superficially real, and they often played minor or comic roles. Now the humble, the downtrodden, and the ordinary people took a central position on stage. They were revealed as complex individuals with conflicting psychological drives, products of heredity and environment. The playwright dramatized these people at critical moments of their lives, not those of violent physical action so much as the inner crises, thus penetrating the surface and giving insight into their desires, aspirations, and frustrations. The realist seemed especially concerned with presenting women on the stage, and created such memorable feminine characters as Strindberg's Laura and Julie, Chekhov's Madame Ranevsky and Nina, Shaw's Candida and Pygmalion, and Ibsen's Nora, Hedda, Rebecca West, and Mrs. Alving. Hamlin Garland, a contemporary of Ibsen, was particularly impressed with his creations:

Dramatically Ibsen's women are centres of action. Not passive dramatic "bones of contention" but active agents in their turn. Indeed they take the play in their own hands at times. Witness Lena in *Pillars*, Nora in *The Doll Home*, and Mrs. Alving in *Ghosts*. They re-act upon men, they rise above men at times in the perception of justice, of absolute ethics, as Lona above Bernick, Mrs. Alving over Manders. These women are out in the world, the men's world. They may not understand it very well, but they are at least in it and having their opinions upon things, and voicing their emotions. . . . They are grappling not merely with affairs but social problems.

As the result of the realist's emphasis on observation, the new dramatist carefully detailed the external aspects of character. His costume, speech, and manners were noted and described so that the actor found numerous clues for his performance.

In placing the contemporary man in the spotlight on the stage, the dramatists limited the possibilities of achieving the elevation and magnitude of classic tragedy with its heroic figures. Furthermore, the deterministic concept of character motivation based on environmental conditioning, ruled out the tragic hero with his free will and spiritual orientation. The protagonist of realism was a man of little stature, who was sometimes shown as the victim of circumstances, incapable of taking action against the forces which pressed against him.

The naturalists, as we shall see in another chapter, carried the mechanistic and bestial aspects of man to an extreme in their overemphasis of the sordid and the bizarre. The realist found it possible to show both sides of men and dealt with many characters who had redeeming qualities— characters who were close to the norm in behavior and outlook.

The realists made significant contributions to drama in the integrity of their characterization, their concern with sound psychological motivation, their cumulative technique of character revelation, and their treatment of protagonists drawn from the common walks of life.

THOUGHT

As we have suggested earlier, realism was an outgrowth of the intellectual revolution of the nineteenth century; the emphasis on science and materialism was reflected in the new drama.

Since the change in speculative thinking depicted man as a superior animal, rather than a child of God, his behavior was conditioned by the physical forces about him. Hence, the new playwright took an interest in these forces and showed how man's conduct was determined not by his free will but rather by the environment which impinged upon him. The scope of drama was lowered from the idealism and heroic stature of the romanticist and classicist, but it was broadened to include subject matter which preceding generations had ignored or disdained. The realist dealt boldly with new themes, many of them growing out of his awakened interest in the social sciences—economic conflicts, sex, domestic difficulties, social strife, and the interrelationships of men one upon another. Emulating the ways of science, the playwright attempted to record life objectively, so he pulled no punches, honored no taboos, found no material too commonplace or sordid for his probing. He became absorbed in the facts of man's existence here and now—commonplace facts about contemporary commonplace people. His observations of life caused him to discard everything that smacked of the theatrical, the artificial, the contrived, the sentimental. Like the late-nineteenth-century painters who went out of the studio to draw directly from life, the dramatist recorded what he saw, rather than what he imagined or wished to see.

The result was to open the doors of the theater to the dramatization of the day-to-day struggles of ordinary life. In insisting on the right to select his dramatic materials from all walks of life, the realist brought about a franker, freer stage. The theater audience sometimes found itself challenged to think as it was confronted with bold new themes. Dramatic literature had found a connection with the intellectual life of the time. Melodrama became *drame*.

DICTION

The realist's interest in accurate observation and reporting prompted him to capture an exact transcription of speech from life. Since he centered his attention on the common man in everyday circumstances, the playwright's dialogue frequently was ungrammatical, fragmentary, and disturbingly frank. To make the dialogue as exact a referent to life as possible, the realist abandoned the theatrical devices of asides, soliloquies, unmotivated "purple passages," and the inflated bombast of "paper speeches." Even in scenes of strong emotional climax, the dramatist avoided rhetorical display, having learned the eloquence of a broken phrase, a small gesture, and silence. Stage dialogue became strictly utilitarian, serving to advance the plot or delineate character, rather than to call attention to itself. In attempting to record environment accurately, the playwright noted the use of dialects and provincialism as a part of local color.

The frankness of the uncompromising realist burned too many polite ears; the new freedom of speech won its way slowly in the theater. Nearly half a century after Ibsen's *Ghosts*, Laurence Stallings and Maxwell Anderson found it necessary to warn their audiences in a program note about the forthrightness of their dialogue in *What Price Glory?* (1924).

What Price Glory? is a play of war as it is, not as it has been presented theatrically for thousands of years. The soldiers talk and act much as soldiers the world over. The speech of men under arms is universally and consistently interlarded with profanity. Oaths mean nothing to a soldier save as a means to obtain emphasis. He uses them in place of more polite adjectives.

The authors of *What Price Glory?* have attempted to reproduce this mannerism along with the general atmosphere they believe to be true. In a theatre where war has been lied about, romantically and effectively—and in a city where the war play has usually meant sugary dissimulation—*What Price Glory?* may seem bold. The audience is asked to bear with certain expletives, which under other circumstances, might be used for melodramatic effect, but herein are employed because the mood and the truth of the play demand their employment.

As George Bernard Shaw pointed out, another benefit which resulted from realism was the possibility of introducing "discussion" into drama. The new dramatists were concerned with ideas, and they took pains to stimulate the audience's thinking about their ideas by giving them expression on stage. Ibsen's and Shaw's characters not only act, they think —and they discuss their thoughts. Their dialogue becomes action—an investigation, an adventure, a verbal tug-of-war.

Critics of the realism lamented that the speech of the new drama drove poetry out of the theater. It is true that the playwright turned his ear in another direction, and sacrificed the use of poetic speech, and lost particularly the richness of imagery, but it is also true that much of the embellished dialogue of nineteenth-century writers of romanticism and melodrama was poor stuff—sentimental, pretentious, vapid, an unkempt garden of luxuriant and overgrown clichés. Moreover, in the hands of skillful playwrights, realistic speech had a clarity and intensity which went directly to the heart of the matter. Garland found much to admire in Ibsen's dialogue: "How true and unconventional his style. We hardly realize how false and stilted current stage conversation is, till we hear the real word spoken there. His words come to us at times like the thrusts of the naked fist. They shake the hearer with their weight of real passion. In one sense it is astoundingly direct, and then again it is subtly indirect— as in life."

The realist's point of view toward diction was clearly expressed in a letter which Ibsen wrote to Edmund Gosse, explaining why he did not use verse in writing *Emperor and Galilean:*

You are of opinion that the drama ought to have been written in verse, and that it would have gained by this. Here I must differ with you. The play is, as you will have observed, conceived in the most realistic style: the illusion I wished to produce is that of reality. I wished to produce the impression on the reader that what he was reading was something that really happened. If I had employed verse, I should have counteracted my own intention and prevented the accomplishment of the task I had set myself. The many ordinary insignificant characters whom I have intentionally introduced into the play would have become indistinct and indistinguishable from one another, if I had allowed all of them to speak in one and the same rhythmical measure. We are no longer living in the days of Shakespeare. . . . Speaking generally, the style must conform to the degree of ideality which pervades the representation. My new drama is no tragedy in the ancient acceptation; what I desired to depict was human beings, and therefore I would not let them talk "the language of the gods."

SPECTACLE

Although realistic scenery was employed in the theater in the past, its appeal was based on novelty and picturesqueness. The realist had quite a different purpose. Since he learned from the scientist that the environment conditions man's behavior, it became important to show the environment in order to understand the man. Thus, realistic scenery is not a mere accompaniment of the action; it is a causal force of the action. It shapes and molds the characters. The scenic background is an essential part of the symbolic configuration. In such plays as *Dead End, Street Scene,* and *Beyond the Horizon,* the setting assumes the importance of a major source of character motivation, and there is the sociological implication that to improve the man, you improve his circumstances.

The realist's observation of actuality and his concern with the commonplace prompted him to locate the action in a setting crammed with the domestic details of everyday life. He filled the stage and action of his plays with properties, but in the hands of the genuine realist these were not mere clutter for verisimilitude; they were selected because of their organic and symbolic relationship to the characters such as Hedda's pistols, Nora's macaroons, and Oswald's pipe. The use of props illustrated the notion of the significant trifle. Incidentally, the props were an enormous help to the actors in achieving naturalness in performance.

Just as the realist rejected the cardboard cut-out stock figures of the past, likewise he discarded the "painty" two-dimensional wing and groove, and backdrop setting. The "box set" (a setting with three continuous walls, often capped with a ceiling) which had been introduced earlier in the nineteenth century now became a standard requirement for realistic drama. Practical doors and windows, appropriate furniture, and genuine props were added to give the illusion of actuality. The environment became real. The actor was now surrounded by scenery, and played *within* a locale rather than in front of it. As a logical accompaniment of the new scenery came the convention of the "fourth-wall,"—a tacit agreement with the audience that the opening framed by the proscenium arch was the fourth wall of the set, thus giving the illusion of a solid room instead of a platform. The fourth-wall defines the downstage limit of the acting area and confines the actor to the setting; he pretends not to see or communicate with the audience.

This effort to represent a realistic environment was a mixed blessing as Arthur Hopkins' criticism in his book *How's Your Second Act?* (1918) suggests:

Realistic settings are designed wholly for conscious appeal. An attempt at exact reproduction challenges the conscious mind of the audience to comparison. . . . Unfortunately while the audience has been doing its unconscious checking up, the play has been going, and going for nothing, since any form of conscious occupation must necessarily dismiss the play. Further than that the result of the whole mental comparing process is to impress upon the auditor that he is in a theatre witnessing a very accurate reproduction, *only remarkable because it is not real.* So the upshot of the realistic effort is further to emphasize the unreality of the whole attempt, setting, play and all. So I submit that realism defeats the very thing to which it aspires. It emphasizes the faithfulness of unreality.

That Hopkins had a point is evidenced by the increasing tendency of the contemporary scene designer to use *selective* realism, in which he suggests more than he actually depicts, which lends itself more readily to new efforts in playwriting. The important contribution which realism made to spectacle was that scenery became an integral part of the interpretation of the play.

DEPARTURES FROM REALISM

While realism has been the dominating mode of contemporary drama, there have been many voices of protest raised against its commonplaceness of surroundings and character, its prosaic speech, and its lack of scope and scale. The radiant glow of romanticism idealizing the "natural man," has not only appeared in the plays of Rostand, Yeats, Dunsany, Edward Sheldon and Maxwell Anderson, but its spirit has had a generally pervasive influence so that many of our modern plays that are ostensibly realistic, actually are camouflaged romanticism in their emphasis on love, happy endings, and sentimentalism. The playwright with his eye on the box-office finds it difficult to write with uncompromising realism.

The next two chapters deal with two off-shoots of realism—naturalism and expressionism. These three modes by no means encompass all modern drama. Our twentieth century is notable for its freedom of experimentation as the playwright has sought to respond appropriately to the powerful and often bewildering forces at work in our contemporary culture. As a consequence, the dramatist has not felt obliged to confine himself to a single way of writing, but may, like Arthur Miller in *The Death of a*

Salesman, attempt to create a modern tragedy utilizing realistic characters and situations, but sometimes employing expressionistic techniques, or like Tennessee Williams, place his characters in sordid surroundings, while treating them with the lyrical touch of a poet. Our present playwrights seem to be increasingly impatient with the literal narrowness of realism and have struck off in many new directions, even to the extent of current "absurdists" who write "antidramas" in which they exaggerate realistic techniques to parody realism itself. Recent technological advances, particularly in lighting, have encouraged the writer to explore the possibilities of nonrealistic staging. But despite the eclecticism of modern playwriting and production, the impact of science with its stress on observation and our materialistic preoccupation with things have weighed the scales heavily in the balance toward realism.

Questions and Exercises

1. How does realism reflect contemporary society?
2. What changes in nineteenth-century thought laid the groundwork for realism?
3. What techniques and points of view does the realist attempt to borrow from the scientist?
4. What is the importance of environment in character motivation?
5. How did realism affect dialogue? Spectacle?
6. What changes did realism make necessary in acting?
7. What new subject matter did realism introduce to the stage?
8. What are the limitations of realism?

Realistic Plays to Read

IBSEN, Henrik: *A Doll's House, Hedda Gabler*
STRINDBERG, August: *The Father*
HOWARD, Sidney: *They Knew What They Wanted*
SHERIFF, R. C.: *Journey's End*
O'CASEY, Sean: *Juno and the Paycock*
CHEKHOV, Anton: *The Cherry Orchard, The Sea Gull*
WILLIAMS, Tennessee: *The Glass Menagerie*

Suggested Reading

BROWN, John Mason, *The Modern Theatre in Revolt* (New York, W. W. Norton and Co., Inc., 1929).

CHANDLER, Frank W., *Modern Continental Playwrights* (New York, Harper and Brothers, 1931).

DICKINSON, T. H., *The Contemporary Drama* (Boston, Little, Brown & Co., 1931).

HENDERSON, Archibald, *The Changing Drama* (Cincinnati, Stewart and Kidd Co., 1919).

SHAW, G. B., *Dramatic Opinions and Essays* (New York, Brentano's, 1907).

9

Naturalism

Naturalism is an exaggerated form of realism. As a specific aesthetic movement, Naturalism was short-lived, first gaining attention under Émile Zola's messianic leadership in the 1870's and flourishing briefly during the following decade in a period referred to by one critic as that of *"la litera-ture brutale."* As a literary style, naturalism waned quickly, but it con-tinues to have a leavening influence in the modern theater.

In part, the rise of naturalism was a reaction against the popular theater of the late nineteenth century which was at such low ebb that Matthew Arnold was prompted to say, in 1879 "In England, we have no drama at all." The successful box-office plays which catered primarily to the lower classes, wallowed in cloying romanticism, contrived "cliff-hang-ing" melodrama, and vapid farce, all of which were essentially dishonest, affecting the pulse and the tear ducts, but offering no sustenance to the mind. The naturalist made it a personal crusade to expose this shoddy material by presenting as frankly as he could, the problems and condi-tions of *"la bête humaine."* Zola flung out the challenge in his preface to his play *Thérèse Raquin:*

I am absolutely convinced that we shall next see the Naturalist movement imposed on the theatre and bringing to it the power of reality, the new life of modern art.

I defy the last of the Romanticists to put upon the stage a heroic drama; at the sight of all the paraphernalia of armor, secret doors, poisoned wines and the rest, the audience would only shrug its shoulders. And melodrama, that middle-class offspring of the romantic drama, is in the hearts of the people more dead than its predecessor; its false sentiment, its complication of stolen children and discovered documents have finally rendered it despicable, so that any attempts to revive it proved abortive.

157

The experimental and scientific spirit of the century will enter the domain of the drama and in this lies the only possible salvation of the drama.

The naturalist's primary stimulus was science as Zola's contemporary, Berenson, the art critic, observed: "A naturalist is a man with a native gift for science who has taken to art. His purpose is research, and his communication consists of nothing but facts."

Although he shared with the realists a similar approach and background, the naturalist made quite a different use of his materials. The naturalist is dedicated to the mechanistic and deterministic view of life; he stresses the animal in man and views him as a product of a callous nature. The heart is a muscle. He selects only the unsavory, the sordid, the somber aspects of life. His point of view is suggested in the criticism that was made of the Russian naturalist, Maxim Gorki, who was accused of "looking at life from a sunless basement, seeing only garbage pails and men's feet." The naturalist breaks sharply from the realist in his preoccupation with only the ugly and squalid aspects of character and action.

The naturalistic movement is inextricably linked with the name of Émile Zola who not only wrote the first naturalistic play but also bombarded the senses of his contemporaries as he clamored for a new dramatic method—the method of science.

I am waiting for them to rid us of fictitious characters, of conventional symbols of vice and virtue, which possess no value as human data. I am waiting for the surroundings to determine the characters, and for the characters to act according to the logic of the facts. . . . I am waiting until there is no more jugglery of any kind, no more strokes of the magical wand, changing in one minute persons and things. I am waiting, finally, until this evolution takes place on the stage; until they return the source of science to the study of nature, to the anatomy of man, to the painting of life in an exact reproduction, more original and powerful than anyone has so far dared to place upon the boards.[1]

Zola attempted to set the example with his own play, *Thérèse Raquin* (1873), an intense study of violence and crime in the lower depths. Thérèse and her lover drown her unwanted husband. They seek in vain to live down their crime under the accusing eyes of the dumb and paralyzed mother. Their unremitting remorse leads them to take poison on the night of their marriage. The play was located in a petty bourgeois background, well supplied with commonplace realities. *Thérèse Raquin* failed to attract an audience in the theater but the play and Zola's challenging preface led others to write in a similar vein. Becque, in *The Vultures*

[1] Émile Zola, *The Experimental Novel* (1880).

(1882), attacked the idea of the survival of the fittest in the economic jungle in dramatizing the destruction of a family and their fortune as the result of the preying activities of a dead man's business associates. Hauptmann, in *Before Sunrise* (1889), depicts the degradation of a Silesian coal-mining family suddenly grown rich in a story of misery and death. In his *Weavers* (1892), Hauptmann uses a mob as the protagonist in presenting the struggle between capital and labor with striking realism unrelieved by a love story or sentimental reconciliation. Tolstoi, in the *Power of Darkness* (1886), tells a grim story of illicit love, drunkenness, and murder, although he tempers the gloomy atmosphere with spiritual overtones. Strindberg's *Miss Julie* (1888), is a story of lust and suicide. Shaw in attacking slum-landlordism in *Widower's Houses* (1892), and prostitution in *Mrs. Warren's Profession* (1898), indicates his motivation for writing as he did: "I felt the need for mentioning the forbidden subjects, not only because of their own importance, but for the sake of destroying taboo by giving it the most violent possible shocks."

These playwrights, not all disciples of Zola, although sharing in many of his ideas, demonstrate the naturalist's efforts to introduce new attitudes and subject matter into the theater. While the audience soon tired of a steady diet of misery, crime, and disintegration, the naturalist, stimulated by the scientist's methods and attitudes, succeeded in injecting into drama, new characters and materials treated with honesty and forthrightness that characterize much of the best of our contemporary playwriting.

PLOT

As the playwright worked with new ideas and subject matter, it was inevitable that his dramaturgy should change too. During the first half of the century, Scribe and his followers had perfected the techniques of the *"pièce bien faite"* (well-made play), a highly ingenious machine; and while the well-oiled gears meshed smoothly enough beneath the shiny surface, the engine never served any purpose or produced anything except the fascination of watching the wheels go around. As someone observed, "Scribe is fine if you like clockwork." Plays built around props such as the letter, the glass of water, and the jewels, slid neatly off the assembly line in prefabricated packages, but the interest was in exterior wrappings and not the significance of the contents nor the characters. Less skillful writers of melodrama and farce manipulated formula devices and situations in an effort to evoke the maximum number of thrills, tears, and laughs. The plots were made up of a series of climaxes and episodes rigged by the playwright for eliciting excitement rather than an inevitable progression of events growing naturally out of character.

When the naturalistic playwright began to write plays from a scientific point of view with emphasis on observation and carefully documented details, he was forced to break with the plotting techniques of the writers for the popular theater. But unlike Ibsen who borrowed Scriban techniques and altered the purpose of playwriting to reveal character and induce thought, the naturalist tried to disregard all sense of form and technique. He argued that the action must be natural, not contrived. Thus he did not build climaxes or thrilling curtains. He simply put characters into a situation and observed them. Potentially dramatic scenes were underplayed, suggested or even avoided altogether. The ultimate effect of this approach was the *"tranche de vie"* (slice of life) play in which theatricality and skillful dramaturgy were negated in an attempt to give the impression that what happened on stage was actuality unorganized, without a beginning, a middle, or an end. The result of this approach was to challenge the shopworn trickery of the past and to cultivate a taste for playwriting which was simple in form and penetrating in its delineation of character. But the plotting practices of the naturalist did not make for a popular appeal since the plays often lacked excitement and suspense as well as a sense of form.

CHARACTER

As the result of his observation of contemporary life, the naturalist opened the doors of the theater to an entirely new collection of characters, many of them drawn from the seamy side of life—black sheep from across the tracks. It was in keeping with the naturalist's volatile attitude toward life, for him to show the debilitating effects of unfavorable environment and heredity by bringing on stage characters who were twisted, wayward, and grotesque. The heroic protagonist of romanticism who worked out his own salvation by exercising his will, was replaced by leading characters who were victims of circumstance such as the Vignerons in Becque's *The Vultures,* Nikita in Tolstoi's *The Power of Darkness,* and the downtrodden mob in Hauptmann's *The Weavers.*

As in his plotting methods, the naturalist developed an unobtrusive technique in the delineation of characters, revealing them cumulatively bit by bit and showing complex motivations frequently at odds with one another. The protagonist does not move in a straight line toward his goal from conscious intent but is bedeviled by doubts and frustrations, torn by inner conflicts, ridden by passions. This technique of complex characterization was clear to Strindberg who wrote in his preface to *Miss Julie:* "People are not character. They are conglomerates made up of past and present stages of civilization, scraps of humanity, torn-off pieces of Sunday clothing turned into rags—all patched together as is the human soul itself."

In his insistence on freedom to choose bold new themes and subject matter, the naturalist utilized emotional drives which previous writers had neglected or considered too degraded for the public stage. And when the audience hissed his play and the critic Sarcey protested that "this fellow, Zola, makes me a little sick," Zola argued stoutly that his purpose was highly moral, inasmuch as he was demonstrating that evil is caused by conditions, and that he was actually pointing the way to the elevation of man.

There are no more lustful men, there are only hearts of flame who dream of the infinite in the joy of love. There are no more wrathful men, avaricious men, deceitful, gluttonous, slothful, envious or proud men, there are only men whose inner forces, whose untamed energies, whose desires for activity, for battle, and for triumph have been misdirected. A miser can be turned into a careful steward, a wrathful, envious, arrogant man can be made a hero, devoting himself to the last drop of blood for the sake of a little fame.

In his attempt to imitate the objectivity of the scientist, Zola justified his choice of characters and situations in *Thérèse Raquin* by claiming that he was serving only as a dispassionate observer, honestly recording facts: "Given a strong man and an unsatisfied woman, to seek in them the beast, to see nothing but the beast, to throw them into violent drama and note scrupulously the sensations and acts of these creatures. I have simply done on two living bodies the work which surgeons do on corpses."

Gorki, in a similar vein, described the writer's obligation to character in his preface to *The Judge:*

The characters of a drama should all act independently of the volition of the dramatist, in accordance with the law of their individual natures and social environment; they must follow the inspiration of their own destiny, and not that of any other destiny arbitrarily imposed upon them by the writer. They must be driven by their own inner impulses, create the incidents and episodes —tragic or comic—and direct the course of the play, being permitted to act in harmony with their own contradictory natures, interests and passions.

Other naturalistic playwrights were as much concerned with the secret, silent, inner forces of man as they were with such overt and sensational action as murder, suicide, violence, and sex. The naturalists profoundly affected contemporary drama in gaining new freedom for the introduction of all kinds of characters, and in their interest in and techniques for character revelation that plumbed the very depths of men's behavior.

THOUGHT

Naturalism was not a novelty or a quirk of Zola's imagination, but it was a by-product and the natural accompaniment of the materialistic and scientific development of the nineteenth century. It was caused by the culture from which it came. The intellectual revolution, of course, was the result of many divergent forces at work, but Charles Darwin's hypothesis of evolution was the great ignescent idea of the period which kindled new sparks and fanned into flame all manner of conjecture and controversy. The far-reaching effects of Darwin's ideas is indicated by the following statement from the *Encyclopedia of Social Sciences:*

By placing man wholly within the organic realm, he upset creationism, raised doubts as to the unique spiritual nature of man, undermined belief in miracles, revelation and answer to prayer, destroyed the myths of the fall and original sin and compelled a complete recasting of the argument from design and theology in general. In addition, his emphasis on continuity and naturalism stimulated extensive inquiries into the origin, nature and evolution of ideas of the soul and of religious beliefs and practices.

Karl Marx likewise made considerable impact on nineteenth-century thought since his ideas extended and reinforced implications of the new science, especially his emphasis on the influence of environment and its conditioning effect on behavior. Marx taught that not only were men shaped by their environment, but more importantly, the social scientist and political thinker should bear in mind that "circumstances are changed precisely by man."

From these views the naturalist took courage to expose the shameful side of life and the depravity of character. Since, as the biological scientist taught, disease, crime and poverty are caused by conditions, then as the social scientist teaches, the solution is to change the conditions—and the first step is to focus attention on the rottenness of society—which is exactly what the naturalist set out to do. And when people criticized Maxim Gorki for his *The Lower Depths,* he replied:

Why do I relate these abominations? So that you may know, kind sirs, that it is not all past and done with. You have a liking for grim fantasies: you are delighted with horrible stories well told: the grotesquely terrible excites you pleasantly. But I know of grimmer horrors, everyday terrors, and I have an undeniable right to excite you unpleasantly by telling you about them, in order that you may remember how we live. A low and unclean life it is and that is the truth.

Although the naturalist professed to be as objective as the scientist, his selection of materials and the social implications back of the pictures that he drew made it clear where his sympathies lay.

The naturalist attempted to translate into concrete images what he had gained from the changing thought of the late nineteenth century. The hard shell that protected the traditional views of love, authority, duty, honor, and morality was shattered when the playwright probed beneath the surfaces of life into the relation of the individual to his mate, his employer, and his family as he sought to lay bare his innermost desires and passions. A new blow was struck for freedom of thought in drama.

DICTION

Since the naturalist took his cues from life and was particularly zealous in depicting environment in accurate detail, it was essential that the characters on stage should speak the speech of everyday life. Moreover, the emphasis on the dregs of society, made it necessary for the playwright to use dialogue that would characterize the low-born and humble. It was this sort of speech which the playwright now sought to recreate on stage. When Arno Holz and Johannes Schlaf wrote *Die Familie Selicke* (1891), Ludwig Lewisohn reported that the audience was struck by the authentic speech of real men: "Not speech rewritten and rearranged in its order, but the humble speech of our daily lives with its elisions, its hesitations and iterations, its half-articulate sounds and cries, but also its sting and sob and clutch."

In his introduction of bold new themes, the dramatist found it necessary to discuss openly subjects which had hitherto been considered too controversial or salacious for the delicate ears of the theater-goer, but the naturalist pulled no verbal punches, flailing away with direct and frank dialogue that brought cries of shocked protest. The outraged critic, in order to make his vehemence sufficiently emphatic, was forced to borrow the imagery of naturalism as one English reviewer did in expressing his reaction to Ibsen's *Ghosts:* "A mass of vulgarity, egotism, coarseness and absurdity. . . . An open drain, a loathsome sore unbandaged, a dirty act done publicly."

While it is true that the naturalist debased stage diction, it is also true that he performed a valuable function in a negative way in ridding the stage of bombast, inflated rhetoric and sentimentality, even though the new style opened the way for speech that was nonliterary, ungrammatical, and disturbingly frank.

SPECTACLE

When the naturalist set the scene for his plays, he was motivated by the desire to show the environment as a causal force in the behavior of his characters. Hauptmann, Tolstoi, and Gorki utilized scenes of poverty and squalor not as mere novelties for their picturesque qualities, but because the physical surroundings were an integral part of the drama, necessary for understanding the way the characters lived and moved and had their being. Gorki's setting for *The Lower Depths* epitomizes the psychological atmosphere of the play.

A cavelike basement. A heavy vaulted ceiling, blackened with smoke, with patches where the plaster has fallen off. The light comes from the direction of the audience and from a square window high up the wall, right. The right corner is cut off by a thin partition behind which is PEPPEL's room. Near the door leading into it is BUBNOV's plank bed. In the left corner is a big Russian stove. In the stone wall, left, is a door to the kitchen, where KVASHNYA, the BARON, and NASTYA live. By the wall between the stove and the door stands a wide bed screened off by a dirty cotton-print curtain. Everywhere along the walls are plank beds. Near the left wall, downstage, stands a block of wood with a vise and a small anvil mounted upon it. Sitting before it, on a smaller block of wood, is KLESTCH, who is busy trying keys in old locks. On the floor lie two bunches of keys strung on wire rings, a battered tin samovar, a hammer, and some files. In the center of the basement stand a big table with a samovar, two benches, and a square stool—all unpainted and dirty. At the table KVASHNYA is serving tea, the BARON is munching black bread, and NASTYA, seated on the stool and leaning on the table, is reading a battered book. ANNA, lying on the bed behind the curtain, is heard coughing. On his plank bed the capmaker BUBNOV, holding a hat block between his legs, is fitting a ripped pair of pants over it, figuring out the best way to cut the cloth. Scattered about him are a torn hatbox containing cap visors, scraps of oilcloth, and cast-off clothing. SATIN, just awake, lies on a plank bed emitting loud guttural sounds. On top of the stove, unseen by the audience, the ACTOR is puttering around and coughing.

It is morning in early spring.[2]

From this example it is evident that just as the naturalist built character and plot by the accumulation of significant details, so the stage setting utilized a collection of properties to give the illusion of actuality. This led to an excess of clutter, an obsession with the solidity and authenticity of material objects which at its extremes caused Antoine to hang sides of beeves on stage, and Belasco to bring into the theater actual parts of houses and restaurants. The lack of moderation doomed the naturalist's efforts to failure, although they were a contributing force in replacing ostentatious display with scenery that functioned as an integral part of the play, and in establishing the appropriate environment for the action of the drama.

[2] Maxim Gorki, *The Lower Depths,* translated by Alexander Bakshy (New Haven, Yale University Press, 1945). Reprinted by permission of the publisher.

Scene from Gorki's *The Lower Depths*, first produced at the Moscow Art Theatre in 1902

Questions and Exercises

1. What is the importance of heredity and environment in naturalism?
2. What is the importance of spectacle in naturalism?
3. What changes occurred in the nineteenth-century intellectual revolution that influenced naturalism?
4. What is a "slice of life" play?
5. How does naturalism affect dramatic structure?
6. What services did naturalism perform for the theater?
7. What is the naturalist's point of view toward character?
8. What are the weaknesses of naturalism?
9. Compare the use of scenery in melodrama with that in naturalistic drama.

Naturalistic Plays to Read

STRINDBERG: *Miss Julie*
GORKI: *The Lower Depths*
BECQUE: *The Vultures*
HAUPTMANN: *The Weavers*

Suggested Reading

BENTLEY, Eric R., *The Playwright as a Thinker* (New York, Reynal and Hitch-cock, 1946).

CHANDLER, Frank W., *Modern Continental Playwrights* (New York, Harper and Brothers, 1931).

CLARK, B. H., *A History of Modern Drama* (New York, Appleton-Century-Crofts, Inc., 1947).

FILON, P. M. A., *Modern French Drama*, translated by Janet E. Hogarth (London, Chapman and Hall, 1898).

SMITH, H. A., *Main Currents of Modern French Drama* (New York, Holt, 1925).

10

Expressionism

ONE of the persistent and frustrating limitations of the playwright is his inability to get inside of his characters' heads. We all know that people are not completely or accurately represented by what they do or say. The novelist may pry beneath the surface into his characters and reveal their private feelings, their unconscious motivations, their unspoken desires, but the playwright has been hamstrung because at the time the psychologist unearthed the rich and confusing interior world of man, the dramatist was perversely trying to acquire techniques to suggest the maximum surface reality. A century ago, the dramatist might use a soliloquy to let the audience know what was going on inside, but realism discarded that device as too artificial. But the need to externalize the inner life continues. It is interesting to observe the ingenuity of various modern writers in their efforts to project psychological action in their plays. Pirandello was one of the most ingenious writers in employing such devices as the mask, insanity, feigned and real, and the character who is acting. Strindberg utilized dream-like sequences, T. S. Eliot worked through a psychiatrist, Evreinoff splits a character into several aspects of personality, Miller uses a character talking to himself. All manner of techniques have been tried to explore the possibilities of revealing the inner man.

One of the most interesting experiments has been that of the expressionists who had the wit to recognize their problem and the courage and ingenuity to make bold efforts to deal with psychological reality, the subconscious, the man beneath the skin.

The expressionist is a superrealist. He insists that actuality is within. The true character is masked by conventional behavior. Beneath the social façade, there is a vast jungle of primitive feelings and desires to be explored. And it is here that man really lives. It is this aspect of life and character that the expressionist seeks to reveal in as frank and striking a way as possible. In order to do so, the expressionist found it necessary to reject the traditional ways of the theater and develop his own special techniques and conventions.

Long before the twentieth century, playwrights occasionally had utilized the point of view and methods of expressionism in their plays. We recall Cassandra's whirling words in *Agamemnon*, the hallucinations in *Macbeth*, and Richard III's ghostly vision. For a moment, the playwright lifted the veil and allowed us to see into the workings of a tormented mind. But these are sporadic outcroppings within the play, rather than a sharp break with conventional styles.

Strindberg, in his preface to *The Dream Play* (1902) indicated the expressionist's approach to drama: "Anything may happen; everything is possible and probable. Time and space do not exist. On an insignificant background of reality, imagination designs and embroiders novel patterns; a medley of memories, experiences, free fantasies, absurdities, and improvisations." A drama, Strindberg says, may have the "disconnected but seemingly logical form of a dream." He gave substance to his theory in writing such works as *The Dream Play, The Spook Sonata* and *To Damascus.* For a time, Strindberg was an isolated innovator in his approach, but from 1912 to 1925, expressionism became an important and striking style, especially in Germany. Kafka and Joyce paralleled the experiment in drama in their novels. In America, expressionism found its voice in the 1920's, notably in O'Neill's *The Emperor Jones* and *The Hairy Ape,* Rice's *Adding Machine,* and George Kaufman and Marc Connelly's *Beggar on Horseback.*

Expressionism as a specific aesthetic movement began in Germany and made its first appearance in painting when the expressionist strove to report the inward vision by use of nonrepresentational symbols or by the juxtaposition of objects whose relationship set up a kind of tension. Oskar Kokoshka, a pioneer expressionist, both as a playwright and as a painter, stated the experimenter's point of view: "We must hearken closely to our inner voice. . . . All that is required of us is to release control. . . . One's soul is a reverberation of the universe."

From painting, the impetus swept into the theater, at first through stage design, and then in playwriting. Frank Wedekind led the way and was followed by others, most notably by Ernst Toller and Georg Kaiser, who became the outstanding expressionists of the theater. Following World War I, expressionism became a rallying point for those creative souls who were rebelling against war and materialism. It was a form of releasing their frustrations and yearnings. Expressionism became the revolutionary style of faddists and cultists of all kinds who were dissatisfied with the world which they inherited. Their purpose was to show the disintegration of modern man and twentieth-century society, and to challenge their contemporaries to find a new way of life.

THE EXPRESSIONIST'S POINT OF VIEW

The expressionist insists that reality is not represented by the surface of things. A man is more than his external behavior and appearance. To get at the truth, the mask must be torn away, the façade pierced. Genuine reality is inner reality. To really understand a man is to know the private, inner world where dwell his secret and sometimes unconscious desires, aspirations, conflicts, frustrations, hallucinations. It is this strange and confusing subjective reality that the expressionist wished to explore. Moreover, he saw beyond the immediate act and the momentary response to the larger essence of an idea. A bridge is not merely an engineer's creation of steel and concrete—it is a means of joining people together. A madonna and child are not merely two of the Holy Family; they are maternity. A pool hall is not just a room in a building; it is a glare of green and yellow. The expressionist strives to project the essential qualities of objects, experiences and people from the inside out. He is not concerned at all with copying what meets the eye. Accurate representation of shape, size, and appearance hold no interest for him. He wishes to plumb the depths where man really lives.

In his approach, the expressionist is somewhat analogous to the composer. Like the musician, he wishes to convey the feelings that have been aroused in his inner being without any consideration of their reference to reality. He wants to present the essential qualities of an experience through imaginary and fanciful analogues to indicate the texture and quality of life within.

Expressionism faded very quickly in the theater; by the 1930's it was seldom used except fragmentarily. It never succeeded in capturing a large segment of the theater audience because of its confusing distortions, its lack of story value, its bizarre and oftentimes thin characterization, and because of the author's insistent message. However, the expressionist did provide the theater with half a dozen examples of effective plays, it challenged the tenets and methods of external realism, and it encouraged playwrights and designers to find new ways of working in the theater.

PLOT

Because of his desire to reveal inner reality, the expressionist suppresses the details of actuality and discards conventional theatrical techniques to develop his own style of writing and production. He is not bound by time and space, nor does he pretend to follow a logical sequence of action. The narrative thread is not his concern. He experiments freely with ways of conveying his feelings, sometimes in small fragments, sometimes by implication rather than through direct statement. As a result, his effect is often fantastic and bewildering.

For example, Nikolai Evreinoff's *The Theatre of the Soul* has but a single character. The action takes place within one-half second inside his chest. A conflict splits the character of the Professor into three entities— the Rational, the Emotional and the Subliminal. Projected on the stage from the Professor's mind are four Concepts of the Wife and Dancer. When the conflict is resolved by the Professor's suicide, his heart in the chest of the stage figure shoots forth streams of blood-red ribbon.

The expressionist rejects conventional dramatic structure since he wishes to center his attention on the essential actions no matter when or where they occurred without being obliged to provide for the gradual development of exposition and the close-knit articulation of antecedent and consequent relationships. The expressionist shows the important high points of an experience without being bogged down by small-talk or the machinery of plotting. As a result, his structure is generally fragmentary and episodic. The playwright expresses with sharp immediacy the associations and implications stirred up by an object or character before him. He allows his feelings to carry him where they will. He is driven by intuition rather than logic. The expressionist utilizes any method that occurs to him in order to provoke the audience's imagination into understanding.

The techniques of expressionism are the results of the dramatist's point of view which is from the inside out. Actuality is important only insofar as it evokes associations and reactions in the spectator's mind. The expressionist's creation is thus a subjective response to the stimuli which impinge upon him, and his concern is not with the nature of the stimuli *per se*, but in the nature of the response. He flings open the windows of the mind and allows the spectator to look in upon the private, disordered associative processes of his characters. The playwright makes subjective explorations into the realm of the spirit which defy precise representation. The reader and theater-goer does not get an exact description of an event but the effect and feel of it on the protagonist. James Joyce makes use of this approach in his novel, *Ulysses.* A typical passage occurs when Leopold Bloom takes his place in the hearse and the reader is given access to his private world:

Mr. Bloom entered and sat in the vacant place. He pulled the door to after him and slammed it tight till it shut tight. He passed an arm through the armstrap and looked seriously from the open carriage window at the lowered blinds of the avenue. One dragged aside: an old woman peeping. Nose white-flattened against the pane. Thanking her stars she was passed over. Extraordinary the interest they take in a corpse. Glad to see us go we give them such trouble coming. Job seems to suit them. Huggermugger in corners. Slop about in slipper-slappers for fear he'd wake. Then getting it ready. Laying it out. Molly and Mrs. Fleming making the bed. Pull it over to your side. Our windingsheet. Never know who will touch you dead. Wash and shampoo. I believe they clip the nails and hair. Keep a bit in an envelope. Grow all the same after. Unclean job.

Because of his point of view, the expressionist's play structure is frequently chaotic and disconnected. He contends that life is experienced in spurts and snatches rather than in logically organized patterns, hence a plot may be one of fragmentary actions and events. Experience is shattered into its elements and reformed to suit the playwright's purpose. The critical moments of a man's career are shown in a jagged series of explosive scenes. In *The Adding Machine,* Mr. Zero's crime and punishment are shown; *The Hairy Ape* dramatizes Yank's quest for status; *From Morn to Midnight* tells the story of a bank clerk's theft, spending orgy and death; in *Transfiguration* a series of dream pictures demonstrate the horror of war. These plays are constructed in a series of scenes in a montage of kaleidoscopic action. Climaxes and crises appear without preparation; exposition is simplified to direct communication or neglected altogether; the emotional impact of the play is a cumulative result of scene piled on scene. The action is caused by the effect desired, rather than the necessary or probable consequence of an integrated series of events. The expressionist's method of working, then, is not a clear and orderly arrangement of the parts in an organic or consecutive fashion, but rather a jumble of fragments which suggest, rather than describe, the experiences of the play.

CHARACTER

Characters in expressionistic plays are usually depersonalized. They are not individuals but types who are given such names as the Gentleman in Black, the Billionaire, the Young Woman in Taffeta, Mr. Zero, the Blues and the Yellows. They show little or no psychological complexity except for the protagonist through whose eyes all of the action may be seen, thus providing us with an intimate experience of his world. To reveal the inner state of the character, playwrights revived the technique of the soliloquy so that the character has a means of expressing what goes on inside of him. These soliloquies may be of considerable length, some of them as in *The Adding Machine* constituting entire scenes. When the play is seen through the eyes of the protagonist, his subjective point of view may be confusing to the spectator because of the kind and degree of distortion

and the use of bewildering symbols. The viewer of the outstanding expressionist motion picture *Dr. Caligari,* for example, may be slow to
realize that he is seeing the people and the world around him through
the eyes of a demented man, which accounts for the distortion and
grotesqueness of the visual aspects of the film.

Sometimes, the protagonist is the voice of the author as in Toller's
Transfiguration, in which the hero, Friedrich, is clearly the playwright
protesting against militarism and embittered nationalism. Friedrich is
something of an individual with a specific background of race and country, but he is also an abstract symbol of man appearing in many different
forms as a soldier, professor, sculptor, judge, priest, and working-man. In
From Morn to Midnight the theater-goer sees a personal account of a
clerk who absconds with the bank's funds and goes on a wild orgy ending
in suicide. In *The Adding Machine,* we see Mr. Zero's dismal home life, his
loss of his job and the murder of his boss, the trial, and then we follow
him to the Elysian Fields and finally to the refurbishing department where
he is made over. In working from the subjective point of view, the playwright presents an intimate experience of the protagonist, but the surrounding figures often become automatons.

Because he rejects the usual plot structure, the expressionist does not
employ the ordinary means of building up substantial characters bit by
bit through a consecutive sequence of action. Instead, he simplifies and
exaggerates the characterization to suit his purposes. He quickly establishes characters as types by speech and behavior in scenes selected for
their significance to the protagonist. Character itself is often handled
symbolically and with great freedom as Strindberg indicates: "The characters split, double, multiply, evaporate, solidify, diffuse, clarify. But one
consciousness reigns above them all—that of the dreamer; it knows no
secrets, no incongruities, no scruples, no law."

In presenting the hero's subjective point of view, which may be a distorted one, the playwright may place his action quite often in surroundings that are bizarre and grotesque—a mummy comes out of a closet,
skeletons arise from the grave and perform a weird dance, a corpse climbs
out of his coffin with eyes fixed in hypnotic stare, a madman kidnaps a
girl and escapes with her through a nightmarish landscape, a shrieking
chorus cries out in staccato patterns of sound. Such characters are not
merely the agents for advancing the story, but they also create atmosphere
and are symbolic representations of the protagonist's state of mind.

THOUGHT

In general, expressionists have had an axe to grind. Their plays have
been linked to social causes. Their dramas often have been protests against

Scene from Elmer Rice's *The Adding Machine* as produced at The Theatre Guild, 1923, New York. Set by Lee Simonson.

the status quo. The German expressionists, in particular, utilized the new style not simply as a novel way of attempting to project inner states, but they also developed their plays as an effective means of attacking contemporary political and social ills. Kaiser and Toller were men with a social purpose, dedicated to overthrowing contemporary evils.

The intellectual content of expressionism is not especially striking. The themes of the Germans were mostly well-worn ideas of protest against materialism, mechanization, and militarism, and a plea for a new set of values which would elevate man. American expressionists, similarly, worked over familiar ideas. O'Neill's *The Hairy Ape* is a criticism of our materialistic society and of human disorientation; *The Emperor Jones* dramatizes man's inability to escape from his primitive past; *The Adding Machine* is a merciless satire on the plight of the little man trapped in a mechanical world; and *Beggar on Horseback* lampoons Philistinism in America. The expressionists were not notable for their advanced thinking, but rather their merit was in their ability to give new shape and expression to familiar ideas.

German expressionists were frankly didactic, injecting forthright statements of their social bias. In Kaiser's *Coral*, the Billionaire's Son revolts against the injustice of capitalism: "We are rich, and these others who stifle in torment and misery are men like us." Similarly in *Gas*, Kaiser deplores the effect of industrialization upon mankind: "Are your thundering trains and vaulting bridges and flying motors sufficient recompense for your fever? You brother, are more than a hand!" Again in Kaiser's *From Morn to Midnight*, the author makes a direct attack on materialism: "Not with all the money from all the banks of the world can one buy anything of value. . . . Money is the crowning deceit of all."

In war-weary Germany in the 1920's, all of the elements of revolt went into expressionism. The frustrations and yearnings of a people tormented by guilt and despondency were unleashed. Expressionism was not merely a style of drama; it was a cause, a desperate and agonized plea for some kind of salvation. As Professor Edwin H. Zeydel said: "It denies the world; it boldly maintains that the only true being is the Ego. . . . It is pacifistic by its nature and humanitarian. . . . Recently, it has become even communistic, yes messianic. It has gone so far as to venture to revolutionize not only art but mankind."

In *Masses and Man*, Toller attacked militarism and materialism. The seven scenes of his play are linked together by music and changes of lighting. The plot concerns a woman, who opposed by her husband, joins the workers in a protest against war. They attempt to liberate those who slave in the mines and munition factories. The masses are swept into a frenzy for a war of their own against the State. When the Woman tries to dissuade the masses from violence, they turn upon her and make her the scapegoat for the revolt. She is sent to her death. Such a plot was used by Toller as a springboard for his message which he stated in his autobiography:

Can a man not be an individual and a mass-man at one and the same time? . . . As an individual a man will strive for his own ideals, even at the expense of the rest of the world. As a mass-man social impulses sweep him toward his goal even though his ideals have to be abandoned. The problem seemed to me insoluble. I had come up against it in my own life, and I sought in vain to solve it.

DICTION

The expressionist freely experimented with language, using it to create effects and atmosphere as well as to advance the thought. One of the most interesting efforts was in the expressionist's use of short bursts of staccato speech which sometimes exploited the possibilities of rhythm and sharply marked tempo. Such telegraphic speech created an unreal effect, reinforcing the off-beat atmosphere and the strange characterization. Walter Hasenclever, in his *Beyond*, uses clipped fragments in this fashion:

> JEANE: This is my house.
> This is my window.
> This is the sky.
> The sun shines.
> I know that I live.
> I am happy.
> This is my house.
> This is my window.

Another striking example of staccato speech occurs in Kaiser's *Gas*, part one:

(*The door to left is flung open. A* WORKMAN—*naked—stained by the explosion totters in*).

WORKMAN: Report from Shed Eight—Central—white cat burst—red eyes torn open—yellow mouth gaping—humps up crackling back—grows round—snaps away girders—lifts up roof—bursts—sparks! sparks! (*Sitting down in the middle of the floor and striking about him*). Chase away the cat—Shoo! Shoo! —smash her jaws—Shoo! Shoo! bury her eyes—they flame—hammer down her back—hammer it down—thousands of fists! It's swelling, swelling—growing fat—fatter—Gas out of very crack—every tube! [1]

---

[1] G. Kaiser, *Gas I*. Reprinted by permission of the publishers, Verlag Kiepenheuer, & Witsch, Cologne.

Rice, in *The Adding Machine,* uses this device to lampoon the inanities of social conversation. Toller in *Masses and Man* likewise shows bankers in the stock exchange talking in staccato lines of broken, fragmentary speech. Kaufman and Connelly also make effective use of another technique in ridiculing hackneyed small-talk by the empty chatter of four characters talking at once.

The expressionist revived the soliloquy, utilizing it as a means of penetrating the exterior of character to present his innermost thoughts and feelings directly to the audience. We have mentioned previously Rice's *The Adding Machine* in which two entire scenes are made up of single speeches. Another long soliloquy occurs in the final scene of Toller's *Transfiguration* which ends with Friedrich's impassioned plea to the spectator:

FRIEDRICH: Now, brothers, now I bid you march! March now in the light of day! Go to your rulers and proclaim to them with the organ tones of a million voices that their power is but illusion. Go to the soldiers and tell them to beat their swords into ploughshares. Go to the rich and show them your heart, your heart that was once buried alive beneath their rubbish. Yet be kind to them, for they too are poor and straying. But the castles —these you must destroy; destroy them laughing, the false castles of illusion. Now march! March forward in the light of day.
    Brothers, stretch out your tortured hands,
    With cries of radiant, ringing joy!
    Stride freely through our liberated land
    With cries of Revolution, Revolution.[2]

The final curtain closes with all of the people joining hands reciting the last four lines together. Here, of course, it is obvious that Toller makes use of the soliloquy to state his case and make his appeal to the audience as forthrightly as possible. The above example is also noteworthy for showing the use of a crowd chanting choral passages together and for the introduction of lyrical passages into the play.

It will be recalled that the Greeks made similar use of dialogue patterns in *stichomythia* for the purpose of building excitement. Another effect of telegraphic speech is to remove the human content and to give the speaker and the dialogue a sense of automatism. George Kaufman and Marc Connelly use this device in *Beggar on Horseback* to satirize the mechanical effect of big business men:

(*Four business men, all with hats and newspapers, and all looking just alike, enter one at a time and step into the imaginary elevator.*)

---

[2] From *Seven Plays,* by Ernst Toller. By permission of Liveright, Publishers, New York. Copyright ©, by Ernst Toller.

CADY: Good morning! Made it in twenty-eight minutes this morning!
FIRST BUSINESS MAN: Good morning! I got the eight-six this morning!
SECOND BUSINESS MAN: Good morning! I missed the seven-forty-three.
THIRD BUSINESS MAN: Good morning! I always take the nine-two.
FOURTH BUSINESS MAN: Good morning! I thought you were on the eight-sixteen.

SPECTACLE

The expressionist relies on theatrical devices for a large amount of his effect. An expressionistic play is enhanced in production since it makes unusual demands of theatricalism in its assaults on the ear and eye. The designer, taking his cue from the expressionistic painter, sought to set the action of the play in a scenic environment that not only intensified the emotional content but also established the playwright's point of view. He attempted to bring out the meaning by emotional, rather than imitative, means, not only acknowledging the limitations of the stage, but frankly and deliberately creating in a theatrical way. The phantasmagoria of weird landscapes, of dreams where images and symbols are projected in bewildering and exaggerated shapes, colors, and patterns, made of expressionistic drama a designer's holiday. His efforts to present in visual form the aberrations of a distracted mind, encouraged the designer to experiment freely. For example, in Kokoshka's fantastic play, *Hiob*, a parrot suddenly explodes and rises in the shape of a rosy cloud to heaven; in Kaiser's *From Morn to Midnight*, a tree struck by lightning becomes a human skeleton; and in Strindberg's *A Dream Play*, eerie landscapes appear, merge and alter in the disconnected sequences of a nightmare. Theatricalism was vividly exploited in such scenes as in the opening of Toller's *Transfiguration* which is set in a vast military cemetery at midnight. The skeleton figure of Death-by-Peace enters wearing a top-hat; his companion, Death-by-War, wears a steel helmet and carries a human thigh bone as his Field Marshal's baton. The weird atmosphere of expressionism is clearly indicated in the following excerpt from O'Neill's *The Hairy Ape*. Yank has emerged from the fireman's forecastle of a ship to confront the social set on Fifth Avenue, New York—an environment which completely baffles and frustrates the protagonist:

(*The crowd from church enter from the right, sauntering slowly and affectedly, their heads held stiffly up, looking neither to right nor left, talking in toneless, simpering voices. The women are rouged, calcimined, dyed, overdressed to the nth degree. The men are in Prince Alberts, high hats, spats, canes, etc. A procession of gaudy marionettes, yet with something of the relentless horror of Frankensteins in their detached, mechanical unawareness.*)

VOICES: Dear Doctor Caiaphas! He is so sincere!
What was the sermon? I dozed off.
About the radicals, my dear—and the false
doctrines that are being preached.
We must organize a hundred per cent American
bazaar.
And let everyone contribute one one-hundredth
per cent of their income tax.
What an original idea!
We can devote the proceeds to rehabilitating
the veil of the temple.
But that has been done many times.

(YANK *after vainly trying to get the attention of the Easter Paraders*)

(*He turns in a rage on the men, bumping viciously into them but not jarring them the least bit. Rather it is he who recoils after each collision. He keeps growling.*) Git off de oith! G'wan, yuh bum! Look where yuh're goin', can't yuh? Git outa here! Fight, why don't yuh? Put up yer mits! Don't be a dog! Fight or I'll knock yuh dead!

(*But without seeming to see him, they all answer with mechanical affected politeness: I beg your pardon. Then at a cry from one of the women, they all scurry to the furrier's window.*)

THE WOMAN: (*ecstatically with a gasp of delight*) Monkey fur! (*The whole crowd of men and women chorus after her in the same tone of affected delight*) Monkey fur!
YANK: (*with a jerk of his head back on his shoulders, as if he had received a punch full in the face—raging*). I see yuh, all in white! I see yuh, yuh white-faced tart, yuh! Hairy ape, huh? I'll hairy ape yuh!

(*He bends down and grips at the street curbing as if to pluck it out and hurl it. Foiled in this, snarling with passion, he leaps to the lamp-post on the corner and tries to pull it up for a club. Just at that moment a bus is heard rumbling up. A fat, high-hatted, spatted gentleman runs out from the side street. He calls out plaintively: Bus! Bus! Stop there! and runs full tilt into the bending, straining YANK, who is bowled off his balance.*)

YANK: (*seeing a fight—with a roar of joy as he springs to his feet*). At last! Bus, huh? I'll bust yuh!

(*He lets drive a terrific swing, his fist landing full on the fat gentleman's face. But the gentleman stands unmoved as if nothing had happened.*)

GENTLEMAN: I beg your pardon. (*Then irritably*) You have made me lose my bus.

(*He claps his hands and begins to scream: Officer! Officer! Many police whistles shrill out on the instant and a whole platoon of policemen rush in on* YANK *from all sides. He tries to fight, but is clubbed to the pavement and fallen upon. The crowd at the window have not moved or noticed this disturbance. The clanging gong of the patrol wagon approaches with a clamoring din.*) [3]

In striving for effect, the expressionist sometimes was carried away in an excess of fantastic experiments as Mordecai Gorelik observed:

In scene design there developed an hysterical environment. Leaning walls, doors and windows at impossible angles, writhing trees in human shape, gave an unearthly aspect to the once familiar world. In Max Slevogt's design for Mozart's *Don Giovanni* at the Dresden Staaatstheater (1924), a Baroque palace seems kneaded out of dough. The setting of C. T. Pilartz for the throneroom in Hamsun's *Queen Tamara* (Vereinigte Stadttheater, Cologne, 1924) is constructed on diagonal prisms, while the thrones have forked and jagged outlines.

In Fritz Schoefler's settings for *Much Ado About Nothing* (Residenz Theater, Munich) the stage is filled with huge, grotesque flower-shapes leaning at all angles. Ernest Stern's design for *Die Wupper* (1919) shows a mass of houses like crumpled cardboard. In *From Morn to Midnight* (1916) the stage directions of George Kaiser read, "The wind shakes the branches of a tree and the snow clings to it, forming the shape of a skeleton." [4]

The problem with expressionistic staging is that it often sacrifices communication for shock appeal, and that as a style of design it is appropriate only to expressionistic plays, which in recent years have constituted a small and decreasing percentage of dramatic literature. On the other hand, the expressionists' bold theatricalism demonstrated new and effective ways of using light and color, it cleared the stage of the rigid three walls and replaced the conventional clutter with a few simple forms picked out by light on a relatively bare platform giving the actor the appropriate psychological climate for his performance. Expressionistic staging did not replace realistic scenery in our theater, but its influence continues, especially in the décor for ballet, dance dramas, musical comedies and occasionally in motion picture sequences.

Questions and Exercises

1. How is expressionism superrealism?
2. How important is spectacle in expressionism?
3. What dialogue devices does the expressionist use?

[3] From *The Hairy Ape,* by Eugene O'Neill. Copyright ©, 1922, by Random House, Inc. Reprinted by permission of the publishers.
[4] *New Theatres for Old.* Copyright ©, 1940, by Mordecai Gorelik. All rights reserved. Reprinted by permission of the author and Samuel French, Inc.

4. Why does the expressionist employ distortion?
5. How does expressionism affect plot?
6. What is the purpose of expressionism?
7. What is the expressionist's point of view?
8. What are the weaknesses of expressionism?
9. What did the expressionist contribute to the theater?

Plays to Read

KAISER, George: *From Morn To Midnight*
RICE, Elmer: *The Adding Machine*
KAUFMAN, George and CONNELLY, Marc: *Beggar on Horseback*
O'NEILL, Eugene: *The Emperor Jones, The Hairy Ape*
MILLER, Arthur: *Death of a Salesman*

Suggested Reading

CHENEY, Sheldon, *Expressionism in Art* (New York, Liveright Pub. Corp., 1934).
DOWNEY, J. E., *Creative Imagination* (New York, Harcourt, Brace & World, Inc., 1929).
DUKES, Ashley, *Youngest Drama* (Chicago, Dramatic Publishing Co., 1923).
GASSNER, John, *Form and Idea in the Modern Theatre* (New York, Holt, Rinehart and Winston, Inc., 1956).
STUART, Donald Clive, *The Development of Dramatic Art* (New York, D. Appleton and Co., 1928).

I I

The Director

LONG AGO, when Aeschylus staged his earliest extant Greek tragedy, *The Suppliants* (*c.* 492 B.C.), he must have learned that producing a play is a complex and tricky business. Like directors who followed him, he had scores of problems to solve and decisions to make. Roles had to be assigned, costumes designed and constructed, entrances and exits marked out, and rehearsals conducted until the play was ready for presentation before the discriminating Athenian audience.

Even a cursory glance at *The Suppliants* indicates the need for painstaking planning and rehearsal. The play tells the story of the fifty daughters of Danaus who seek sanctuary at Argos from the pursuing sons of Aegyptus. At the climax of the play, the Herald and his attendants attempt to carry off the maidens by force, but they are rescued by the king, who refuses to release them.

Perhaps the most difficult task which Aeschylus faced in producing his play, was training the chorus of fifty maidens, who recite and chant more than six hundred lines of poetry, sometimes combining words with dance, and sometimes engaging in vigorous action when they cling to the altar in terror, pleading for asylum. In addition to the careful preparation of speech and choreography of the chorus, it was necessary to provide them with appropriate costumes—striking Egyptian robes, dark masks and linen veils fastened to their heads with gold bands. In the action of the other performers, two entrances required special care. In the first, the king and his retinue make a dramatic entrance—probably using horses and chariots. The second complicated entrance occurs when the Herald and his coterie appear and threaten to tear suppliant maidens away from the altar. Although this play has a simple plot, its implicit demands for the movement of a large group of performers, required

181

arduous rehearsal. We may be sure that Aeschylus was grateful for his military experience when he prepared *The Suppliants* for performance.

Throughout the history of the theater, the manifold tasks of play production have been handled in a variety of ways. The assigned archons and Greek playwrights were in charge of the presentation of tragedies. In the medieval cycle plays, with their fragmentized episodes, many of them requiring realistic staging, an enormous amount of organization was necessary, much of which was parcelled out to various participating groups. In the Elizabethan theater, with its permanent professional companies of actors and playwrights, the theater manager selected the plays and assigned the casts. Undoubtedly, the playwrights took considerable interest in seeing that their works were performed as they intended them to be. And just as Hamlet found it expedient to advise the players about their style of acting in the play-within-the-play, it requires little stretch of the imagination to believe that Shakespeare made a similar effort in the performance of his dramas at the Globe. Molière, in the seventeenth-century French theater, labored for twelve years with his troupe in the provinces, polishing and perfecting the performance of his plays before returning to Paris. That Molière not only set an example for his company but took care to improve the quality of his productions is suggested by his wry comment that, "actors are strange creatures to drive."

In the eighteenth and nineteenth centuries, such stars as David Garrick and William Macready attempted to make play production less haphazard, but in general, many of the responsibilities of organization were delegated to underlings, or ignored altogether. Oftentimes, plays were patched together with "typed" characters assigned to roles with little or no genuine rehearsal, and almost no concern for ensemble acting. Stock sets were refurbished on a makeshift basis and there was little attention paid to lighting. Costuming was mostly a matter of individual taste, and apparently no one worried about the resulting incongruities. There were, of course, a few notable exceptions to these practices. Charles Kean, in the 1850's, staged remarkable productions of Shakespeare, for which special scenery was designed and painted with accurate geological and botanical detail. In his production of *A Midsummer Night's Dream* in 1856, Kean was praised for the harmony of effect which resulted from music, scenery, and choreography especially created for the occasion. A decade later, the Bancrofts introduced rehearsal reforms which were in the direction of greater unity.

THE MODERN DIRECTOR APPEARS

The Duke of Saxe-Meiningen in Germany performed an invaluable service for the theater through his exemplary staging of Shakespeare and

Schiller, in which he emphasized ensemble acting and the use of appropriate scenery and costume. The tour of the Duke's troupe through the major cities of Europe (1874-1890), inspired theater workers elsewhere to emulate his synthesis of production.

With the appearance of realism and naturalism in the latter part of the nineteenth century, actors and directors became increasingly concerned with unifying all elements of the performance. The new plays demanded a new approach to staging. André Antoine led the way with his Théâtre Libre in Paris; Otto Brahm followed his example in the Freie Bühne in Berlin; and Constantin Stanislavski worked along similar lines at the Moscow Art Theatre.

In addition to the independent theater pioneers, two visionaries championed the concept of unity in play production in a series of notable stage designs, as well as in their writings. These men were Gordon Craig and Adolphe Appia, whose contributions are discussed in Chapter 13 on Design. At this juncture in our discussion of directing, the point needs to be made that there were several forces at work in the late-nineteenth-century theater which led to the guiding principle that all aspects of play production should grow from a central interpretation. The corollary of this idea was that in order to secure such unity, there must be a single creative intelligence responsible for designing the whole production, namely, the director. This idea is widely accepted in the contemporary theater, and a number of men have assumed this dominating role to set the example, notably Max Reinhardt, Alexander Tairov, Stanislavski, Vsevolod Meierhold, and Leopold Jessner.

Directors work under many different conditions of rehearsal depending on the type of theater which they serve. A Broadway director may find it necessary to throw a play together in three weeks; in Russia, some plays have taken two years of rehearsal. Joshua Logan auditioned nearly a thousand actors in a few days for the sailor roles in *Mr. Roberts;* Meierhold, after two months of rehearsal had not settled on any one of the three characters for a one-act play. Max Reinhardt preplanned his performances to the last detail so that the rehearsal period was one of teaching the actors what he wished them to do; Arthur Hopkins simply turned his actors loose with occasional stimulation and encouragement, his idea of direction being to "put on a play without anyone realizing how it was done." Some directors find that the law of diminishing returns sets in on rehearsals lasting longer than three hours; David Belasco was known to rehearse for twenty hours at a stretch. Meierhold gave his actors every piece of business and read every line for them; Bertolt Brecht sat and waited for his actors to show him the meaning of his own plays; and Eugene Vakhtangov conducted round table discussions with his casts, trying to arrive at a common interpretation. Directors even vary in their concept of the actor's function. Huntley Carter reported that: "Stanislavski told the actor he must forget that he is on the stage. Taïrov told the actor he must remember nothing else. Meierhold told him he must remember that he is one of the audience."

KINDS OF DIRECTING JOBS

The tasks of the director vary with the situation in which he works. On Broadway, the professional director is hired to produce a specific play. A particular assignment may last a month, during which time he has taken the play from the initial auditions through the final dress rehearsal. He may have absolute control over the preparation of the play, even to the point of persuading the playwright to make major revisions in the script as Kazan did with Tennessee Williams' *Cat on a Hot Tin Roof*. Or the director may work under the shadow of a star or dramatist who is powerful enough to assume the dominant position. The professional director in Europe usually is employed by a permanent theater organization and is paid an annual salary to direct a company of actors in a series of plays. The director in the American college or university theater, ordinarily is a member of the regular academic staff. In addition to teaching courses and directing plays, frequently he selects the plays for the season and supervises all phases of production, giving continuity to the educational policy of the campus theater. The community theater director in this country works on a salary to direct a season of plays produced by amateurs. His job may include that of organizing and promoting civic interest in dramatic activities. In any one of these assignments, the director may become the dominant figure of the production—so much so that the critic George Jean Nathan found cause to complain that "the Broadway theater was becoming a director's theater."

Whatever conditions the modern stage director works under, his job is a complex one requiring the solution of multifarious problems. Although the following description of a day in the life of a director is not altogether typical, it illustrates the breadth of his activity. This is an account of a day with George Abbott, a noted New York director, when he was working on a musical comedy.

Take, for instance, a day's work for the director of a musical comedy. At ten o'clock he goes to the office to meet the authors and read the revisions of a scene upon which they have been working during the night. While he is there, the costume designer calls to say that one of the actresses says she can't wear green—it makes her so nervous she won't be able to remember her lines. It takes about ten minutes to insist that she will have to wear green whether she's allergic to it or not.

Just as the director is starting for rehearsal, the press agent calls to ask if he can take some pictures during the lunch hour. When the director gets to the theatre, he finds the business manager waiting to say that they have just found that the scenery can't be hung on time to open on Monday in Boston—will it be all right to postpone until Tuesday? He rehearses with the principals from eleven til one.

Lunch hour is spent with his associates, talking over the problems of the play. In the afternoon, rehearsals are resumed for two hours but have to be interrupted because some of the principals are needed to work with the choreographer.

The director then goes to another theatre, where the singers are rehearsing under a separate supervision. Here he discovers that a new musical arrangement is so effective that he must find a way to introduce it in further scenes, and he gets in touch with the authors to find if they will not agree to writing it in that fashion.

He then goes to a third theatre, where the choreographer is working with the dancers. There is a terrible fight going on between the composer and the choreographer. The former feels that his music is being unjustly distorted to fit dances. The director is the umpire.

That evening, musical numbers are worked on and the principals are coached in their acting of the songs as differentiated from the acting of the script proper.[1]

THE FUNCTION OF THE DIRECTOR

As the unifying force in the production of a play, the director has a number of specific assignments. From the time that the script is placed in his hands until the curtain rises on opening night, it is the director who initiates and controls all aspects of the presentation of the play. He analyzes the script, auditions actors, casts the roles, sets the basic floor plan for the sets, supervises the design of costumes, scenery and lighting, instructs the cast in the meaning of the play, and conducts rehearsals during which he blocks out the action, assists the actor with his interpretation of his character and the reading of his lines, and finally polishes, times, and unifies the play into a cohesive whole. Everything about the interpretation and performance of the play is his business.

The director's function may be indicated by quoting representative statements of three outstanding men of the contemporary theater. John Mason Brown said that the "director is a critic in action." Arthur Hopkins, a prominent American director, phrased it this way: "The director is the guide. The play is the unknown region through which he leads the actor. He must know the paths and the turnings so well that he never hesitates.

[1] George Abbott, "A Director's Lot," *New York Times,* April 15, 1951. Reprinted by permission of the author.

For once he falters, wondering if he is headed right, the actor inevitably begins to look around for his own way out." [2]

Harold Clurman, another outstanding American director, summed up the job in these words: "To put it as simply as possible, the function of the stage director is to translate a play text into stage terms: that is, to make the play as written, clear, interesting and enjoyable by means of living actors, sounds, color and movement." [3]

Implicit in these statements are two root ideas: The director is an interpreter, and the director is a theater craftsman.

THE DIRECTOR AS AN INTERPRETER

As we have indicated in our previous discussion, the function of the director as the interpreter of the play is a contemporary concept. When such playwrights as Aeschylus, Shakespeare, and Molière, experienced theater men, worked directly with the actors, the shape and meaning of the performance was undoubtedly determined by the writer. But where the dramatists were not trained in the ways of the theater, or not available (some of them being dead), the individual actor was left to his own devices, which usually meant in the case of a star that he was concerned only with presenting himself in a favorable light, regardless of his colleagues, except as they affected his performance. With the coming of contemporary drama, the director assumed the responsibility for integrating the production, and his most important influence was that of interpretation.

The director begins by working with the script. He must have a complete understanding of the play. This goes far beyond a mere acquaintance with the story line or even an intimate knowledge of the play's structure. Drama shows men in action—men making choices, reaching for objectives or withdrawing, attacking or resisting. And all of this action is about something. There is a residue of meaning beneath the surface of the physical action. The play is a commentary on the characters' attitude toward life. *Death of a Salesman* is more than a story of a tired old man; it is also an attempt to re-examine the values that many contemporary men live by; *Juno and the Paycock* is not only the story of a brave woman and her incorrigible husband; it is also an attack on the ignorance and narrowness of the slum-dwellers of Dublin; *A Streetcar Named Desire* is not merely a case study of the deterioration of a weak woman; it is a disturbing picture of sensitivity being ground under by brutality. The director must search for the core of the action, the "spine," the larger

[2] Arthur Hopkins, *How's Your Second Act?* (New York, Philip Goodman Co., 1918).

[3] From *Lies Like Truth* by Harold Clurman. Copyright ©, 1958 by Grove Press, Inc.

implications and significance of the externals of the plot. The director's first task then, is to gain insight into the play which the dramatist has created.

Now let us consider some specific examples of directors at work on the interpretation of the play.

Norris Houghton in *Moscow Rehearsals,* a fascinating account of his visit to Rusia in the 1930's, describes Meierhold's approach to directing a play. He read it through a single time, trying to grasp the meaning of the author, noting the first impression which the script gives to him. When he produced a play, Meierhold often changed the text to suit the interpretation he gained from his first reading. Once Meierhold determined the motivating idea, he visualized a tentative plan for the scenery and lighting. He came to the first rehearsal without any notes or promptbook, but apparently with his head swarming with ideas, which he released spontaneously as he worked with the actors on their interpretation of the lines and their invention of movement and business. A staff of eight to twelve assistants recorded in detail every aspect of each rehearsal, so that by the time the play reached production, there was an accumulation of a vast body of material about the play and its performance.

Norris Houghton describes Meierhold's interpretation of Chekhov's *The Proposal,* which he gave to the actors at the first rehearsal:

"Two things are essential for a play's production, as I have often told you," Meierhold begins. "First, we must find the thought of the author; then we must reveal that thought in a theatrical form. This form I call a *jeu de theatre* and around it I shall build the performance. Molière was a master of *jeu de theatre*: a central idea and the use of incidents, comments, mockery, jokes— anything to put it over. In this production I am going to use the technique of the traditional vaudeville as the *jeu*. Let me explain what it is to be. In these three plays of Chekhov I have found that there are thirty-eight times when characters either faint, say they are going to faint, turn pale, clutch their hearts, or call for a glass of water; so I am going to take this idea of fainting and use it as a sort of leit-motif for the performance. Everything will contribute to this *jeu*.[4]

After this introduction Meierhold read the script to the cast and dismissed the rehearsal.

The noted German director, Max Reinhardt, famous for his theatricalism, like Meierhold, dictated every detail of the production. However, he did not depend on the inspiration of the moment. Reinhardt's presentations were the results of months of careful preparation during which time he developed a complete annotated account of the play. The purpose of

[4] From *Moscow Rehearsals,* by Norris Houghton. Copyright ©, 1936, by Harcourt, Brace & World, Inc., and reprinted with their permission.

his rehearsals was to teach his interpretation line by line to the actor. R. Ben-Ari, who worked with Reinhardt, describes his methods in this fashion:

Reinhardt comes to work with his secretaries and his assistant directors all laden with books. They are volumes with interpretations and explanations, with various data, drawings and symbols relating to the production—the evidence of colossal artistic and technical work which was done in preparing the manuscript for the stage. In these books the working out of every scene, every phrase, is recorded exactly and in detail—precisely when this or that player, when this or that group has to move to another part of the stage; how many musical intervals they have before they move; how much space they have to move in; the exact moment when the light is to go on. All this put together gives birth to the Reinhardt production. Reinhardt, himself a wonderful actor, influences his actors in such a way that they are compelled to do everything that he shows them. Reinhardt's personality dominates one to such an extent that one must copy all his intonations, all his emphases. These are wonderful in themselves, and of the deepest and most convincing sort, but they come to life through Reinhardt and not through the actor.[5]

Just as Reinhardt felt free to mold the actor into a preconceived image, he also assumed the power to interpret the play as he wished, with the result that in some of his productions, the original play was merely a point of departure, which he embellished and enlarged upon, like a musician improvising on a theme.

Although not as extreme in his domination of the interpretation as Meierhold and Reinhardt, Tyrone Guthrie, a celebrated contemporary English director, takes a good deal of latitude in his ingenious interpretations of Shakespeare, moving around freely in time and space. Guthrie does not preplan his productions, although his preliminary study of the play leads him to an underlying mood. Once in a rehearsal, he shapes the play to his preconception, usually through persuasion rather than outright dictatorship.

Two American directors who owe a good deal to Stanislavski in their method of approach to the directing of plays are Harold Clurman and Elia Kazan. Both of these men make a careful study of the script in advance, searching for a basic interpretation, their interest centering on the psychological backgrounds of the characters in the play. As they analyze the play, Clurman and Kazan make notes to guide their thinking during rehearsals. These personal notes are interesting for revealing the ways in which these directors arrive at their interpretations.

[5] R. Ben-Ari, "Four Directors and the Actor," *Theatre Workshop*, Jan.-March, 1937. Reprinted by permission of the author.

Here are a few sample notes from Clurman [6] when he was preparing for a production of *The Member of the Wedding:*

The *main action of the play:* to get "connected."

It all happens in a hot summer atmosphere, the world is "dead"—the people suspended. Everything is slightly strange, not altogether real.

A mighty loneliness emanates from this play. It is as if all the characters were separated from the world—as if the people were only a mirage in a vaporous space making wraiths of the people.

More decisive than any of these notes is my line by line "breakdown" of the script, which indicates the aim of each scene and what particular actions and adjustment (mood) moment by moment the actor must carry out and convey. These actions—what the character wants to do and why—together with any physical action (or "stage business") which might result from the character's purpose are duly noted by the director, or, in most cases in my own work, they may be left to the actor's nature and imagination—under the director's guidance—to accomplish.

These sample notes record Kazan's [7] interpretation of the stage production of *A Streetcar Named Desire:*

Theme—this is a message from the dark interior. This little twisted, pathetic, confused bit of light and culture puts out a cry. It is snuffed out by the crude forces of violence, insensibility and vulgarity which exists in our South—and this cry is the play.

Style—one reason a "style," a stylized production is necessary is that a subjective factor—Blanche's memories, inner life, emotions are a real factor. We cannot understand her behavior unless we see the effect of her past on her present behavior.

This play is a poetic tragedy. We are shown the final dissolution of a person of worth, who once had a great potential, and who, even as she goes down, has worth exceeding that of the "healthy," coarse-grained figures who kill her.

To keep his interpretation of each scene clearly before him, Kazan broke the play down into its component parts and placed a label on each scene:

> *Scene 1:* Blanche comes to the last place at
> the end of the line.

[6] Quotations from the notebooks of Harold Clurman and Elia Kazan, from *Directing the Play,* by Toby Cole and Helen Krich Chinoy (Indianapolis, The Bobbs-Merrill Co., Inc., 1935). Reprinted by permission of the authors.

[7] *Ibid.*

Scene 2: Blanche tries to make a place for
herself.

Scene 3: Blanche breaks them apart, but when
they come together, Blanche is more
alone than ever. (etc.)

Just as they searched for the core ideas of the plays as the basis for their
interpretations of the total meaning, similarly Clurman and Kazan probed
for the "spines" of action which determined the character's behavior.

These are some of the notations which Clurman made about the character of Frankie in *The Member of the Wedding:*

Her main action—*to get out of herself.* Getting out of herself means *growth*
. . . She has "growing pains": she is both tortured and happy through
them . . . The juices of life are pouring through her. She is a fragile con-
tainer of this strange elixir.

Growth twists and turns her—as it does us—gives us new shapes. Frankie
twists and turns. The play is the lyric drama of Frankie's growth. At the
end of the play, she runs or twirls out—"to go around the world." She has
achieved her aim—imaginatively. She is ready "to get out of herself."

Clurman follows this analysis with a list of eight main characteristics
which begins like this:

1. Frankie is tomboyish. (She puts on no show with kissing. Her father is a
   "widowman" with his nose to the grindstone. She has no mother, no "social
   environment.")
2. Frankie is crazy with first love; literally head over heels; the love of the
   wedding.

He continues detailing her chief qualities, each one suggesting clues to
her actions and behavior on stage.

Kazan made similar notations, but he is even more explicit, his comments on the character of Blanche alone, run more than five pages. These
notes are extremely significant in revealing the way in which a director
studies the play and the characters' motivations before he brings the play
to life on stage. These are a few of Kazan's observations about Blanche:

Blanche is a social type, an emblem of a dying civilization, making its last
curlicued and romantic exit. All her behavior patterns are those of the dying
civilization she represents. In other words her behavior is *social.* Therefore
find the social modes! This is the source of the play's stylization and the production's style and color. Likewise Stanley's behavior is *social* too. It is the
basic animal cynicism of today. "Get what's coming to you! Don't waste a day!
Eat, drink, get yours!" This is the basis of his stylization, of the choice of his

props. All props should be stylized: they should have a color, shape and weight that spell: style.

Her problem has to do with her tradition. Her notion of what a woman should be. She is stuck with this "ideal." It is her. It is her ego. Unless she lives by it, she cannot live; in fact her whole life has been for nothing. Even the Alan Gray incident as she now tells it and believes it to have been, is a necessary piece of romanticism. Essentially, in outline, she tells what happened, but it also serves the demands of her notion of herself, to make her *special* and different, out of the tradition of the romantic ladies of the past: Swinburne, Wm. Morris, Pre-Raphaelites, etc. This way it serves as an excuse for a great deal of her behavior.

Because this image of herself cannot be accomplished in reality, certainly not in the South of our day and time, it is her effort and practice *to accomplish it in fantasy.*. Everything that she does in *reality* too is colored by this necessity, this compulsion to be *special.* So, in fact, *reality becomes fantasy too.* She makes it so!

An effort to phrase Blanche's spine: to find *protection,* to find something to hold onto, some strength in whose protection she can live, like a sucker shark or a parasite. The tradition of *woman* (or all women) can only live through the strength of someone else. Blanche is entirely dependent. Finally the doctor!

Directors not only vary in their methods of working with the actor on his interpretation, but they also vary in their approach to the script itself. A play exists on many levels at the same time, and the director's interpretation may, therefore, stem from many sources. Craig based his interpretation on color, Reinhardt on spectacle, Stanislavski on characterization. A director may find justification for his analysis in the imagery of the poetry, in significant symbols, or in the atmosphere of the locale. He may find inspiration for his point of view in music, movement, scenery, speech, theme, or social milieu. Whatever the approach, the director is the ultimate interpreter of the play.

THE DIRECTOR AS A CRAFTSMAN

The director begins as an interpreter of the play. Secondly, he is a skilled craftsman capable of revealing in tangible theatrical terms, the full meaning of the play to an audience.

Although this text is not a manual of play production, nor is it our intent to discuss in detail every phase of the director's function, it may be helpful in understanding his contribution to the presentation, if we indicate the use of at least one of his tools—stage movement.

A play in the theater is dynamic. It is in a continual process of ebb and flow, action and reaction, adjustment and readjustment. Through its characters, changes take place—the frustrated boy finally gets the girl; by suffering, a woman comes to understand herself; a hero falls from a high place to catastrophe; the downtrodden little man achieves status.

Because of the primacy of action, the director regards movement as a basic tool. When he analyzes a play, he searches for its *main action,* the "spine." We have just observed that Clurman in his study of *The Member of the Wedding* found that the main action in the play was for the characters "to get connected," and that Kazan's interpretation of his protagonist was based on Blanche's "spine," or "superobjective." "She was trying to find protection; to find something to hold onto."

The director concentrates a good deal of his attention on blocking out movement, inventing business, and grouping his characters. The playwright may provide directions for such essential plot actions as entrances and exits, duels, love scenes, death scenes, etc., and the context of the lines may provide clues for movement. For instance, it is clear in Act I, Scene 1 of *Hamlet* that Horatio joins the soldiers in their vigil, that the ghost enters, and the three watchers attempt unsuccessfully to restrain it. But the director must go far beyond this bare framework of action to devise movement and groupings which will bring out the full dramatic content of the scene. The director is not only concerned with *what* happens; he is also interested in *how* an action is performed. How does the ghost make his appearance? How does Horatio's expression of fear differ from that of the soldiers? How does Horatio attempt to stay the ghost?

Since a play is dynamic, the attention of the audience must be shifted constantly from one character to another to another. Unlike the motion-picture director who can concentrate the camera on a specific person or object at will, eliminating from the screen all extraneous matter, the stage director must find other means to evoke and sustain a steady flow of attention. One of his most important means for this purpose is the use of movement. For example, the opening scene of *Hamlet* is a rather simple one since it is short, relatively uncomplicated and requires only five characters, and yet, the movement and grouping need careful planning. See pages 58-67. The director's primary consideration probably will be to establish the audience's acceptance of the ghost. Most likely it will be kept remote from the audience, played in dim light and deep shadow, and perhaps elevated in position. The actor must be able to move freely and without noise so that his entrances and exits create the illusion of an apparition in space. The attempts of Horatio and the soldiers to strike at the ghost must not destroy the feeling of majesty and dignity of the dead king. In the grouping of the three watchers, Horatio must be given the dominant position since the others look to him for counsel. Moreover, he carries the burden of the dialogue and has several long speeches, so that he must be placed in an advantageous position to project his lines to the audience. The director may find it desirable to place him in the center of a triangle, perhaps with more elevation and light than that of his companions. Thus, the stage director works his way through the play, line by line and scene by scene, leaving nothing to chance, endowing every gesture and movement with significance that will help the audience to understand the playwright's meaning.

The director uses his blocking to create atmosphere, the appropriate emotional background for the action. In many plays, the environment is very important for understanding or reinforcing the conduct of the characters. Referring again to Clurman's analysis of *The Member of the Wedding* it will be recalled that he wished to create a "hot summer atmosphere" in which the world is "dead" and everything "strange and unreal." Some playwrights give the director very specific directions which help to create the emotional climate for the play. Hauptmann, the German playwright, was especially painstaking in his description of atmosphere. For example, the stage directions for the beginning of Act II of *The Weavers* gives a very complete picture:

A small room in the house of Wilhelm Ansorge, weaver and house-owner in the village of Kashbach, in the Eulengebirge.

In this room, which does not measure six feet from the dilapidated wooden floor to the smoke-blackened rafters, sit four people. Two young girls, Emma and Bertha Baumert, are working at their looms; Mother Baumert, a decrepit old woman, sits on a stool beside the bed, with a winding-wheel in front of her; her idiot son, August, sits on a footstool, also winding. He is twenty, has a small body and head and long spider-like legs and arms.

Faint, rosy evening light makes its way through two small windows in the right wall, which have their broken panes pasted over with paper or stuffed with straw. It lights up the flaxen hair of the girls, which falls loose on their slender white necks and thin bare shoulders, and their coarse chemises. These, with a short petticoat of the roughest linen, form their whole attire. The warm glow falls on the old woman's face, neck and breast—a face worn away to a skeleton, with shriveled skin and sunken eyes, red and watery with smoke, dust and working by lamplight; a long goitre neck, wrinkled and sinewy; a hollow breast covered with faded, ragged shawls.

The room is full of sound—the rhythmic thud of the looms, shaking floor and walls, the click and rattle of the shuttles passing back and forward, and the steady whirr of the winding wheels, like the hum of gigantic bees.[8]

Few playwrights give such detailed assistance to the director and actor in establishing mood. Usually, the director, with the assistance of the actor, must rely on his own ingenuity to create atmosphere. Sometimes, a director will invent an entirely new scene in order to provide the appro-

[8] From *The Weavers*, by Gerhart Hauptmann, translated by Mary Morison. Copyright ©, 1913 by B. W. Huebsch, 1941, by Ludwig Lewisohn. Reprinted by permission of The Viking Press, Inc.

priate mood for his interpretation. An example of this reveals Stanislavski's ability to devise movement and business. Gorchakov, a visiting director at the Moscow Art Theatre, was directing a student production of *The Sisters Gerard*. After witnessing a rehearsal, Stanislavski gave Gorchakov the following suggestions:

My advice to you is not to present the first scene of the play as it is written. Don't begin with the revolt. You rob yourself of a much better moment for it later in the play—in the prison. My advice is to create an alarming mood in the first scene. We remember from history of the period that there was scarcely any bread in Paris. And because of that just before the revolution, bread was hidden from the people. Naturally there were groups of people who always tried to be near the bakery in case bread was brought in or taken out. In your direction of the first scene you have a long line tell each other about their misfortunes. I find this scene too static and too obvious. There is nothing in your scene that arouses the audience's imagination.

Here is how I advise you to do the scene. Divide your bread line into two groups. The actors who are in these groups should live with all the thoughts and relationships that I assume you worked out with them. Spread your groups in different places on the square. Within each group there will be conversation. Within some there will be arguments about certain questions. Establish the movement of people from one group to another and the motives for their changing places. For this kind of grouping you can use certain spots, such as the fountain, cafe, tables, the arch, the pillars, and the statue. Five or six people should come in as the scene begins; some people should leave and then return. All this has to be done without any excitement, rather slowly. The basic physical problem is waiting; perhaps they will bring the bread. The inner action is preparation for the great events and discussion of the situation in the city and of the debate in the National Assembly. Once in awhile, in one or another of the groups, someone bursts out with a loud sentence. Choose several phrases, serious and meaningful. Don't let your people declaim, and whatever people say in the group should come as the result of the discussion or arguments they are having. Let them speak mostly with their eyes. The object of their attention should be the bakery, the baker who appears at the window, the policeman walking on the streets, those who do not agree with the majority opinion that things are wrong in Paris.[9]

Stanislavski went on from this general outline to detail the movement of the individuals in the scene. Although this lengthy invention is rather exceptional for a stage director to add to a play, the description above is an illuminating example of how Stanislavski's specific movement and business stemmed from a basic physical problem and the "inner action" which serves as the spine for the scene as a whole.

[9] Reprinted from *Stanislavsky Directs* (New York, 1958), by Nikolai M. Gorchakov, translated by Miriam Goldina. By permission of the publishers, Funk & Wagnalls, New York.

The director blocks the action of the play to indicate character relationships. Congenial people draw together; enemies keep their distance until there is a showdown when they are brought face to face in open conflict. The director shows the moment by moment psychological interrelationships of his characters by graphic representation. Performers must be given opportunities to act out their emotions, to give pictorial evidence of the psychological climate of the social environment. A dominating figure may be given an elevated position, face front, emphasized by a bright light, a striking costume, visual focus, movement; a subservient character may grovel on the floor, in dim light, in a drab costume, closed in from the audience. The director composes a series of constantly changing pictures which present the emotional states of the characters. He is concerned with all aspects of movement—its extent, speed, shape, direction, length, the position of the mover, his manner of moving, and the relationship of his action to the furniture, scenery, and other characters.

The first scene in *Hamlet* suggests that Bernardo, Marcellus, and Horatio are closely allied; they are friendly men sharing a common objective. The cold night and the atmosphere of foreboding draws them together. The ghost enters and they recoil in fear from the dreadful sight. Horatio recovers himself, bravely assumes command, and advances on the ghost pursuing it until it disappears in the darkness. Then the watchers are joined together again trying to find answers to the questions which the appearance of the ghost has raised. This opening scene with its homogeneity of grouping makes an interesting contrast to the one which follows in which Claudius and Gertrude are holding court. They make overtures to soothe the troubled and alienated Hamlet, but he spurns their efforts and isolates himself from the King and Queen and those who seek royal favors.

Another function of the director closely allied to the blocking of movement is that of inventing and assisting the actor in creating "stage business," by which we mean the detailed actions of the individual characters such as in their use of a cane, the opening of a letter, pouring tea, smoking a pipe, etc. Stage business is similar to movement in its uses. In general, it is the director's and actor's way of giving life and verisimilitude to the acting of a play. Again, like movement, business may be inherent in the playwright's script such as Hedda burning Lövborg's manuscript, Juliet drinking the potion, and Captain Boyle cooking his "sassige." However, much of the business which is not essential to the plot but necessary for enriching the performance, is imposed on the presentation by the inventiveness of the director and actor. This is especially true in comedy where one of the marks of the skilled performer is his ingenuity in creating original business. (The example of Charlie Chaplin's performance cited on pages 138-140 is a case in point.)

Ordinarily the director allows his actors to create as much of their own business as possible, but he will find it necessary to guide and edit their contributions as well as to stimulate their inventiveness. For example, Kazan in his notes to *A Streetcar Named Desire* indicates how he helped Brando by selecting his props: "Choose Marlon's objects . . . the things he loves and prizes: all sensuous and sensual—the shirt, the beer (how it's poured and nursed, etc.)."

An extreme example of a director who dictated the business down to the last detail is described by Houghton is his account of Meierhold's rehearsals of Chekhov's *The Proposal:*

The next rehearsal I attended was devoted to setting "business." The stage was crowded. The center part of it was set for the action. Meierhold sat at one table at the edge of it; his assistants sat at two other tables; the usual crowd of onlookers filled the wings and footlights. The actors took their places for the opening scene. "Let us begin!" said Meierhold. The first two speeches were read. Meierhold was at once on his feet.

"As you say "Ivan Vassilyevich!" the second time, clap your hands—so," he directed. "And you, Ivan, turn your head slightly to the left . . . just a little further . . . There! And at the same time, distend your neck. Watch me do it. . . . That's it. Now let us try it again . . . That was better. Only your handclap, Stepan Stepanovich, must be more affectionate. Place your wrists directly opposite each other as you clap, instead of side by side. That will make a smoother, more sliding clap." etc. . . . [10]

At a later rehearsal, Houghton comments on Meierhold's amazing flow of ideas which seemed to come to him spontaneously. His invention of a piece of comic business is especially interesting:

Meierhold had been inventing a dozen pieces of business to point his *jeu,* the fainting-water-drinking motif. Ivan Vassilyevich had done as much with the glass and carafe of water as he could. Finally as the rehearsal drew near its close, Meierhold rose suddenly. "Watch me and do likewise," he ordered. Then he read the line: "If it were not for these terrible agonizing palpitations, Madam, if it were not for the throbbing in my temples—" He paused, looked about him wild-eyed, seized the carafe, held it in his outstretched hand a moment, then lifted it and emptied its entire contents over his head! With his hair and nose streaming water, he finishes the line: "I should speak to you very differently!" [11]

A final example of a director at work shows the detailed care of a theater craftsman as he translates his interpretation of the play into concrete images. If he is to achieve a complete and unified performance, the

[10] Houghton, *op. cit.*
[11] *Ibid.*

director must labor through his play line by line, weighing every detail of movement and business, every word spoken, every nuance of meaning.

The following example records Stanislavski's preparation for a projected performance of *Othello* at the Moscow Art Theatre in 1929. This excerpt shows Stanislavski's way of interpreting the first few lines of the scene in Act IV when Othello, his suspicions aroused, comes to Desdemona's bedchamber. The first line is spoken by Emilia, Desdemona's nurse.

EMILIA: Look, where he comes.

(*In the last pause Emilia hears steps below. She rushes to the stairs, sees Othello coming and then hurries to Desdemona so as not to be compelled to call out. Her movement shows alarm and excitement.*)

Emilia thinks differently from Desdemona. She did not like Othello's behavior during the day. It does not seem the way to spend one's time during the first days of one's marriage.

Hearing that he is coming and thinking of last night's wonders, Desdemona wants to meet him suitably. She runs to the mirror to touch up her hair.

Emilia waits respectfully at the stairs to disappear at the first opportune moment and not to disturb the husband and wife.

DESDEMONA: I will not leave him now till Cassio
              Be call'd to him.

She speaks these words while smartening herself up. Her hair done, she runs to the banisters to meet Othello.

(*Enter* OTHELLO)

Pause. Othello's entry should be delayed to underline its significance. He enters trying to seem cheerful and cordial at all costs and not make Desdemona see how he feels inside.

                    How is 't with you, my lord?

She speaks, leaning over the banisters. Thus their meeting takes place as follows: flirting lightly, Desdemona at the banisters looking at him questioningly and trying to find out how he is, while Othello stops on the stairs, having had not time to come up yet. Their heads are on a level.

OTHELLO: Well, my good lady. O, hardness to dissemble! (*Aside*)

He tries to sound cheerful. Desdemona suddenly puts her arm round him over the banisters, leaving his head uncovered. His face is turned to the audience, she is showing the back of her head.

                    How do you, Desdemona?

Desdemona stops dead still in the embrace. He starts at it. The embrace is intolerable, but he restrains himself. One can see by his arms how he would like to, but he cannot make himself, put them around her. His face shows suffering. The embrace over, however, he will try again to seem, if not gay, at least calm.

By the way—it would be better were the actor to make it his task to be cheerful; should he not succeed in being sincere about it, even better: this failure will accentuate the artificiality which Othello requires at the moment.

Pause. This scene of meeting and embrace must be played right through to the end; do not be afraid of prolonging the pause.[10]

Questions and Exercises

1. How does the director interpret the play?
2. Trace the evolution of the modern director.
3. What are the functions of the director?
4. Discuss the director's use of movement.
5. Watch a motion picture, play, or television drama paying special attention to the grouping of characters. What principles were applied in designing the groupings? Describe some of the most effective moments of the production.
6. Study the opening scene of a modern play. Make a ground plan and block out the action.

Suggested Reading

ALEKSEEV, Konstantin Sergeevich, *Stanislavsky Produces Othello*, translated by Helen Nowak (London, G. Bles, 1948).

COLE, Toby, and CHINOY, Helen Krich, eds., *Directing the Play* (Indianapolis, Bobbs-Merrill Co., Inc., 1953).

DEAN, Alexander, *Fundamentals of Play Directing* (New York, Farrar and Rinehart, Inc., 1941).

HEFFNER, Hubert C., SELDEN, Samuel, and SELLMAN, Hunton D., *Modern Theatre Practice*, 4th ed. (New York, Appleton-Century-Crofts, 1959).

SELDEN, Samuel, *First Principles of Play Production* (Chapel Hill, Univ. of North Carolina Press, 1937).

STANISLAVSKY, Constantin, *The Sea Gull Produced by Stanislavsky*, edited by S. D. Balukhaty, translated by David Magarshack (New York, Theatre Arts, Inc., 1952).

[10] From *Stanislavsky Produces Othello* (London, 1948), by Konstantin Sergeevich Alekseev, translated by Helen Nowak. Reprinted by permission of Geoffrey Bles, Ltd., London.

I 2

The Actor

THE ACTOR'S CONTRIBUTION

THE LIFE FORCE of the theater is the living actor playing before an audience. Our mechanical age may find ways to record his voice and movement on film and ship his likeness from here to there in a small can, and his image may be projected in an enormous colored enlargement on a wide screen in an immense drive-in lot, or his range of action may be reduced to a twenty-one inch frame within our living-room, but genuine theater begins and ends with the actor's living presence. His creation and interpretation give the theater its special quality. More than the stage settings, the director's skill in organization, sometimes, more than the drama itself, it is the actor who gives to the theater its reason for existence. It is his "histrionic sensibility" which induces the audience to live imaginatively in the characters and drama before them. It is the actor who ignites the spark and fans the flame that warms and illuminates the audience.

As we have seen in an earlier chapter, the impulse to imitate, to impersonate, to act is a very old one in the race and a very early one in our own lives. Because of its peculiarly subjective and intimate nature, the creative processes of the actor are difficult to explain and describe. Since acting is a private creation, the actor may work through his intuition and subconscious, or by means which he himself does not fully comprehend. Actors, like other artists may vary widely in their methods of approach. Some actors insist that the performer must have complete emotional identification with the character he is playing; others are equally adamant that acting is a matter of technique. Interestingly enough, exponents of both extremes have brilliant examples of actors who succeeded by utterly

199

diverse methods. The actor's approach to his role varies with the individual.

Furthermore, the actor is a prisoner of his times, and especially of the kind of drama in which he appears. Although a modern actor like Laurence Olivier may play in many styles of drama from Sophocles to Shakespeare to Wilde, an Elizabethan actor like Richard Burbage was obliged to play according to the style of his own period. And no one approach serves all actors in all styles. An Athenian actor in the fifth century B.C., might be called upon to play several roles (some of them feminine) in a relatively short play, speaking verse before an outdoor audience of thousands. Compare the Greek actor's task with that of a performer in Japanese Noh drama who plays in an intimate theater seating several hundred people at the most. He performs in an elaborate costume, speaking the archaic language of the old aristocracy, chanting, singing, and dancing within an eighteen-foot-square stage, his every sound and gesture based on tradition, striving to give a performance worthy of his ancestors who played the same role six or seven generations before him. Consider the differences in demands placed upon a contemporary actor as he moves from the stage to the screen. In a "hit" show on Broadway, his chief problem may be how to keep his performance as spontaneous and credible on the 300th night as it was on the first. The same actor working in motion pictures may satisfy the director if he can give a series of satisfactory performances of a few seconds' duration in two to six takes over a period of weeks. There is no one approach which can be universally applied to all acting roles from Oedipus to Willy Loman, Scapin to Cyrano, Lady Macbeth to Candida, Mrs. Malaprop to Lady Bracknell. There is no one acting style suitable for the naturalism of Gorki, the stylized Kabuki drama of Japan, the neoclassicism of Racine, the romantic comedy of Shakespeare, the sophisticated comedy of Congreve, the expressionism of Strindberg, and the "Epic" style of Brecht. The actor's task varies with the conditions under which he works, and there is no rigid formula which can be applied in all cases.

THE ACTOR CREATES

The actor is creative, not merely imitative. He does not simply reproduce a faithful copy from life. He selects, heightens, expands. Moreover, his creation is endowed with the stamp of his own personality, unique and valid, while remaining true to the playwright's outline. The actor creates a complete entity—not a static portrait which hangs in a fixed frame and position on the wall. His creation is fleeting, evanescent, constantly changing and adjusting, forming a flow of images which communicates to the audience the essential character. The actor creates his

role with expressive movement and vocal interpretation; he makes clear
his relationship to the other characters on the stage who are frequently
entangled in a complex web of emotional involvements. The symbols by
which he projects his meaning must be dynamic and interesting. His
external behavior must reveal the inner life of the man. Finally the actor
must be able to create and sustain a character not only for the length of
the evening, but he must have his resources so well controlled that he is
able to repeat his performance again and again at specific times without
losing the "illusion of the first time."

THE ACTOR INTERPRETS

The actor is an interpretative artist who stands as a middleman between
the original idea and its final effect. He works with emotional characters
and situations which must, in most plays, elicit a sense of participation
and belonging on the part of the theater-goers. If he leaves them cold
and remote, the play does not succeed. The real business of the actor,
then, is to make the audience act—to evoke in them an empathic response.

The word *empathy* means "feeling into." It may be defined as *imitative
motor response*. Notice the word, motor. An empathic response is more
than sympathy, more than an attitude of the mind; it involves actual physical identification and participation. When we escape into the open countryside, a part of our sense of relaxation comes from the fact that we feel
out with our bodies the lines of the wide horizon. Conversely, when we
are cramped down in a low-ceilinged cellar, our musculature responds to
the environment. We have had the experience of listening to an un-
sure soprano trying desperately to hit a high note beyond her range,
and have felt some of her tension in our own throats. When an actor for-
gets his lines, we may blush and perspire along with him, borrowing some
of his humiliation. This is empathic response. And it is very important in
the theater because it is one of the means by which the actor elicits audience response. Probably one of the reasons that farce and melodrama
have such wide popularity is because they are built on frameworks of
physical action which provide the audience with an ample opportunity
to respond empathically to the characters and situations.

As an interpreter of the dramatist's creation, the actor works within
circumscribed limits to develop the values of the play. The actor of integrity is faithful to his sources. He does not, as many actors have done,
use the script as a point of departure to free-wheel in outer space. The
play remains his constant frame of reference. Under the guidance of the
director, he is related to the other characters who make up the whole. He
is as much a re-actor as he is an actor. He does not break the back of the
play to display his own ego. He is not merely an exhibitionist who, like a

basketball player, puts on a one-man fancy shooting-and-dribbling show. He passes the ball to his teammates; he supports, feeds, assists, and unites with the others in a total effort toward a common goal.

REQUISITES OF THE ACTOR

The first requisite concerns the actor's physical equipment. With the wide variety of roles available in drama, an actor may be almost any size and shape, but whatever his physical endowments, he must have his body under as precise a control as the violinist has over his fingers and instrument. The actor should move and gesture easily and in a variety of ways to fit the demands of different kinds of characters and plays. He should look and feel as at ease in tights or a toga, as he does in slacks. He should be as comfortable playing on a bare stage picked out in a cone of light as he is in a modern living-room with chairs, cocktails, and cigarettes. He must have a feeling for movement that is expressive and meaningful, not only in his overt gestures but in a constant stream of subtle, nearly hidden images that reveal his full character and motivation to the audience. His movement is not mere posturing. The first law of stage deportment is that every movement should have a meaning and purpose. The actor should be imaginative in the invention of business by which he enriches the character, indicates the mood, creates atmosphere, or reveals his emotions. He should be able to handle his props and costume not only in authentic ways, but by their use, he reinforces the meaning of his lines and character. Stanislavski, who is generally thought of in terms of character motivation, was thoroughly insistent on the actor's training of his body so that he possessed a supple and expressive instrument. In a class session with his students he demonstrated his skill with a fan in order to convince them of the need for gaining control over the "language of objects." Gorchakov, a visiting director in Moscow, describes Stanislavski's demonstration in these words:

Then he showed us how one should talk with a fan. The fan quivered in his hand like the wings of a wounded bird, revealing his excitement. Stanislavsky's figure, face, and half-closed eyes were seemingly calm. Only the movement of his hand and a slight trembling of the closed fan showed his inner excitement. Then the fan opened with a sharp impulsive movement, flying up and hiding his face for an instant, and just as suddenly it lowered and closed. We understood that in this brief moment the face hidden by the fan had time to give vent to feeling and time for a deep sigh or a short laugh. And it was possible that the hand lightly brushed away a tear with the aid of the fan. Then the fan, with scarcely a noticeable movement, ordered someone supposedly nearby to come closer and sit next to him. The fan stopped trembling. It opened calmly and began to sway softly in his hand as though listening attentively to the the person sitting next to him. Then the fan smiled and even laughed. "We swore to him later that that's exactly what we heard." The fan closed again for a second and lightly struck the hand of the person next to him as though saying, "Oh, you are mean!"—and then suddenly covered the blushing face. Now his eyes entered the conversation. First they sparkled under the lace-edged fan; then they looked over the fan and half hid behind it.[1]

A second requisite of the actor is a voice that is easily understood, free from tension and unpleasantness. He must be able to read a variety of materials from the verse of Romeo and Orestes to the grunt and groan dialogue of the Hairy Ape. He must understand and be able to communicate the full intellectual and emotional content of each line of dialogue as it relates to his character and to the play as a whole. He must be able to sustain and make effective a long narrative passage or soliloquy, or engage in the rapid repartee of smart comedy with such precise timing that he maintains the pace, without stepping on the laughs. He must read his lines in context with other players creating the appropriate action and reaction, and setting the exact mood and emotion of the moment.

Finally, the actor must possess a quality difficult to define, which the great French actor Talma referred to as an "excess of sensibility." He meant by this a vivid imagination and an acute awareness which is indicated by the actor's insight into the role, an understanding of what the play and the character are all about, and in performance, a keen sense of his effect on the audience and the other members of the cast. One of the deadliest defects of an actor is the inability to assess the effect of his performance, especially in comedy when in striving too hard to "milk" laughs, the insensitive actor unconsciously destroys himself. The actor's sensibility enables him to perceive the response he is receiving and gives him the means of projecting the playwright's full meaning in a performance that is highly personal and unique, yet one that is fitting and compelling, merging smoothly into the total effect of the production.

Beyond these three attributes, many people would suggest that the actor needs to possess a spark, a magnetism, a personality that projects out into the audience and woos and wins it. In many cases of our popular stars, especially in motion pictures, this may be their sole talent.

EVOLUTION OF MODERN ACTING

Up until modern times, the actor learned his trade mostly by observation and experience. In the past, the stage-struck youth watched the stars in action, became an apprentice and worked his way up from a spear-

[1] Reprinted from *Stanislavsky Directs* (New York, 1958), by Nikolai M. Gorchakov, translated by Miriam Goldina. By permission of the publishers, Funk & Wagnalls, New York.

carrier to a speaking part, assimilating what he could by his contact with the veterans. The beginner might be taken under the wing of an experienced actor or a sympathetic manager and be given "pointers" about acting, but in general, the newcomer was left pretty much to his own devices, which meant his inspiration, imagination, and his powers of observation. A number of published works appeared from time to time on elocution, oratory, rhetoric, and stage deportment, chiefly emphasizing oral interpretation and the use of the voice, and there were occasional attempts to define characteristic emotional states and to relate them to specific postures, gestures, vocal qualities and facial expressions, but these were entirely subjective and mechanical. The great teacher was the theater itself, where through trial and error, the actor groped for his interpretation and perfected his technique for achieving effects. Those who struck the public's fancy at first attempt in the major theater centers were fortunate. Others, like Molière and Mrs. Siddons, two of the greatest performers of all time, met with initial failure and had to spend years in the outlying provincial theaters, mastering their craft before making their triumphant returns to Paris and London.

In the latter half of the nineteenth century, as a part of the scientific revolution in which nearly everything was examined, classified and catalogued, a Frenchman, Delsarte, devised an elaborate system of acting based on purely mechanical techniques. He found in man a trinity consisting of the torso, the "vital zone"; the head, the "intellectual zone"; and the face, "the moral zone." Each zone and every part of the mechanism was in turn divided into trinities, each producing its own specific expression. The student of Delsarte learned to act by memorizing and utilizing the appropriate gestures, vocal qualities and inflections. For example, in order to depict fear, the actor followed this description:

When violent and sudden, terror opens very wide the mouth, shortens the nose, draws down the eyebrows, gives the countenance an air of wildness, covers it with deadly paleness, draws back the eyebrows parallel with the sides, lifts up the open hands—with the fingers spread to the height of the breast, at some distance before it, so as to shield it from some dreadful object. One foot is drawn behind the other putting the body in posture for flight. The heart beats violently, the breath is quick and short and the whole body is thrown into a general tremor.

This artificial and external school of acting was counteracted by another approach based on the inner life of the character being portrayed. In part this resulted from the contemporary interest in psychology, but the strongest impulse came from the new drama of realism and naturalism, in which the playwright took his cue for his methods and his point of view from the scientist, attempting to record with strict fidelity the

observed facts of man's existence even though they showed him in commonplace or sordid surroundings. Because the new science taught that
man was conditioned by his environment, the naturalistic playwright
depicted the physical surroundings in accurate detail as a causal force in
his characters' motivation and behavior.

In 1877, Henri Becque, responding to the new influence, wrote a
naturalistic play called *The Vultures,* a somber study of what happens to
domestic life when the forces of the economic jungle are unleashed to
prey on helpless and unsuspecting victims. In 1882, the Comédie-Fran-
çaise was persuaded to give the play a production, but unfortunately, it
was played in the traditional style of acting in which the performers declaimed with exaggerated gestures and inflections, rising from their chairs
for their speeches and directing much of their dialogue to the audience,
thus destroying the atmosphere of Becque's play. It was not until 1887
that Antoine at the Théâtre Libre gave *The Vultures* a sympathetic and
effective performance that the full impact of the drama was realized.
Antoine recognized the need for a new way of acting in the new plays
as he indicated in a letter to the French critic, Sarcey:

The fact is that this new drama required interpreters who are new or renewed.
Plays founded on observation should not be played in the same way as stock
plays are played or as fanciful comedies are produced. To understand these
modern people one must leave behind all old conventions; a realistic drama
must be played realistically . . . the characters in *La Parisienne* or *Grandmere*
are people like us, living not in spacious halls with the dimensions of cathedrals, but in rooms like our own, by their firepaces, under the lamp, around
the table, and not as in the old repertory, close to the prompter's box. They
have voices like ours, their language is that of everyday life, with its contrac-
tions, its familiar tricks of speech, and not the rhetoric and lofty style of our
classics.

Antoine demonstrated his ideas in performances in which he, and other
members of his casts, attempted to secure complete absorption in their
roles using such unconventional stage behavior as turning their backs on
the audience and speaking in a conversational manner with the fragmentary gestures of real life.

Antoine's ideas took root and a revolution occurred in the theater,
driving out the old inflated bombastic acting with its pyrotechnic displays
of the stars. The ground was ready for the modern style of acting, but
it was not a one-sided victory.

While the old exhibitionist school of acting had its faults in an over-
flow of sentiment, wallowing emotionalism, and florid display, on the
other hand, the traditional actor could make verse sing, and he knew how
to win and hold an audience in the palm of his hand. The virtues which

Antoine brought to modern acting were a style that was simple, re-strained, and uncluttered with mannerisms and posturing. But in relin-quishing the old traditions and becoming a mere "cog in the machinery of realism," the contemporary actor lost much of his unique flair and flavor back of his blank mask. John Mason Brown has aptly referred to the new style as the "transom school of acting" in which there are "tea-cup comedians and gas-jet tragedians." He defines the "transom school of acting" in these words: "By that I mean that the modern actor in order to achieve his naturalistic effects, has largely confined his acting zone to his face. He has kept his body carefully closed to the expressive freedom he might have drawn from it, and let the light of understanding, his emotion, his pain and comedy, appear only through that limited area of his body that is safely above his Adam's apple. In other words, he has shut the door, but left the light on in the transom."

The new playwrights who wrote in a naturalistic or realistic manner introduced a whole new gallery of characters to the theater audience. The protagonists were no longer picaresque heroes, romantic adventurers, or highbrow ladies and gentlemen in evening clothes. They might be the outcasts of society—drunkards, criminals, the insane—victims of their environments or of the passions which raged within them. Many of these characters became psychologically complex. The new dramatist might have as his primary purpose the revelation of the conflicting desires which resulted in conduct that was an aberration from the norm. Strindberg indicates the complex motivation of his protagonist in *Miss Julie:*

And what will offend simple brains is that my action cannot be traced back to a single motive, that the viewpoint is not always the same. An event in real life—and this discovery is quite recent—springs generally from a whole series of more or less deep-lying motives, but of these the spectator chooses as a rule the one his reason can master most easily. A suicide is committed. Bad busi-ness, says the merchant. Unrequited love, say the ladies. Sickness says the in-valid. Crushed hopes say the shipwrecked. Now it may be that the motive lay in all or none of these directions.[2]

THE STANISLAVSKI METHOD OF ACTING

With the demands of this new kind of characterization, it was in-evitable, as Antoine insisted, that new methods of acting should be de-vised. The most famous and important innovator was Constantin Stani-slavski, who not only wrote at length about his method of acting but also demonstrated his ideas through his teaching, his directing, and his own acting. The great Russian director and actor worked out his system of acting at the Moscow Art Theatre, of which he was one of the founders.

[2] John Mason Brown in *Theatre,* edited by Edith J. R. Isaacs (New York, 1927).

As the result of years of experience in the theater, and of his self-analysis and the observation of others, he formulated his method of acting during the first decade of the twentieth century. His ideas were made known by his three books, *My Life in Art, An Actor Prepares,* and *Building the Character,* and through his work with his students and actors, a number of whom became teachers, spreading his gospel throughout the theatrical world.

The Stanislavski "method" is not a beatnik style of acting for hopped-up performers who are off on an emotional jag. It is not based on sheer raw feeling without consideration of the techniques and skills of movement and speech. These common misconceptions about the method are the result of the notoriety of some of the actors who have misapplied, misunderstood, or distorted the basic tenets which Stanislavski formulated.

Stanislavski's purpose was to devise an objective, regularized technique by which the actor could gain control of his body and emotions for the appropriate interpretation of his character and the play. Instead of depending upon haphazard inspiration, Stanislavski searched for a system with basic principles by which the actor could discipline his art. Much of his emphasis was in *preparing to act* by means of a conscious technique for causing inspiration as a conditioned response. His books are full of examples by which he sought the practical application of his techniques as he worked with students and actors.

In order to make clear his basic principles, the following explanation in Stanislavski's own words sums up his thinking. He is explaining his method to Gorchakov, a director who was working with Stanislavski in Moscow.

Now what are these basic principles of my method? First, my method gives no recipes for becoming a great actor or for playing a part. My method is the way to the actor's correct state of being on the stage. The correct state is the normal state of a human being in life. But it's very difficult for an actor to create this state on the stage. He must be physically free, must control his muscles, and must have limitless attention. He must be able to hear and see on the stage the same as he does in life. He must be able to communicate with his partner and to accept the given circumstances of the play completely.

I suggest a series of exercises to develop these qualities. You must do these every day, just as a singer or pianist does his scales and arpeggios.

My second principle concerns the correct state of being on stage. This calls for the correct actions in the progressive unfolding of the play: inner psychological actions and outer physical actions. I separate the actions in this manner intentionally. It makes it easier for us to understand each other during rehearsal. As a matter of fact, every physical action has an inner psychological action which gives rise to it. And in every psychological inner action there is always a physical action which expresses its psychic nature; the unity between these two is organic on the stage. It is defined by the theme of the play, its idea, its characters, and the given circumstances. In order to make it easier for himself, an actor must put *himself* into the given circumstances. You must say to yourself, "What would I do *if* all that happens to this character, happened to me?" I believe this *if* (I call it jokingly, the magic *if*) helps an actor to begin to *do* on the stage. After you have learned to act from yourself, define the differences between your behavior and that of the character. Find all the reasons and justifications for the character's actions, and then go on from there without thinking where your personal actions end and the character's begins. His actions and yours will fuse automatically, if you have done the preceding work as I suggested.

The third principle of the method—the correct organic (inner plus outer)—will necessarily give rise to the correct feeling, especially if an actor finds a good basis for it. The sum of these three principles—correct state of being, actions and feelings—will give to your characters an organic life on' the stage. This is the road which will bring you closest to what we call metamorphosis. Of course this takes for granted that you have understood the play correctly—its idea and its theme—and that you have analyzed the character accurately. And beyond all this, the actor must have a good appearance, clear and energetic diction, plastic movement, a sense of rhythm, temperament, taste and the infectious quality we often call charm.[3]

Another helpful statement comes from Lee Strasberg, who as head of the Actors' Studio in New York City, is one of the chief exponents of the method. Says Strasberg:

The aim of the modern method is to turn the actor away from a concern with what he, the actor is doing, thus ridding him of his fundamental self-consciousness; and to create for him those proper elements of what the *character* is doing which becomes the impulses for behavior. The actor thus becomes concerned with acting the *causes*, and not the *results*, permitting the latter to occur as they do in life. The actor's concentration is on the *object* which creates fear, rather than the worry over what to do to express fear.

Each person who experiences fear expresses it. But not each person can experience it when he so desires. This the actor learns to do. He learns to live at the command of his will and his imagination. He is not playing at something—but being; he is not "acting"—but doing. He is not imitating—but creating. Thus he holds "as 'twere, the mirror up to nature." [4]

In order to develop the ability to control the state of being, it is noteworthy that Stanislavski and other "methodists" prescribed a rigorous program of training, which, in addition to dance, fencing, movement,

---

[3] Gorchakov, *op. cit.*

[4] From *The Theatre Handbook* and *Digest of Plays,* edited by Bernard Sobel. Copyright ©, 1940, 1948, by Crown Publishers, Inc. Used by permission of the publishers.

and voice and diction, included a series of exercises on the memory of emotions, concentration, observation, imagination, and improvisation. In addition there was considerable emphasis given to the analysis of plays and characters, seeking out the basic meanings and objectives as the so-called "spine" of interpretation.

Too often the "method" actor in this country has displayed a tendency to exaggerate emotional identification, as if the only procedure the performer needed to follow was to feel the feeling, become the character, let the role possess him. This has given rise to the "sweat-shirt" school of acting whose cardinal aim is to become so involved in the character that the actor "tears a passion to tatters," and whose logical result would be that in playing *Othello*, a new Desdemona would be needed each evening. (There is historic precedent for such complete emotional identification, for we are told that the Roman actor, Aesop, actually murdered a slave during an outburst of passion in a performance.)

Some of the blame for misunderstanding and misapplication of the method must be credited to Stanislavski himself and to his followers. While he ostensibly devised an objective method of acting, some of his techniques for stimulating the inner life are clearly subjective, if not in the realm of the metaphysical. This is particularly true when the exponents of the method concern themselves with "radiation," "currents" and "imaginary centers." An example illustrates how the unwary might be led astray. This passage on the use of "radiations" comes from Michael Chekhov, who, before coming to America, worked for a number of years in the Russian theater, and who devised his own conception of the method which he describes in his book, *To the Actor*.

Imagine that within your chest there is a center from which flows the actual impulses for all your movements. Think of this imaginary center as a source of inner activity and *power* within your body. Send this power into your head, arms, hands, torso, legs and feet. Let the sensation of strength, harmony and well-being penetrate the whole body. See to it that neither your shoulders, elbows, wrists, hips nor knees stanch the flow of this energy from the imaginary center, but let it course freely.

So long as the center remains in the middle of your chest (pretend it is a few inches deep), you will feel that you are still yourself and in full command, only more energetically and harmoniously so, with your body approaching an "Ideal" type. But as soon as you try to shift the center to some other place within or outside your body, you will feel that your whole psychological and physical attitude will change, just as it changes when you step into an imaginary body. You will notice that the center is able to draw and concentrate your whole being into one spot from which your activity emanates and radiates. If, to illustrate the point, you were to move the center from your chest to your head, you would become aware that the thought element has begun to play a characteristic part in your performance. . . .

Try a few experiments for a while. Put a soft, warm, not too small center in the region of your abdomen and you may experience a psychology that is self-satisfied, earthy, a bit heavy and even humorous. Place a tiny, hard center on the tip of your nose and you will become curious, inquisitive, prying and even meddlesome. Move the center into one of your eyes and notice how quickly it seems that you have become sly, cunning and perhaps hypocritical. Imagine a big, heavy dull and sloppy center placed outside the seat of your pants and you have a cowardly, not too honest, droll character. A center located a few feet outside your eyes or forehead may invoke the sensation of a sharp, penetrating and even sagacious mind. A warm, hot and fiery center situated within your heart may awaken in you heroic, loving and courageous feelings.[5]

It is in such statements as these that the seeds of misunderstanding have been sown about the method.

While the central idea of the Stanislavski system is control, an admirable objective for any actor, it should be kept in mind that there are serious doubts as to the application of the method carte blanche for all kinds of drama and all styles of production. The method may be ideal for working under conditions which permit long months of rehearsal and experimentation in which the actor strives for maximum identification with the character he is playing, but the method is quite inappropriate for the training of a Japanese Kabuki actor whose objective is to suggest the traditional movement and gesture of a puppet. Nor was the method applicable to meet the requirements of Meierhold's "biodynamics," a kind of acting devised to meet the acrobatic and athletic requirements of mechanized platforms, ramps, and steps. Brecht, the modern German playwright, had little use for Stanislavski's approach in the production of "Epic" drama in which the playwright sought to achieve his "alienation" effect to avoid audience identification with the character and the play in order to preserve a critical attitude in the spectator, rather than an emotional response. Hence Brecht strove to *prevent* the illusion of reality from occurring by requiring his actors to drop in and out of character, by interrupting the continuity of performance, and by having them address the audience directly at times. Nor does it seem likely that the Stanislavski system is ideal for performance in those kinds of comedy in which the actor avoids emotional involvement. The limitations of the method of acting are that it may be inappropriate in some styles of production, and that it may be misinterpreted to the extent that the actor regards every role as that of a clinical case study in abnormal psychology.

The value of Stanislavski's ideas have been discussed widely. Most of the criticism of the method centers about its abuse. Too many disciples and performers have exaggerated feeling and inspiration and paid too

[5] Michael Chekhov, *To the Actor* (New York, Harper & Bros., 1953).

little attention to the originator's insistence on the importance of technique. Those who emphasize technical training, point out that the actor must have complete mastery of his voice and body so that he is free to move and speak in a way that is expressive, projectile, and appropriate. It is not enough for Romeo to feel like fighting a duel; he must know how to fence. In reading a comic line, it is not enough to think that the dialogue is funny; the delivery requires skillful timing. Generations of outstanding actors who gave brilliant performances in the theater long before Stanislavski testify to the fact that their acting was mostly a matter of cool and calculated technique or personal intuition. Every actor must find his own procedure. The value of the Stanislavski system is that it provides one way by which the actor may regularize his approach to his art.

THE ACTOR'S TRAINING

In any kind of training, the actor begins working on himself. While there may be considerable divergence as to the degree of emotional identification necessary or desirable, modern textbooks on acting are generally agreed that the actor needs disciplined training for his body and voice. Most acting books set up a series of exercises for developing sensory responses, pantomime, improvisation, oral interpretation, and body movement. Many of them include scenes from plays for experimental performance.

The beginning actor learns to respond at first to such sensory stimuli as touching a piece of fur, tasting a lemon, seeing a flashing light, listening to a distant bell and smelling a subtle perfume. He works on such elementary pantomimes as cooking an imaginary dinner, exploring a haunted castle, or repairing an old car. He is assigned scenes to play from a variety of standard dramas. For example he may be called upon to perform Cyrano's death scene, the stage manager in the drugstore scene in *Our Town*, or Lord Porteus in the bridge game in *The Circle*. Another typical assignment is to improvise acting scenes, making up characters, situations, and dialogue spontaneously. Later on, the student actor works on building characters in complete plays. The objective of the actor's training in such a program is to develop his skill in speech and movement so that he possesses an expressive and controlled instrument.

In many countries of the world today, there are permanent residential acting companies in major cities where the aspiring actor can learn his business. Many countries have national academies of dramatic art for the instruction of the young. Sixty years ago in the United States, there were several thousand professional theaters where legitimate drama was played. In many of these theaters, the new actor found his training. Today our theater has shrunk to a few blocks on a small island, where a few dozen playhouses are regularly devoted to the production of drama. Less than 5 per cent of our total population ever see a professional play! The beginning actor in America now finds his training in community theaters or on the campuses of our college and universities. At least four hundred institutions of higher learning now offer majors in drama, a few of them leading to the doctorate. The typical curriculum in a college drama program includes such courses as Acting, Directing, Play Production, Playwriting, Scene Design and Lighting, Costuming, Oral Interpretation, Voice and Diction, Theater History and a number of courses in Dramatic Literature. Academic classwork is augmented by a regular program of play production in which outstanding contemporary and historical plays are performed by student actors, usually under trained faculty directors. Some of the campus theaters are fine pieces of architecture, and frequently the stage design is of a highly professional quality.

Although the educational theater offers excellent facilities for instruction in dramatic production, when the aspiring actor attempts to make a living in the profession, he faces a hazardous task. Less than sixty new productions are given annually on Broadway. Thus the opportunities for new talent are meager. The beginning actor may eke out an existence in off-Broadway plays, or he may find employment in summer stock or community theaters, but in general he must face up to the economic fact of life that only a small percentage of American actors can make a living in the legitimate theater. Even the established professional hopes for a long-run hit in order to raise his standard of living. Or he may turn to motion pictures or television in order to increase his income. In any case, both economically and artistically, the actor in this country has unfavorable working conditions because our theater is sadly lacking in tradition or continuity.

THE ACTOR'S WAY OF WORKING

The way in which an actor approaches a new play and builds a character has been the subject of endless conjecture and controversy. Actors themselves freely acknowledge their inability to describe what actually happens to them in performance. The literature on the art of acting is filled with conflicting statements which indicate that the process is too personal for clear-cut intellectual analysis. As a matter of fact, most actors seem to distrust intellection, especially during performance. Sir Cedric Hardwicke, a prominent English actor, emphasizes this point in recounting his experience on stage: "You have an awareness of what you're doing, but it's instinctive. The best effects are the ones you are not conscious of. Actors decay when they begin to *understand* what they are saying." [6] Hardwicke goes so far as to add: "The great Shake-spearean actors didn't have the vaguest idea what the hell they were saying. Ellen Terry didn't know what it was all about, but she never made a mistake." [7]

The actor places his faith in his feelings. This point is made again and again in a series of interviews which Lillian Ross conducted with outstanding stage and motion picture performers for *The New Yorker* [8] in which are found such representative statements as these:

It's when you start to rehearse, with other people, that things begin to hap-pen. What it is exactly I don't know, and even don't want to know. I'm all for mystery there. Most of what happens as you develop your part is uncon-scious. Most of it is underwater. (KIM STANLEY)

Once you set things you do and make them mean certain things, you then respond to the stimuli you yourself set up. Then you *feel*. (MAUREEN STAPLE-TON)

What you try to do in the theatre is to give a universal picture, through your own eyes and feelings, of the person you play. You try to be, in your way, what that person would be. You have a feeling about the thing. If you don't feel strongly about a part, or if it doesn't appeal to you, it's a mistake to do it. (KATHERINE CORNELL)

When I'm building a role, I start with a series of mental pictures and feel. (HUME CRONYN)

Every actor has, as a gift from God, his own method. My particular method is to go first by the sense of taste—physical taste. I actually have a physical taste for every part. Then I go to the other senses—hearing, seeing, touching. Thinking comes much later. (VLADIMIR SOKOLOFF)

In working on a new play, many actors testify to an initial period of trial and error before the image becomes clear. Geraldine Page, one of the outstanding American actresses, sees her role developing like a jig-saw puzzle, a small piece at a time. Henry Fonda says, "I baby up on a part. I get the feeling gradually." [9] Katherine Cornell comments, "Some-times you read a part over and over and you get lost in many things you think about it. You flounder around struggling with it. Little by

---

[6] Lillian Ross, "Profiles: The Player," *The New Yorker*, October 21, 1961, October 28, 1961 and November 4, 1961. Reprinted by permission. Copr. ©, 1961 The New Yorker Magazine, Inc. October 28, 1961.

[7] *Ibid.*

[8] *Ibid.*

[9] *Ibid.*, Oct. 28, 1961.

little, some line emerges, and you've got it." [10] Apparently many actors
go through a similar experience until all at once "a bell rings," or there
is a "spark," or "suddenly there is a click." Henry Fonda describes this
phenomenon in this way: "I always know when it feels real to me. . . .
When my emotion takes over in a part, it's like a seaplane taking off
on the water. I feel as if I were soaring. If five times out of eight a week
the emotions take over, you've got magic." [11]

Geraldine Page makes an interesting observation concerning character identification:

When you take the character over and use the character, you wreck the fabric
of the play, but you can be in control of the character without taking the
character over. When the character uses *you*, that's when you're really cooking. You know you're in complete control, yet you get the feeling you didn't
do it. You have the beautiful feeling that you can't ruin it. You feel as if you
were tagging along on an exciting journey. You don't completely understand
it, and you don't have to. You're just grateful and curious.[12]

This statement suggests the interesting dichotomy of the actor who,
while assuming the role of another character, still remains in complete
control of himself. Whether the actor's approach to his craft is sheerly
technical or by means of emotional involvement, it must be recognized
as a very personal and highly individualized process that defies complete definition or understanding. Nevertheless, there are certain general
steps that may be followed.

Like the director, the actor's initial task in approaching a play is that
of analysis. He searches for the core idea, the "spine." What does the play
mean? What is the effect supposed to be on an audience? What is the
desired emotional impact? What gives the play its dramatic tension? The
actor, under the guidance and stimulation of the director, analyzes the
play to establish its basic interpretation.

The actor may begin by examining the play's structure. Is the play an
episodic one like *Waiting for Lefty, The Private Life of the Master Race*
or *From Morn Till Midnight?* Or does the play progress steadily toward
a sweeping climax as in *Ghosts* or *Oedipus Rex?* The actor may find it
profitable to break the play down into fragments so that he can determine
the dramatic purpose and effect of each sequence.

The actor will want to know what kind of a play it is. Is it a mixture
of forms like *Juno and the Paycock* which has both comic and tragic elements? Is the play a comedy? If so, is it a smart sophisticated play like
The Second Man or is it the source of laughter to be found in the physical

10 *Ibid.*, Oct. 28, 1961.
11 *Ibid.*, Oct. 28, 1961.
12 *Ibid.*, Nov. 4, 1961.

antics of type characters involved in ludicrous situations as in *The Doctor in Spite of Himself* or *The Taming of the Shrew?* Or is the comic writer attacking contemporary foibles and follies as in *Doctor Knock* and *Volpone?*

As he analyzes the play, the actor must consider its style of performance. While the basic interpretation and style will be governed by the director, the actor must realize the implications of the style in his manner of speaking and moving. Is it a highly artificial style like *Yellow Jacket* or *The Importance of Being Earnest?* Or does the play require an elevated scale, a feeling of dignity and grandeur as in *Agamemnon* or *Phaedra?* If the play is a period piece, will the acting style be an attempt at complete historical accuracy, or will it simply be suggested? Or perhaps the original style may be satirized.

The analysis of the play should lead the actor to an understanding of the pervading atmosphere of the play. Does the locale suggest a hot, tropical, exotic quality like *Rain?* Does the environment require the tempo and flavor of big city tenement life like *Street Scene* or *Dead End?* The dominating atmosphere of the play provides the actor with clues to his interpretation and method of playing—the tempo, his use of props and business. From his study of the total play, the actor sees not only the relationship of his character to the action as a whole, but he also finds many sources of inspiration for the interpretation of the spirit and quality of the playwright's creation.

After the actor has a clear comprehension of the play's structure, atmosphere, style, and basic interpretation, he studies his individual character. He may begin by approaching the character from the outside, making an inventory of his race, age, occupation, appearance, manner of speaking and moving, physical condition, posture, movement, carriage, and dress. He may take his observations directly from life, or if it is a period play, he will find it profitable to study historical pictures showing the costume, architecture, and manners of the time.

The actor will find four main sources of information about his character in the script. In modern drama, the playwright frequently provides a character description which will give him some of the details listed above. Some playwrights, like Shaw, provide very complete portraits down to the color of the eyes and shape of the nostrils. Other contemporary playwrights may simply give the actor the barest hint, such as "a waiter," "a young man of twenty-four," or "a tramp." In period plays, the dramatist usually gave no character description at all.

A second source of information comes from the lines which the actor speaks. The playwright has usually taken great pains to write dialogue which represents and delineates the character. Lines, of course, are susceptible to a variety of interpretations and it is obvious that two different actors playing the same role may find marked differences in the reading of the dialogue. Indeed, the same actor may give a variety of interpretations of lines in different performances. The skillful playwright goes beyond the literal meaning of the words and uses dialogue as a means of revealing his characters as well as advancing the plot. The actor, therefore, must search his lines for their essential meaning, not only in reference to the immediate context, but also to the revelation of the total character.

A third clue in the actor's analysis of the role is found in what he does. Is the character an active agent or is he acted upon? What change does he undergo during the course of the play? What emotions are aroused? What is his primary objective and how does he go about reaching it? How much of the inner man is revealed by what he does? To what extent does he understand his own motives? What choices and decisions does he make and how do they affect him? Do his actions make him a sympathetic character?

Finally, the actor learns a good deal about his role from the reaction of other characters to him—what they say and do. The actor must understand his dramatic purpose in the struggle which is frequently revealed by the reaction of other characters to him. Shakespeare sometimes delineates his characters sharply in the lines of another character: "Yon Cassius hath a lean and hungry look"; Coriolanus was captured in a sentence: "When he walks he moves like an engine, and the ground shrinks before his treading; he is able to pierce a corselet with his eye, talks like a knell, and his hum is a battery." But it is mostly in the action and reaction of one character upon another that the playwright indicates the motivations of his characters. From their behavior toward one another, the audience learns that they are in love, or they are bitter enemies, or that one is plotting to destroy the other.

It is from this kind of preliminary analysis of the script that the actor determines the broad outlines of his role. Suppose he is cast in the part of Horatio in *Hamlet*. Let us glance at a single scene and consider the hints that Shakespeare has provided for playing the character. See pages 58-67.

Shakespeare provides no character description and no stage directions, but we may make a good many inferences about Horatio and his behavior. Marcellus helps to establish him with the line, "Thou art a scholar, Horatio." He is obviously a young man—a scholar, an intellectual, a friend of Hamlet's. He is probably well dressed, wearing a doublet, tights, possibly a cloak or cape, and carrying a sword. He brings to this soldier's post an air of courtly polish by his aristocratic bearing. His voice and speech should be refined and flexible, showing his authority, blurting out commands to the ghost and fellows of the watch, and bringing out the full beauty of the poetic lines at the end of the scene. Physically, he is strong and vigorous.

Within a very few lines, Shakespeare provides considerable information about Horatio. His first speech, "A piece of him," shows a touch of good-natured humor despite the fact that he has been persuaded by the fearful soldiers to come out late at night in the bitter cold to see something which he regards as a mere fantasy. "Tush, tush, 'twill not appear," shows his scholar's skepticism. But sixteen lines later, Horatio having seen the ghost is compelled to say, "it harrows me with fear and wonder," key lines of the scene. He "trembles and looks pale." Thus, Shakespeare in dramatizing Horatio's conversion from skepticism to belief has established the credibility of the ghost.

Despite his "fear and wonder," Horatio takes the initiative as he attempts to question the ghost. It disappears and Horatio says, " 'Tis strange," and he immediately seeks for the significance—not merely the personal one, but Horatio is concerned about the larger meaning of the appearance of the apparition and any possible political implications. "This bodes some strange eruption to our state." Then Horatio explains to the soldiers the threatened conflict with Fortinbras. His feeling of foreboding as he recalls the fall of Julius Caesar is good preparation for the later action of the play as well as an indication of Horatio's scholarship and of his concern about the welfare of his country.

With the second appearance of the apparition, Horatio takes more vigorous action. "I'll cross it, though it blast me. Stay illusion!" Horatio's poetic passages at the end of the scene are a change of pace showing his sensitivity. Then he becomes a man of action again as he goes to tell Hamlet what he has seen.

During the few lines of this opening scene, Horatio's actions reveal his skepticism, his change to belief when he confronts the ghost, his attempt to force it to speak, and finally Horatio's determination to seek further for the solution to the mystery.

The reactions of the soldiers to Horatio show that they respect him and look to him for assistance and assurance. They have confidence in him, asking Horatio to come with them and share their vigil in an attempt to solve the mystery.

Horatio has a number of dramatic functions in this first scene. He helps to establish the validity of the ghost, thus reinforcing the "fear and wonder" atmosphere. His exposition provides the framework of the political background of the play, and Horatio's action carries the progression of the plot forward as he goes to tell Hamlet about the strange apparition which he has seen.

An actor playing Horatio, would of course make a complete study of the play, searching for all of the evidence he could find that would help him to create a fully-realized character. He would work in conjunction with the director who would see the part of Horatio in terms of the larger design of the entire production. During the rehearsal period, he would experiment with the reading of the lines, the movement and business, and the interaction with the other members of the cast until the character became a substantial person with a life of his own.

The art of acting is really the art of reacting. It is not alone through the recital of his lines that the play comes to life, but in the response of the actor to the words and actions of others, and his reaction to objects. A mere reading of Horatio's lines aloud gives an incomplete and flat version of this dramatic scene. Shakespeare cries out for movement: "How now, Horatio? You tremble and look pale." "I'll cross it, though it blast me. Stay illusion!" "Stop it, Marcellus." "Shall I strike at it with my partisan?" These lines are cues for action. This scene, with its interplay among the characters must be projected by living actors to realize the full content of Shakespeare's creation. This interaction among the characters and the emotional overtones which accompany and reinforce the lines—these constitute the theatric elements which the reader is liable to miss in his armchair. The memorable moments in the theater are often the result of the actor's particular and expressive way of reaction: Claudius's blanching as he sees the re-enactment of his crime, Lady Macbeth rubbing her guilty hands, Mrs. Alving's horror when Oswald asks for the sun—these are key moments which only the actor can express.

It is in the creation and enrichment of the performance that the actor makes his unique contribution. A good deal of his effect results not so much from what he says or does, but rather from his way of saying and doing. As an example of what the actor contributes to his performance, we may cite John Gielgud's production of *Hamlet* which he played in New York in 1935. This was acknowledged to be one of the finest Hamlets of the century. Rosamond Gilder made an attempt to describe and record as accurately as possible exactly what Gielgud did during the performance. The following excerpt is typical for showing what the actor did during the soliloquy, "Now I am alone . . ." (Act II, Scene 2)

"Now I am alone . . ." It is, once again, that desperate cry of nerves too highly strung. His head goes back in a gesture of physical suffering as though the accumulated weight could be thrown off in this moment of release. "O' what a rogue and peasant slave am I" follows in an explosion of rage and self-scorn. He turns a little toward the spot where the Player had stood, and the burning words pour out. "He would drown the stage with tears"—Hamlet swings around facing front, his clenched fist thrust down, his head back, his voice rising in a tornado to the crest of *"amaze indeed* the very faculties of eyes and ears." Then, suddenly, a drop—voice, body, carriage all deflated. He moves slowly to the stool at the left end of the table and falls on it, vanquished.

The bitter challenge of "Am I a coward?" rises in swift, staccato exclamations until "Who does me this?" brings him to his feet with a cry. Again the weary fall, he leans against the table—half sitting—his agitation slowly mounting, this time to a final climax of horror as the hated uncle is excoriated in hissing, virulent words—"treacherous, *lecherous, kindless villain!*" Hamlet is trembling with fury, his body shaking, his voice high. With "Vengeance!" he snatches his dagger from its sheath and rushes to the doorway right, throwing himself against it as the wave of his futile fury crashes to its height and dies. His raised arm falls, the dagger rolls on the ground, his body sways against the door and he sinks, almost crouching on the top step.

The downward sweep of his self-concern is as devastating as the upward sweep of his rage. His voice is broken with a sob of humiliation. He sees himself without kindness and judges himself without pity. His courage deserts him, not in the face of danger, physical or supernatural, but in the face of his own incalculable and uncontrollable impulses. "Fie upon 't! foh!" The silence that follows is Hamlet's nadir; he is beaten down, almost lost.

Then slowly he moves, raises his head, invokes that bright particular particle that shines even in this black night of his soul. "About, my brain!" The idea already seen returns and gives him the needed impulse toward action. He plans the playtrap in a hoarse, whispered voice, rising from the steps, moving a little forward. "I'll have these players play something like the murder of my father"—the voice is low, the tempo uncertain. It quickens a little with the hope of making his uncle blanch. A pause and then very slowly we see in his face that look Ophelia saw, the look of one "loosed out of hell." The pathos of his loneliness, of his fear, of his "weakness and . . . melancholy" are poignantly revealed in the cadence of his voice, in the line of his figure which seems fragile, helpless, all its informing vigour gone.

He stands for a moment absolutely still, weighing the awful possibility of eternal damnation should he be led by ghost or demon or by his own fevered imagination into committing the very crime he is called upon to avenge. "I'll have grounds more relative than this" is a cry of despair and defiance. "The play's the thing wherein I'll catch the conscience of the king" is spoken in a frenzy of excitement, reaching this time in one burst the summit of intensity. His body is galvanized, he hurls himself across the intervening space to the chair at the end of the table where he has sat listening to the Player. He pulls the paper toward him, seizes a pen, the light catches his wildly excited face, then blacks out as he bends forward writing frantically.[13]

Questions and Exercises

1. In what ways is the actor creative? Interpretative?
2. How does empathy affect the playing and reception of a performance?

[13] From Rosamond Gilder, *John Gielgud's Hamlet* (New York, Oxford University Press, 1937). Reprinted by permission of the author.

3. What are the requisites of a good actor?
4. Describe the most memorable performance you have seen in the theater. Account for the effectiveness of the portrayal.
5. How did Delsarte and Stanislavski differ in their approach to acting?
6. What was Antoine's contribution to modern acting?
7. How does an actor study his part?
8. Discuss the evolution of modern acting.
9. What are the limitations of the modern realistic style?
10. Study a one-act play. Make a complete character description of one of the major roles including the character's appearance, manner of speaking and moving, motivation, and social background. What function does the role serve in the play? What are the problems of playing the role?
11. View a performance of a play, motion picture, or television drama centering your attention on one actor. Was his performance credible? How effective was his business? Was his performance in harmony with the rest of the cast? How well did he listen and react?

Suggested Reading

BOLESLAVSKY, Richard, *Acting: The First Six Lessons* (New York, Theatre Arts, Inc., 1933).

CHEKHOV, Michael, *To the Actor: On the Technique of Acting* (New York, Harper & Brothers, 1953).

COLE, Toby and Chinoy, KRICH, Helen, eds., *Actors on Acting: Theories, Techniques, and Practices of the World's Great Actors* (New York, Crown Publishers, Inc., 1949).

EUSTIS, Morton, *Players at Work* (New York, Theatre Arts, Inc., 1937).

McGAW, Charles, *Acting Is Believing* (New York, Holt, Rinehart and Winston, Inc., 1955).

STANISLAVSKY, Constantin, *An Actor Prepares,* translated by Elizabeth Reynolds Hapgood (New York, Theatre Arts, Inc., 1936).

STANISLAVSKY, Constantin, *Building a Character,* translated by Elizabeth Reynolds Hapgood (New York, Theatre Arts, Inc., 1949).

13

Stage Design

YOU WILL RECALL that Aristotle placed the element of spectacle sixth and last, but this does not mean that the visual aspects of dramatic production are inconsequential. It is no mere anomaly of usage that causes us to speak of going to *see* a play. At times, theatrical performances were given which reversed Aristotle's order, exploiting scenery, costuming, and lighting as the chief means of audience appeal. At other times, it was the convention of the theater to use little or no specific graphic representation of locale. However, such stages were not lacking in spectacle. The permanent architectural features of the Greek, Elizabethan, and Noh theaters were enhanced in performance through the use of movement, dance, and elaborate costuming and properties, and the playhouses themselves delighted the eye, as we shall see in the chapter on Architecture.

Our present interest in stage design is two-fold: first to sketch the pictorial tradition which has dominated the Western theater since the Renaissance, including a brief statement about modern experimentation, and second, to consider the scene designer's function and his methods of working.

THE PICTORIAL TRADITION

Our current convention of pictorial representation of the dramatic environment is only a few centuries old. Medieval drama with its manifold station oftentimes was staged with elaborate attention to realistic detail in order to secure the maximum amount of identification from the spectator, as Lee Simonson points out in his excellent book, *The Stage Is Set*. But essentially our scenic tradition stems from the Renaissance innovation of the proscenium arch at the Farnese Theatre in Parma, Italy (1618). This

Farnese Theatre (1618), Parma, Italy

theater exerted an enormous influence on playwriting, and on all phases of production, especially stage design, which continues to affect our practice today.

Two factors were especially influential in the kinds of sets which appeared in the new proscenium-arch theaters. First, the Italian painters were intrigued by the potentialities of design with linear perspective by which they could produce the illusion of depth on a flat surface. This led to the construction and painting of scenery built of wood and canvas in direct imitation of architecture and natural phenomena. Verisimilitude and solidity were given to the settings by making those units nearest to the audience three-dimensional, and gradually reducing the space between set pieces until the upstage area was completely two-dimensional. As time went on, perspective settings became more and more elaborate, until they became astonishing mazes of corridors, fountains, pillars, and buildings so huge and spectacular that the actor was completely dwarfed on stage. The Bibiena family inaugurated the use of several vistas by running their perspective scenery at divergent angles, thus making possible overwhelming visual displays. The second factor influencing stage decoration was the custom of creating extravagant "effects," floats and arches for court pageants and festivals. This taste for ostentatious display and the novelty of perspective scenery were combined in the theaters when designers swamped the stage, not only with eye-filling scenery, but also with all manner of sensational mechanical stunts such as great floating clouds and chariots, dazzling practical fountains, and enormous fires which were frighteningly real. While at first the perspective set served as a neutral background for the production of many plays, under royal and aristocratic patronage, the practice was to create specific scenery and effects for specific plays and occasions. Thus, the tradition was established of illusional picture settings—a tradition from which the theater has not escaped to this day.

As the public stage grew and professional companies were forced to make their own way financially, it was impossible for many theaters to afford the expense of extravagant scenery. Furthermore, the action of many plays demanded scenery that could be shifted rapidly. A mechanical system was developed consisting of backdrops and wing-pieces on which were painted a variety of scenes. Wings were portable screens of wood and canvas which could be slid in and out of grooves at the sides of the stage. Rows of these wings, set parallel to the footlights, lined the acting area. Entrances and exits were made by simply walking between the wings. A series of backdrops was flown at the rear of the stage completing the vista of the setting. Overhead, borders of canvas masked the flies from the spectator. Although these stock pieces were obviously two-dimensional, painted contrivances, they satisfied the audiences' taste for reality.

Design for Stage Set by F. G. da Bibiena (1657-1743)

Not only were individual pieces of scenery standardized, but every theater owned a series of stock sets such as an Italian garden, a prison, a mountain pass, a drawing room, a woodland glade, a kitchen, and a palace. These stock sets were used again and again as the various plays demanded. Occasionally, extra care and money were expended to design and construct scenery for specific productions, at which time this fact became a special point of publicity, such as for Charles Kean's staging of Shakespeare. But by and large, most drama in the eighteenth and nineteenth centuries was performed in stock sets of standardized units of wings and backdrops.

In the chapter on naturalism we have noted the nineteenth-century efforts to achieve appropriateness of environment not only as the visual background of the action but as a conditioning force on character. The naturalists went to great lengths to make their settings as credible as possible. Antoine went so far as to hang real meat on stage for a scene in a butcher shop. The naturalist's excessive concern with imitating the surface aspects of life led to meaningless clutter as he attempted to implement the idea of the "significant trifle." The realist tempered the naturalist's approach with a degree of moderation and simplification. A valuable service was performed for the theater in clearing the stage of its flatness, its fake trim and unreal properties, its shoddy prettiness, and makeshift workmanship. Stage settings began to have a more substantial look, doors slammed and windows could be opened and shut. The wings in the grooves were replaced by flats of canvas representing real walls which enclosed the acting area. Real properties were assembled, and the stage was filled with casual objects of daily living. The painted perspective tradition was wiped out, and there was a new sense of material rightness of things. But most importantly, the idea was advanced and accepted that the scenery should serve as the specific and appropriate environment for the action of the play.

Realism was no sooner the accepted way of staging drama than it was challenged by the appearance of plays written in defiance of realistic practices, as in the works of Maeterlinck, Claudel, Yeats, and Hauptmann. But even more significant was the appearance of two pioneering spirits, endowed with poetic fervor and imagination who led the way toward the new stagecraft.

GORDON CRAIG

Although Gordon Craig was trained and experienced in the English legitimate theater, his contribution does not lie in the practical aspects of scene painting and construction, but rather in his point of view, which was that of a visionary who crusaded for an ideal art of the theater. He castigated the contemporary stage for its shabbiness, its exaggeration of realistic detail, and most of all for its lack of artistic purpose and direction. Craig conceived of the theater as an aesthetic unity in which all aspects of production would be harmonized. Toward this end, he called for a *regisseur* who would give to the production of drama this unified concept. Impatient with the actor, Craig even suggested replacing him with supermarionettes. He saw the theater from the standpoint of design based on the selection of a few simple set pieces and properties which possessed symbolic value as this advice to the designer illustrates:

And remember he does not merely sit down and draw a pretty or historically accurate design, with enough doors and windows in picturesque places, but he first of all chooses certain colors which seem to him to be in harmony with the spirit of the play, rejecting other colors as out of tune. He then weaves into a pattern certain objects—an arch, a fountain, a balcony, a bed—using the chosen object as the center of his design. Then he adds to this all the objects which are mentioned in the play, and which are necessary to be seen.[1]

Craig sought to replace imitation with suggestion, elaboration with simplicity. He insisted on the spiritual relationship between setting and action. He pointed out the emotional potentialities of figures moving in design, of shifting light and shadow, of the dramatic values of color. He emphasized that the theater was above all "a place for seeing." Craig illustrated his ideas with a series of provocative designs, and he sought to demonstrate his theories in production; sometimes these were doomed to failure because of impracticability, but sometimes they were brilliantly successful. Craig's contribution was not, however, in the utilitarian aspects of the theater; his real significance was in his dream, which he persuaded others to see by the compelling force of his enthusiasm and argument.

ADOLPHE APPIA

The other pioneer of modern staging was the Swiss, Adolphe Appia, who in 1899 published his seminal work in which he called for reforms in the theater, *Die Musik und die Inscenierung*. He arrived at his conclusions through his experiences in staging Wagner's operas at Bayreuth. Appia began with the actor, and insisted that the design must be in harmony with the living presence of the performer. When a forest was required on stage, it was not necessary to give accurate representation of a forest, but to create the atmosphere of a man amidst the trees. The attention of the audience should be focused on the characters, and not distracted by detailed branches and leaves. Painted stage settings are incompatible with the actor because of the contrast between his plasticity and

---

[1] Gordon Craig, *The Art of the Theatre* (London, 1905).

Sketch by Gordon Craig for Scene in *Macbeth*

the flatness of his scenic surroundings: ". . . the human body does not seek to produce the illusion of reality *since it is in itself reality!* What it demands of the *décor* is simply to set in relief this reality . . . we must free staging of everything that is in contradistinction with the actor's presence . . . Scenic illusion is the living presence of the actor."

Appia suggested two tenets of good design: (1) the lighting should emphasize the plasticity of the human form, rather than destroying it; and (2) a plastic scene should give the actor's movements all of their value. Implicit in Appia's theories is a fundamental unity of all phases of production, with the major emphasis on the actor. Appia enforced his arguments by applying them to his designs for Wagner, fashioning uncluttered settings of simple forms in which skillful lighting created a remarkably appropriate and effective atmosphere. Appia's theories were well-timed since they coincided with the invention of the electric light, which gave theatrical production a marvelous new dimension in design. Up until this time, stage lighting was an awkward and dangerous aspect of production, in which almost all efforts went into getting enough light on the stage so that the audience could see. Now with electricity, the way was opened up for the use of lighting for its evocative potentialities in creating and enhancing the mood of the play. Appia was the first to demonstrate this new force aesthetically.

The sparks which Craig and Appia kindled, ignited and the "new stagecraft" made its appearance, based on the generally accepted point of view that scenery should augment and reinforce the atmosphere and meaning of the play, and that scenery should be utilitarian in providing the actor with a serviceable environment for his performance. This point of view is apparent from the following representative statements. John Gassner regards the function of the setting is to supply a "psychological frame of reference"; Marc Blitzstein says that scenery "should be used to pull the play along its intended course"; and Harold Clurman stresses its practicability: "A set is a utensil which cannot be judged until its worth is proved in practice by the whole course of the play's development on stage."

Robert Edmond Jones, a moving force in the progress of scene design in America, reflects his debt to Craig in his concept of the purpose of stage scenery:

Stage-designing should be addressed to this eye of the mind. There is an outer eye that observes, and there is an inner eye that sees. . . . The designer must always be on his guard against being too explicit. A good scene, I repeat, is not a picture. It is something seen, but it is something conveyed as well; a feeling, an evocation. Plato says somewhere: It is beauty I seek, not beautiful things. That is what I mean. A setting is not just a beautiful thing, a collection of beautiful things. It is a presence, a mood, a symphonic accompaniment to the drama, a great wind fanning the drama to flame. It echoes, it enhances,

Sketch by Adolphe Appia for Set in Act III of Wagner's *Die Walküre*, 1924

it animates. It is an expectancy, a foreboding, a tension. It says nothing, but it gives everything.[2]

EXPERIMENTS IN DESIGN

The cleavage between various *isms* in our theater today is largely a matter of academic argument, and while there is little profit in trying to separate various styles and modes into confining compartments, it may be helpful to distinguish between two points of view toward theatrical production. On one hand there are those who look upon drama in the Aristotelian tradition that the theater is an imitation of life. This attitude, referred to as *representationalism* by Alexander Bakshy, endeavors to create the illusion of actuality. The characters and events on stage have, for the moment, the authenticity of real life. On the other hand, there is *presentationalism*, in which it is frankly admitted that the theater is make-believe and that the actors are only pretending. Although less familiar to Western audiences, presentational staging has a long tradition on the stage, notably in the Oriental theater where symbolic theatrical conventions are readily accepted. For example, two coolies carrying flags on which are painted wheels, become a carriage; a stick becomes a horse when a rider mounts it; and a table may be a bridge, a bed, or a mountain top. Although in America our traditions and experience are mostly with representational production, we have seen occasional examples of the breaking down of traditional procedures in such plays as *Our Town* in which the atmosphere of a funeral was admirably created on a bare stage by a handful of people carrying wet, black umbrellas. Contemporary playwrights, seeking more freedom for their action, have made use of fragments of scenery, simultaneous settings representing several locales at once, and walls of painted transparent gauze which give the effect of solidity when lighted from the front, only to melt away as the light is brought up behind. While most of our theatrical production continues to be literal and representational, there is a wearing away of the old traditions and more and more theatricalism as playwright and designer seek new forms of expression, as for example they did in expressionism. The theatricalism of presentational staging elsewhere suggests some of the directions which our future theater may wish to explore.

EPIC THEATER

One of the most interesting efforts in experimental drama has been the "epic" theater which began in the 1920's as the result of the work of Erwin Piscator and Brecht. The latter, in addition to being a director,

[2] Robert Edmond Jones, *The Dramatic Imagination* (New York, Duell, Sloan & Pearce, Inc., 1941).

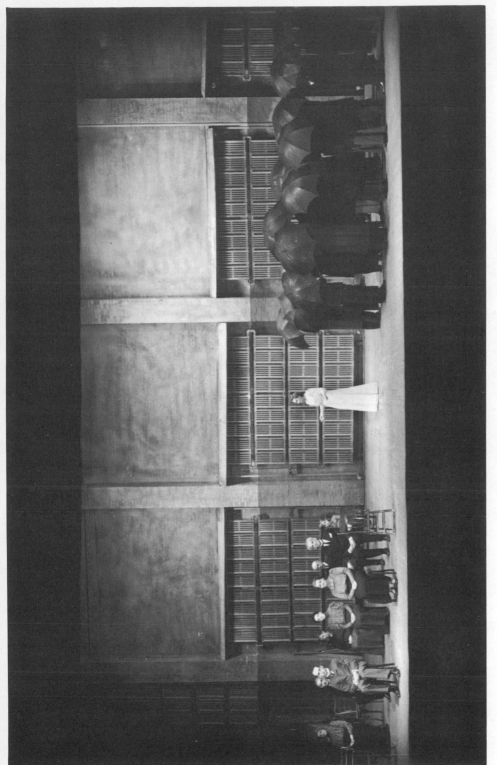

Funeral Scene from Thornton Wilder's *Our Town*, 1938

was also a playwright who put his theories into practice, even to inventing a new approach to acting. The epic theater-worker revolts against the tradition of Ibsenian realism. He is not concerned with the personal problems of a man and his wife in a home; epic drama calls for a larger arena of action which shows the dynamics of social forces at work. Hence, the epic theater playwright and designer pay no attention to the unities, but they demand instead, a stage which will serve for many fragments of action, some of them occurring simultaneously. In 1928, Piscator's production of *The Good Soldier Schweik* offered a brilliant and stimulating example of the new style. A dramatization of a novel, the play concerns the life of a private soldier as he is ground down by the stupidity and brutality of war. His story is told in a kaleidoscopic arrangement of scenes, recitations, songs, and explanations. In addition to the usual facilities of the stage, Piscator utilized slides, posters, charts, maps, graphs, a treadmill for moving scenery and actors, and a motion-picture screen on which were projected cartoons, captions, and film sequences—all joined together in a welter of sights and sounds.

A descriptive excerpt from Gorelik indicates the nature of Piscator's production:

"I'll do my duty for the Emperor to the end," adds Schweik. On the screen a Russian soldier is swimming in a pond. A bush rolls on with the Russian's uniform hanging on it. "A souvenir," thinks Schweik. He puts it on. A shot rings out, and a Hungarian patrol rushes on and seizes him in loud Hungarian tones. "What do you mean, prisoner?" Schweik demands. "I'm on your side. . . ." A shell bursts. Schweik falls. From the upper corner of the screen a procession of crosses starts toward the audience. As the crosses, growing nearer in perspective, reach the lower edge of the screen, a muslin drop, lowered downstage, catches them once more, bringing them still closer to the spectators. A rain of crosses falls upon this wry comedy as the lights begin to go up.[3]

Brecht's *The Private Life of the Master Race,* another epic drama, dramatizes the experiences of a German Panzer crew moving across Europe from the early stages of the war until it is defeated by the Russians. The play is really a series of one-act plays depicting the effects of Nazism and warfare on the crew. The various threads are knit together by lyrical passages. The play begins with this stage direction:

A band plays a barbaric march. Out of the darkness appears a big signpost: TO POLAND and near it a Panzer truck. Its wheels are turning. On it sit twelve to sixteen soldiers, steel helmeted, their faces white as chalk, their guns between their knees. They could be puppets.

The soldiers sing to the tune of the Horst Wessel Song.

There follows a series of scenes such as "The Betrayal," "The Jewish Wife," and "The Informer," dramatizing various phases of Nazi terrorism until the Panzer is bogged down in Russia. The sequences are bridged by voices out of the darkness and the roar of the armored car.

Other notable Brecht plays are the *Caucasian Circle of Chalk,* and *The Good Woman of Setzuan.* In America, epic-theater techniques were used by the Federal Theatre in productions of the Living Newspaper series during the 1930's. The epic style is a deliberate attempt to break with tradition, to move away from the struggles of a single individual and consider instead the dynamics of social change. Since Brecht was a man with a message, he utilized all of the resources of the stage as visual aids to get his ideas across. In his attack on the illusional theater, Brecht called for a new style of acting, one of "alienation" (*emfrendung*) which would emphasize his message and avoid emotional involvement in the story. The playwright avoided creating suspense and identification, because he wanted the audience to retain control of its critical faculties so that they were conscious of the idea.

It is apparent that epic theater is not merely a matter of design, but it is a complete concept of dramatic writing and production whose techniques make use of the theater and scenery in a new and oftentimes startling way.

MEIERHOLD AND CONSTRUCTIVISM

Meierhold presents another example of a theatricalist at work. He was not primarily a designer, but an outstanding *regisseur* whose complete control of all phases of production had important and interesting effects on staging and design. Originally associated with Stanislavski, Meierhold broke with the realistic movement to explore new possibilities of the stage which were sometimes bizarre, but always fascinating. Meierhold's focus of attention was not on the actor but on the audience, and he used his considerable ingenuity to prod and stimulate it in a variety of ways. Some of his methods of captivating audience attention were extraordinary as this passage indicates:

A chair is shot up through the floor, beds actually fly, walls run . . . real automobiles and motorcycles run down the aisles, up over the orchestra rail and then among the populace upon the stage!

There are no lights upon the stage. Two projectors, one from each side of the orchestra, next to the stage, throw light upon each actor in rotation as he plays, or upon the decorations, properties, etc., wherever the accent of the plot falls at that particular moment. . . . Movie captions, slogans . . . appear across the stage when they fit in with the action. As the act ends, the stage gets dark—finish. There is no curtain. . . . Sometimes, if the occasion warrants, an actor comes forward to where our footlights usually are, and shoots into the orchestra with a revolver, shouting "Entre'acte!"—"Intermission!" [4]

In his production of Gogol's *The Inspector General,* Meierhold used a semipermanent background of fifteen doors before which appeared a series of moveable platforms for individual scenes. One of them was a tall staircase with a trap door at the bottom for the spectacular exit of a character who stumbled and fell down the flight of steps! The floors of the platforms were tilted toward the audience so that the action seemed thrust out into the auditorium. This kind of staging exploited the dynamic possibilities of the setting as a machine for acting which had its roots in constructivism, originally an experimental movement among Russian sculptors but adapted for the stage by Meierhold. Inspired by the machine and reacting against the ostentatious décor of the decadent past, the constructivist creates stage settings of skeletonized ramps, stairways, bridges and similar structural forms. The spectator sees the bare bones of the setting against the brick stage-wall, unrelieved by any decorative or aesthetic intention. The constructivist stage is based entirely on its practicability as a tool for action. Its advantages are that it is frankly theatrical, it gives the performer extraordinary opportunities for movement and the use of space, and it is arranged for fluent and uninterrupted action. On the other hand, constructivism is inappropriate for most plays, it is unnecessarily severe and antidecorative, and it is apt to be more of a distraction than an aid in the interpretation of the author's meaning. However, its use of simple forms and frameworks has made some impact on contemporary design for all kinds of plays such as *Cat on a Hot Tin Roof, Death of a Salesman,* and *Two on an Island.*

THE ARCHITECTURAL STAGE

Still another revolt in the modern theater, but in quite a different direction, has been the rejection of scenery altogether. Recalling the simple platform for acting of the Greeks, Elizabethans, and Noh drama, efforts have been made to devise a formal, unchanging "architectural" stage without a proscenium arch or the machinery of the theater except for lighting. It is argued that such a stage provides a more functional and flexible place for the actors' performance. In dropping the pretense of

[4] *Ibid.*

A Constructivist Set by L. Popowa for *Der Gewaltige Hahnrei*, 1922

Sketch by Mordecai Gorelik for Set in Robert Ardrey's *Thunder Rock*

picturing nature, it frees the spectator from visual distractions and the time lags between scenes, and focuses his attention on the play rather than on its surroundings. Moreover, the architectural stage offers exceptional freedom of movement allowing the actor space in all directions rather than restricting him almost exclusively to lateral action as he is in the proscenium-arch theater.

Jacques Copeau's Théâtre du Vieux Colombier in France provided the most notable experiment in architectural staging. With a few portable screens and properties and skillful use of lighting, Copeau's theater proved to be remarkably effective for the production of a wide variety of plays. Other attempts have been made to use architectural stages mostly for the production of Shakespeare, the best examples being at Stratford in Canada and the American Shakespearean Festival Theatre in Connecticut.

Despite the various experiments that have been made and will continue to be made in the production of plays in various kinds of backgrounds, it is apparent that in general, the modern theater is committed to graphic reinforcement of the play through some kind of visual environment, although the rigid restrictions of realistic representation are no longer binding. It is also apparent that the words and deed of Craig and Appia have fallen on fertile ground, for our theater today accepts and demonstrates the philosophy that the scene designer is an important force in the interpretation of the play. Let us now consider his method of working.

THE SCENE DESIGNER AT WORK

The designer begins his work on a specific play by studying the script. He may want to record his initial impression of the play after a first reading, or he may prefer a thorough analysis of the script before he arrives at a central dramatic image. He searches the play for answers to numerous questions which occur to him such as, What is the mood of the play? What is germane to the play's meaning in its geographical location or historical period? What images continue throughout the play? How will the actor move? What are the most important scenes, and what areas will be used for them? Does the play have a unique flavor or style? The designer's preliminary study may give him answers to many questions which will stimulate his imagination and give his mind some problems to solve. During this early preparation, the designer is not primarily concerned with the practicalities of construction, painting, and shifting. At the moment he is after the feel and texture of the play.

The designer then meets with the director who helps him to find the answers to his questions. The director may have very specific ideas of the areas of the stage he wants to emphasize; he may have a definite color scheme in mind; he may even have a preliminary floor plan showing the arrangement of walls, entrances and exits, platforms, and stairways. Or his ideas may be nebulous, a general impression of his production without a clear-cut form. The designer mines the director for his ideas looking for specific instructions on the practical aspects of the setting, and for inspiration that will stimulate his imagination when he creates the visual image.

Ordinarily, the next step for the designer is to make sketches of the impressions that occur to him when he searches for the fundamental creative ideas growing out of the director's interpretation of the play. Gorelik produces numerous small sketches in which he strives to express the "poetic image of the scene." He pays no attention to the practicalities of the stage in these preliminary sketches. For example, in his designs for *Golden Boy*, Gorelik began with the concept of a prize ring, even though there was no scene using such a locale in the play, but this basic image influenced his design of each of the scenes. In his design for *Thunder Rock,* which the author set in the interior of a lighthouse, Gorelik's first impression was of an *exterior* view of a lighthouse against a stormy sky. Ultimately, he created the interior set, but his original concept persisted in the final design. Robert Edmond Jones apparently visualized his designs so clearly in his mind that he was able to set them down completely with little or no revision.

The creative scene designer is not merely concerned with reproducing a faithful copy of a piece of architecture. He is not an interior decorator, nor is he simply a skilled draftsman who follows the director's orders in his arrangement of set pieces on the stage. Like the actor, the designer is also an interpreter who makes his own unique contribution to enhancing the values of the play. Some directors give the designer a fairly free hand, since they find considerable inspiration in the designer's way of solving the visual problems of the scenic environment. At times, the designer has exerted such power that his work completely dominates the production. But in general, the designer keeps his work subservient to the total effect, attempting to reinforce the meaning of the play with his designs.

The manner in which the designer studies the script is interesting. For example, Gorelik looks for a basic motif:

As we study the script, we try to penetrate closer and closer to the deepest significance of the play. For myself, I usually work from the climactic scenes onward. That is, I try to visualize the most poignant or striking scenes. I try to understand the dramatic progression in intensity, or the change in quality, from one scene to another. When I know that I have provided for these essential scenes, I make the other scenes fit in. The climactic moments are like the piers of a bridge, on which the cables are afterward spun. I try, also, to fasten upon a *central scenic motif* for each setting. Does the composition of the room revolve about a door? A table? A view from the window? A color?

A texture? Just as the director must find a central action, so the designer must find a central scenic theme related to the action.[5]

An illuminating example of Gorelik's thinking is indicated in his approach to Chekhov's the *Three Sisters:*

It is the *dramatic metaphor*, probably, which sums up, for each setting, all the thoughts which the designer may have. Thus, the attic bedroom of the *Three Sisters* is not only an attic, not only a bedroom, not only a girls' room, not only a European room, not only a room of the period of 1901, not only a room belonging to the gentlefolk whom Chekhov wrote about. On top of all that, and including all that, it may be for the designer, the scene of a *raging fever.*[5]

Jo Mielziner, another prominent scenic artist, describes his way of working, bearing in mind particularly the actor's use of the stage:

I used to begin working on a play by creating a visual picture of the *mise-en-scène,*" says Mr. Mielziner. "I have since given that up, and nowadays, after reading the play through once, I go over it again, seeking this time to visualize in my own mind the actors in the important situations of the drama. This may give me an idea for a significant piece of furniture, a quality of light or shadow, a color combination; it may not be an entire setting at all—just something that is associated with the dramatic significance of the moment, but which may become the clue to, or indeed the cornerstone of, the whole setting." [6]

Still another example shows how the designer Donald Oenslager seeks to capture the atmosphere of the play:

Hamlet dwells in a dual world, the everyday world of external events which is the life of the Court, and the haunted, brooding world of the imagination which is the inner world of an avenging Prince, who drifts down endless corridors of dark, fir-bordered streams. . . . It is the conflict of these two worlds that unbalances his mind and goads him on to indecisive action and helpless frustration.

The way he distorts the external world through the eyes of his own inner world of the imagination must determine the nature and appearance of the scenes. Just as he sees the events of the Court in the curving mirror of his

[5] Mordecai Gorelik, quoted in John Gassner *Producing the Play*, rev. ed. (New York, Holt, Rinehart and Winston, Inc., 1953). Reprinted by permission of the publishers.

[6] Jo Mielziner, quoted in Norris Houghton, "The Designer Sets the Stage," in *Theatre Arts Anthology* (New York, 1936). Copyright ©, 1936, by *Theatre Arts Anthology;* 1936, by Theatre Arts, Inc.; 1950, by Theatre Arts Books. Reprinted by permission of Theatre Arts Books.

Sketch by Jo Mielziner for Set in Maxwell Anderson's *Winterset,* 1935

own brooding conjectures, so the scenes which he inhabits must appear as in-
definite embodiments of his own inner pre-occupations. The members of the
Court must seem to be resolved into dewy shadows of this "too, too solid flesh"
and cloaked in veiled fragments of reality. . . . For all the Castle scenes
bare, chalky walls are pierced with tall tragic doors—always three, whose depth
beyond is as black as Hamlet's sable suit. They must be high, very high, to
admit his anguish and his spirit. Only flashes of red, the red of blood, livens
the scenes—washed over walls, or splotched on characters' clothing.[7]

The sketches which the designer creates should suggest the appearance of the setting as it will actually appear to the audience. It should
be in proportion, and it must be capable of being reproduced within the
limitations of the stage and theatrical materials. The sketch should also
indicate the color schemes, and it may give some sense of the lighting.

These preliminary sketches are a basis for communication between
director and designer. Once there is common agreement on the basic designs, the designer prepares a model set, which is a scaled replica constructed in three dimensions. It is usually rather rough in form since it is
not intended for display but rather serves important uses in making the
director aware of the plasticity of the set, the spatial relationships of the
various parts, which are very useful to him in visualizing and planning
movement. The model is also helpful to the designer in his preparation of
the lighting, and it is extremely useful in solving difficulties of constructing and shifting scenery.

The next step in design is the preparation of working drawings through
which the sketch and model are translated into actual scenery by the
carpenters and painters. The working drawings usually include a scaled
and dimensioned floor plan, elevations of the walls, a hanging chart of
flying pieces, and detail drawings of special set pieces and properties.
Complete specifications are a part of the drawings. In the professional
theater, the designer may make only the sketches and the model, turning
the preparation of the working drawings over to a draftsman, and the
construction over to professional scene-builders and painters. In the educational and community theater, the scene designer often works through
all steps of the design from the preliminary sketches to the actual construction, painting and mounting of the set. In the European theater,
where a permanent staff and company are employed, it is customary to
construct the scenery in the theater, some of which are astonishingly well
equipped in contrast to most of our Broadway theaters. For example,
Norris Houghton reported that the Moscow Art Theater stage was 62
feet deep with a 55-foot turntable, and 66 sets of lines. The technical staff
of the theater numbered 260. In the American professional theater, where

[7] Donald Oenslager, *Scenery Then and Now* (New York, W. W. Norton & Co.,
Inc., 1936).

productions are usually based on a single play, the scenery is generally built at a scene studio and taken to the theater for the production. The technical staff is a minimal one, organized for one particular play.

Perhaps one of the most interesting ways of showing designers at work is to consider their efforts on the same play. The following are descriptive passages of three designers' approach to *Macbeth*. The first is a celebrated statement of Gordon Craig which illustrates his intuitive and aesthetic feeling for design:

Come now, we take *Macbeth*. We know the play well. In what kind of place is that play laid? How does it look, first of all to our mind's eye? Secondly to our eye?

I see two things. I see a lofty and steep rock, and I see the moist cloud which envelops the head of this rock. That is to say, a place for fierce and warlike men to inhabit, a place for phantoms to nest in. Ultimately this moisture will destroy the men. Now then, you are quick in your question as to what actually to create for the eye. I answer as swiftly—place there a rock! Let it mount up high. Swiftly I tell you, convey the idea of a mist which hugs the head of this rock. Now, have I departed at all for one-eighth of an inch from the vision which I saw in the mind's eye?

But you ask me what form this rock shall take and what color? What are the lines which are the lofty lines, and which are to be seen in any lofty cliff? Go to them, glance but a moment at them; now quickly set them down on your paper; *the lines and their directions,* never mind the cliff. Do not be afraid to let them go high; they cannot go high enough; and remember that on a sheet of paper which is but two inches square you can make a line which seems to tower miles in the air, and you can do the same on your stage, for it is all a matter of proportion and nothing to do with actuality.

You ask about the colors? What are the colors that Shakespeare has indicated for us? Do not first look at Nature, but look in the play of the poet. Two; one for the rock, the man; one for the mist, the spirit.[8]

The second description is of the banquet scene as it appeared in Max Reinhardt's production of *Macbeth,* designed by Ernest Stern. Lewisohn's account of the production emphasizes the over-all severity:

Take the scene of the banquet in *Macbeth*. Every line is a straight line, every angle a right angle. All form is reduced to a barbaric severity. But the two rectangular windows in the background through which the cold Northern stars glitter are narrow and tall—so unimaginably tall that they seem to touch that sky of doom. The torches turn the rough brown of the primitive walls to a tarnished bronze. Only on the rude table lie splashes of menacing yellow. There is something barren and gigantic about the scene—a sinister quiet, a dull presage.[9]

[8] Craig, *op. cit.*
[9] From *The Drama and the Stage,* by Ludwig Lewisohn. Copyright ©, 1922, by Harcourt, Brace & World Inc. and reprinted with their permission.

Stark Young describes the designs of Robert Edmond Jones for a production that appeared in New York in 1921.

This design for *Macbeth* was the most profoundly creative decor that I have ever seen in the theatre. There was a stage enclosed with a background of black, flat so that no light was caught to break the complete darkness of it. Drawings or photographs can give at least a suggestion, and only a suggestion of the gold frames, or sharp gold lines, or the forms like Gothic abstractions, or however we may define them, which standing alone, against the black, defined the scenes. Three great tragic masks were hung to the front, high above the action, and from them vast daggers of light poured down, crossed, pierced, flooded the action below, as in the witches' scene or the banquet. The banquet hall with its gold and light figures moving, and above all else Lady Macbeth's robe, in which by a hidden combination of many shades, an unheard-of-intensity of red was discovered, defied any conveyance in words.[10]

Each of these designs is valid in its own right. We see the designer's efforts to evoke the appropriate atmosphere of the play, to intensify its emotional content through judicious use of line, color, lighting and texture. Each represents the approach to the task of the designer when he assists in the interpretation of a play, illustrating the contemporary philosophy of scene design.

Questions and Exercises

1. What does the stage designer contribute to the production?
2. Discuss scenery as environment.
3. What is constructivism? The architectural stage?
4. What is the relationship of the designer to the playwright? To the director? To the actor?
5. What were the contributions of Craig and Appia?
6. Watch a play on the stage or on television. Evaluate the use of scenery and lighting in the total effect of the play.
7. Draw a ground plan for one of the stage settings illustrated in this book, noting entrances and furniture arrangement. Does it provide satisfactory acting areas?
8. From the stage directions describing the setting of a modern play, make a rough ground plan. Describe the color pattern and the general atmosphere you would create.

[10] Stark Young, *The Theatre of Robert Edmond Jones*, Ralph Pendleton, ed., Wesleyan University Press (Middletown, Conn., 1958).

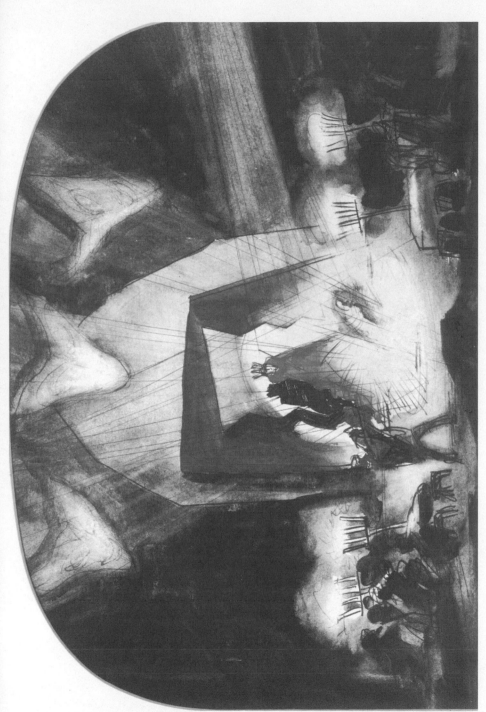

Sketch by Robert Edmond Jones for Banquet Scene in *Macbeth*, 1921

Suggested Reading

ALBRIGHT, H. D., HALSTEAD, William P., and MITCHELL, Lee, *Principles of Theatre Art* (Boston, Houghton Mifflin Co., 1955).

CHENEY, Sheldon, *Stage Decoration* (New York, John Day Co., Inc., 1928).

CRAIG, Edward Gordon, *Scene* (New York, Oxford University Press, 1923).

FUERST, Walter R., and HUME, Samuel J., *Twentieth Century Stage Decoration*, 2 vols. (New York, Alfred A. Knopf, Inc., 1928).

GORELIK, Mordecai, *New Theatres for Old* (New York, Samuel French, Inc., 1940).

HEFFNER, Hubert C., SELDEN, Samuel, and SELLMAN, Hunton D., *Modern Theatre Practice,* 4th ed. (New York, Appleton-Century-Crofts, Inc., 1959).

JONES, Robert Edmond, *Drawings for the Theatre* (New York, Theatre Arts, Inc., 1925).

OENSLAGER, Donald, *Scenery Then and Now* (New York, W. W. Norton and Co., Inc., 1936).

SIMONSON, Lee, *The Stage Is Set* (New York, Harcourt, Brace & World, Inc., 1932).

YOUNG, Stark, *The Theatre of Robert Edmond Jones,* Ralph Pendleton, ed. (Middletown, Conn., Wesleyan University Press, 1958).

I4

Theater Architecture

THE PHYSICAL THEATER exerts a considerable influence on those who work in it. The form, organization, and size of the playhouse affects the conventions of staging, the style of production and the structure of the drama. For example, the Kabuki and Noh drama theaters of Japan with their long passageways to the stage, capitalize on effective entrances and exits in a manner unknown in Western drama. The unlocalized platform of the Elizabethan stage, combined with the inner and upper alcoves, gave to Shakespeare and his contemporaries a stage of exceptional versatility for presenting a complicated and animated plot in a way unknown in our present theater, except in motion pictures. To understand the drama of any period, it is helpful to know something of the characteristics of the theater which housed it.

A theater building, like a play is the result of an interaction of various forces. Architecture is not a mere matter of styles and forms; it has a life of its own. A building reflects the propensities of those who created and occupy it, and they in turn are influenced by the architecture which they have produced. Thus, the variety of theater structures reveals to us something about the cultures in which they were built as well as something about the drama and the audiences which they served.

The size of the auditorium and its relation to the playing area has had interesting and varying effects. Obviously in a large, cavernous auditorium seating several thousand spectators, many of them remote from the performer, all aspects of production must be exaggerated in order to carry to the audience. Conversely, the intimate, conversational style of present-day realism with its restrained underplaying, its fragmentary speech and gestures, would be lost in the Theater of Dionysus. The compact theaters of Elizabethan and Restoration England enabled the play-

245

wright to use complex and subtle speech, and the proximity of the audience encouraged intercommunication between performer and spectator. But we must not be too arbitrary in insisting that the size of the theater will always have a specific effect on the play and playing. Despite the size of the Greek theater, the oral tradition made it possible to exploit nuances of language, while in the intimate Noh drama playhouse, the performance is the essence of aloofness and restraint. In general, however, we can suggest that the larger the audience, the greater the need for increasing projection, which in turn works against the illusion of realism.

We can note from the illustrations of different theaters, the variation in the size and arrangement of the playing area and the space for the audience. While different solutions and conventions work for different kinds of dramas and audiences, there are certain basic requisites that obtain in all playhouses. The audience must be able to see and hear, and the actor must have an area where he can perform. The comfort and convenience of the audience should be considered so that the spectator is freed from distractions and discomfort. The playing area may be of various shapes, sizes, and arrangements as long as it provides the actor with a workable space for his performance. At times, his requirements may be reduced to "bare boards and a passion," although our contemporary taste is for some kind of visual reinforcement of the mood and locale.

At first, performances were adapted to a threshing floor adjoining a hillside, a temporary platform set in an inn-yard, or the altar and stations of the church. But as drama grew more mature and complex, other demands were placed upon the physical surroundings which finally resulted in the design and construction of specific structures for plays. In Greece, when the playwrights added a second and third actor, the resulting development of theater art made it necessary to add to the altar and orchestra, the theatron for the audience, and the stage-house (*skene*) for the actors. And as a corollary, once the theater achieved a satisfactory architectural form, it in turn affected the playwrights' construction of his dramas. An improvised stage in a banquet-hall or inn-yard served well enough for early English plays, but with the full flowering of Elizabethan drama, a complete, permanent structure became essential, whose form and conventions influenced the playwrights. Thus, theater architecture is both a cause and an effect, a stimulus and a response.

The theater must be appropriate to the kind of drama performed in it. We have had to learn this lesson the hard way through trial and error, such as the efforts to produce Shakespeare in the pictorial tradition of the proscenium-arch theater, with the consequent disastrous loss in fluency so essential for Elizabethan drama. Likewise, the production of Greek tragedy in our modern playhouses frequently is awkward, not only because we have no satisfactory way of handling the chorus, but also because our acting style and our taste for illusion are at odds with the conventions of the Greek theater. As a consequence, more and more attention is being paid to the development of a theater structure sufficiently flexible to meet the demands of classic drama as well as the modern.

In order to get some notion of various arrangements of theater buildings, let us now briefly examine four representative playhouses, noting their physical characteristics, and the consequent effects on drama and performance.

THE GREEK THEATER

You will recall that in the chapter on Ritual, Magic and Drama, we sketched the evolution of the Greek theater from the dancing circle to a complete structure which emerged in the latter half of the fifth century B.C. The circular *orchestra* some 75 to 90 feet in diameter repeated the form of the original threshing floor where improvisations took place around the altar of Dionysus. The altar or *thymele* remained in the center of the circle in the permanent theater. The spectators were seated on stone benches in the huge theatron, which was built on a hillside. In the Theater of Dionysus on the Acropolis, 80 tiers of seats were arranged in concentric circles about the orchestra, accommodating an audience of from fifteen to twenty thousand people. The front row of seats was reserved for priests, with the throne of the Priest of Dionysus occupying the center.

Across the back of the orchestra was the *skene* or scene building, originally a temporary structure used for changing costumes and storing properties. Later it became a permanent stone building which was used as a façade for temples, palaces, and houses. The skene was pierced by three doors which served as entrances. It is conjectured that immediately before the skene there was a platform called the *proskenion* or *logeion* where much of the action may have taken place in the later plays. Some scholars think that the platform was a low one, and that the actors performed in the orchestra, but it seems logical to assume that the proskenion must have been high enough to afford the audience a good view of the actors over the top of the chorus who occupied the orchestra. Undoubtedly, some of the action took place in the orchestra, especially in the early plays when the chorus was such an essential part of the plot. On either side of the proskenion, two wings projected, called *paraskenia*. These had doors which may have served as side entrances.

Two mechanical devices are of special interest in the Greek theater. The *deus ex machina* or "god of the machine" was a cranelike device for raising and lowering a god into the scene. Another mechanical contrivance was the *eccyclema*, some sort of portable platform which could

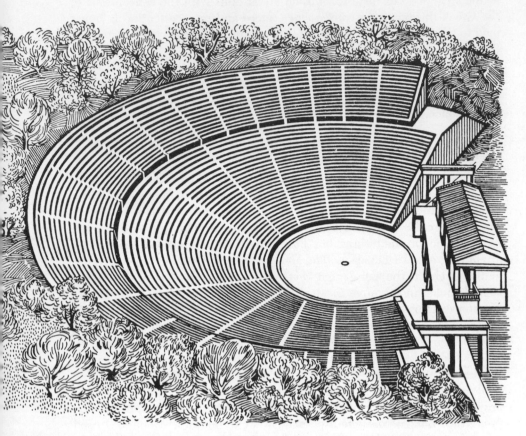

A reconstruction of a Greek Theater from ruins at Epidaurus

be moved out into the audience's view for an interior scene, and for exhibiting dead bodies as in such plays as *Agamemnon* and *Medea*.

While it is difficult accurately to assess the specific influences of the theater on drama and its production, since there is an interaction of all elements, nevertheless, certain general conclusions seem valid from the evidence at hand. The great size of the Greek theater and the long gap between actor and spectator made the drama rhetorical in nature. The actor was a maker of speeches, skilled in the art of recitation and declamation. The members of the chorus required training in movement and singing, but the individual actor was one who spoke. Greek tragedies did not abound in the vigorous action of Elizabethan plays or nineteenth-century melodrama. The clash of protagonist and antagonist in Greek drama was a scene of reasoned discourse. Violence was deliberately kept off stage. The tragic actor's medium of communication was words. Greek drama was performed out-of-doors in the daylight, which meant that once the chorus made its entrance into the orchestra, it was present throughout the remainder of the play. This led to the creation of the dramatic *entrance (parodus)* and *exit (exodus)* of the chorus, as well as the retention and elaboration of choric odes which served to link the episodes of the play. The daylight performances in a curtainless theater were probably responsible for the convention of keeping scenes of violence offstage, since disposition of corpses is often awkward in dramatic production. The fixed architectural façade of the skene and the continuous presence of the chorus may account for the general practice of employing unity of time and place.

The Greek playwright not only was influenced by the physical theater, but he also exerted pressure on it, the most notable instances being the addition of the second actor by Aeschylus and the third by Sophocles, thus enlarging the role of the actors and diminishing the use of the chorus. This transition is reflected architecturally by the evolution of the skene from a temporary hut to a permanent stone structure. Once this complete theater was constructed, it affected the dramaturgy of the playwrights whose dramas were written for this specific architectural design.

The mammoth dimensions of the Greek theater compelled the actor to solve the problems of projection. His style of performance was necessarily enlarged by broad gesture, clear speech, and the use of mask and costume to increase his size and expressiveness. Such exaggeration ruled out the illusion of realistic acting. This does not mean that the audience thought of the style as artificial; the actors' integrity and sense of conviction, and his ability to convey emotion and speak expressively, gave his performance validity despite its conventions. The performance of the chorus, retaining the circular movement of the original improvised dithyrambs performed on the threshing floor, was stylized in the use of dance and song. The length and positions of entrances and exits, and the huge orchestra placed great emphasis on the movement of the chorus and affected its direction and quality.

THE MEDIEVAL THEATER

Medieval drama was first performed in the church when dramatic episodes were used to augment such celebrations as those of Easter and Christmas. The faithful were shown scenes from the Bible—the Three Wise Men coming to the manger, the three Marys discovering the empty tomb. As the re-enactment of the stories became more and more popular, various stations of the cathedral were utilized for each segment of the story, until in the thirteenth century drama became so expansive and secular that it was moved outside of the church, and laymen of the craft guilds took over the responsibility of dramatic production. Three elements of the improvised performances in the church were retained—the episodic structure of the plays, the representation of specific locales, and the convention of moving the action from station to station.

On the continent *stations* or *mansions* were used for *simultaneous staging*. That is to say, separate representational structures were built and painted for each specific locale utilized in the play. At Mons in 1501, *The Mystery of the Passion* employed sixty-seven mansions (stations) and required 48 days of rehearsal. In front of the stations, a common playing area called the *platea* or platform was used by the actor who made his entrances and exits through the appropriate structure. The stations might be arranged in a single line as they were at Valenciennes in 1547 on a stage 130 feet long, with Heaven at one end of the stage and Hell-mouth the other. In between were a variety of other stations such as a Temple, the House of the High Priest and a marketplace. An analogy might be made with the stock setting for a western movie, which consists of a block-long series of stations such as a saloon, a general store, the jail, another saloon, a livery stable, and a saloon. In the street in front of this façade, the actors move about from place to place according to the requirements of the plot. Another arrangement for simultaneous staging was locating the mansions around a central area such as a courtyard, in much the same fashion as separate booths are set up for circus side shows or carnivals. The audience occupied the center area and accompanied the action from one station to another.

Another solution for staging medieval drama was to bring the scene to the spectator by means of a wagon or *pageant stage*. The audience gathered at convenient places through the town, and the pageants appeared one at a time like floats in a parade. This method was particularly popular in England where over a hundred towns and villages used

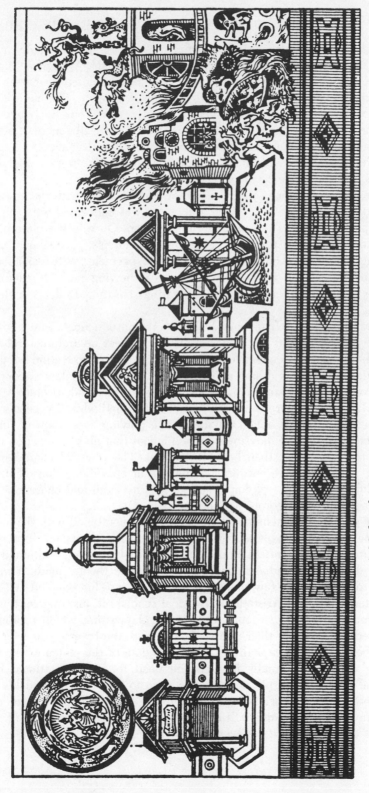

A Medieval Mansion Stage at Valenciennes, France, in 1547

pageant stages for dramatic productions. The wagon was usually a two-story affair representing a specific place such as Noah's Ark or the Manger. The top level was open, but the lower level was enclosed by curtains for changing costumes, and for making entrances and exits. The main action of the plays, however, took place in the street around the wagon. As Thomas Woods Stevens, the eminent teacher and theater scholar, pointed out, the pageant stage anticipates the structure and conventions of the Elizabethan stage with its three acting areas—the upper and inner stages and the unlocalized platea.

The medieval drama sought maximum identification with the audience. As a part of the religious service, the clergy was concerned with impressing upon their flocks the message of salvation. Outside the church, laymen took naive pleasure in achieving realistic effects, particularly in harrowing scenes of torture, legerdemain, and spectacle. With considerable ingenuity and zeal they devised ways for showing miracles, depicting scenes of suffering and dying, and creating sensational effects with fireworks.

Medieval staging had several important consequences. The audience was in close proximity to the performer. There was no architectural separation, no spatial detachment. Furthermore, the introduction of comic material into serious drama and the use of lowly characters encouraged intercommunication and rapport between performer and spectator. Other important effects were the establishment of a method and precedent for putting the essential action on stage. The playing area allowed for unrestricted freedom of movement, which meant that all of the action could be performed rather than be talked about. The physical characteristics of the medieval stage encouraged the use of episodic or loose-knit plot structure, the mixture of comic and serious material and characters, and stories filled with vigorous action.

The graphic representation of specific locale combined with the neutral playing area of the platea, had two interesting effects on subsequent dramatic development. In France, the pictorial tradition continued, but when drama went indoors again, the size of the theater made it impossible to show but a few mansions at one time. This coupled with the misinterpretation of Aristotle by classical scholars in insisting on the unities, imposed a rigid structure on French playwriting which profoundly affected the future of their drama. In England, the reverse was true. The Elizabethan theater capitalized on the freedom of the platea as the main acting area, and virtually ignored the need for representational background. This flexible physical theater gave to Shakespeare and his contemporaries the opportunity to continue the medieval tradition of using a complicated plot, and putting much of the essential action of their stories on stage before the eyes of their audience.

"The handwriting on the wall is seen." Scene from New York Pro Musica production of
The Play of Daniel, Wells Cathedral, England, 1960

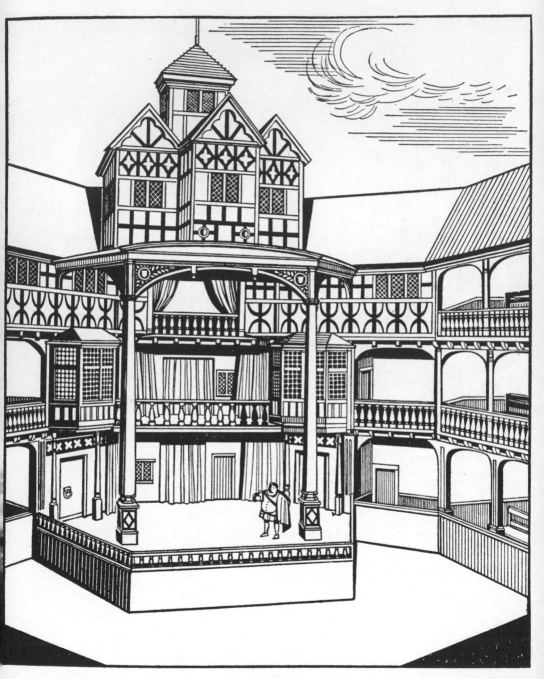

(a) Reconstruction by John Cranford Adams of The Globe, a celebrated London theater originally built in 1599

(b) A Stage for Japanese Noh drama; compare it with the Globe

THE ELIZABETHAN THEATER

Scholars have traced the origin of the architectural features of the Elizabethan theater to many sources—the inn-yards, medieval and Renaissance art conventions, the Spanish and Dutch theaters, banquet halls, and the pageant stage. There is considerable conjecture and controversy over the exact features of the Elizabethan theater, which undoubtedly varied from one structure to another. We do have one specific contemporary source of information in the building contract for the Fortune Theater, which gives these exact dimensions: the exterior walls were 80 feet square, the stage 43 feet wide and 27½ feet deep. There were 3 balconies, 12, 11 and 9 feet high and about twelve feet wide. Note the size of the stage—an acting area more than double the size used for the production of most Broadway plays. A roofed canopy or *heavens*, supported by pillars from the platform, covered the rear of the stage.

The Elizabethan theater which housed professional, residential companies, was usually a three-storied structure consisting of an inner courtyard surrounded by two or three galleries. The chief acting area was a large platform which projected into the courtyard. At the back of this stage were two alcoves used as supplementary acting areas. The remaining galleries were occupied by the audience. The *groundlings* stood in the pit before the platform. We may think of the Elizabethan theater as consisting of a large platea on which most of the action took place without any specific representation of locale other than that suggested by the dialogue of the play. The upper stage was used whenever an elevation was needed, such as in balcony scenes or perhaps for the action of a battle. The inner stage below was probably used for those scenes demanding a specific locale or an unwieldy property, and, no doubt, for the concealment of a dead body. These smaller areas were necessarily limited in use since they were rather small and the angle of vision for many of the spectators would have been very poor. In general practice, no graphic representation of specific locale was used or needed. Furthermore, the problem of sight lines made it impossible to back the actor with scenery since the audience sat or stood on three sides of the performers at various levels. The impression should not be made that the Elizabethan theater was crude or makeshift. On the contrary it was one of the most flexible theaters ever devised. As a means of presenting a story in action, it is only equalled by the motion picture. The Elizabethans were quite capable of making use of spectacle in court celebrations; their theater and its conventions was a matter of choice, not of necessity. It has been only during the last century that we have come to appreciate the merits of the Elizabethan theater which is eminently more suited to the production of

Shakespeare's plays than our own modern proscenium-arch theater with its graphic tradition.

In the Elizabethan theater, scene followed scene without interruption, the action moving from one area or part of the stage to another as characters made their entrances and exits. Perhaps we may gain some idea of the use of the various parts of the stage by suggesting a conjectural use of the theater for Act One of *Hamlet*.

SCENE 1. "A platform before the castle." Upper stage, with characters entering from below.

SCENE 2. "A room of state in the castle." Thrones for Claudius and Gertrude in inner stage. Court audience on platform. Close curtain at King's and Queen's exit to strike thrones.

SCENE 3. "Polonius' house." Enter Laertes and Ophelia through curtain to platform to suggest interior. Play scene at left side of platform.

SCENE 4. "The platform." Upper stage.

SCENE 5. "Another part of the platform." Inner stage below for Hamlet and ghost. Ghost disappears through trap. When Marcellus and Horatio appear, use main platform for cellerage, etc.

The movement is kept continuous. Variety is achieved by the use of various places on the three acting areas, by the flow of action, and the colorful costuming. Where specific locale or atmosphere is needed, the playwright furnishes lines to create the effect. For example, note the atmosphere created by the first few lines of Scene 1, Act I of *Hamlet*, pages 58-59.

The Elizabethan theater was a fortunate architectural creation for the playwright in that it gave him an extremely flexible stage for acting out his story. Furthermore, the intimate quality of the playhouse made it possible for him to exploit the possibilities of the language to the full. Like the motion picture, the stage and its conventions enabled him to move freely in time and space, but without the cinema's compulsion for continuous movement. In Elizabethan drama, the action could pause for speech without violating the medium.

The Elizabethan actor had an excellent place for action and speech. The attention was focused on him, without competing scenery or mechanical intrusion. Moreover, he was thrust out among the spectators enabling him to use rich and refined language, which was immediately expressive despite its complexity. The size and shape of the three acting areas, also gave the actor excellent opportunities for varied movement in both size and direction. He had the dancer's freedom in the use of space. The architecture of the Elizabethan theater was a highly successful achievement in giving the playwright and actor a versatile and fluent stage.

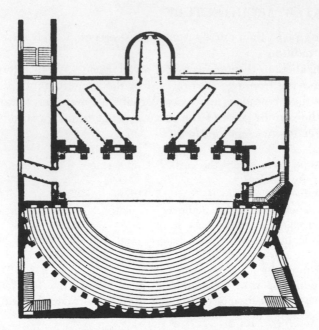

(a) Ground Plan of the Olympic Theater, erected by Palladio in 1579, at Vicenza, Italy

(b) Olympic Theater Interior. Note the perspective vistas.

THE RENAISSANCE PROSCENIUM-ARCH THEATER

In the latter part of the fifteenth century, wealthy Italian noblemen became enamored of the drama with the result that a number of private theaters were designed. Architects were commissioned to adapt large halls, granaries or other commodious buildings for dramatic productions which were given in connection with various social ceremonies. The general public did not attend these theaters except as occasional guests of a generous prince or duke. Drama was available to the lower classes in performances given by touring companies which played on improvised stages in public squares or market places. The association of the private theaters with aristocratic social events led to an emphasis on opulent décor which distinguishes the Italianate theater design.

Two important Renaissance theaters were constructed in "antique" style to satisfy the vogue of reviving things classical. The first was the Olympic Theater at Vicenza built by Palladio in 1579—a roofed-over replica of an ancient Roman theater with the notable addition of a stage façade backed by five entrances through which could be seen vistas of city-scapes in forced perspective. The second was the Farnese Theater at Parma, designed by Aleotti and erected in 1618. This became the first "modern" theater since the central opening of the stage was sufficiently wide so that the audience could see the action through the *proscenium arch*. As George Kernodle points out in his book *From Art to Theatre* the innovation of the framing arch grew out of the conventions of the visual arts. The proscenium arch wielded an enormous influence on dramatic production and composition from the Renaissance to the present.

Up until the Farnese Theater, the acting area was traditionally a platform before an ornamented façade. But with the introduction of the proscenium arch, the acting area was pushed back behind the opening, thus separating the actor from the audience psychologically as well as physically. The proscenium arch provided the Italian scene designer with an opportunity to experiment with linear perspective—an opportunity he was quick to exploit to an amazing degree.

In the early part of the seventeenth century, Italian opera achieved an enormous popularity, profoundly affecting architecture since many of the theaters erected on the continent for the next century and a half were intended for the production of elaborate musical spectacles. Since most of these were public structures, the auditoriums were large, usually accommodating from two to three thousand spectators. The auditorium assumed a narrow horseshoe shape so that spectators could see beyond the proscenium arch. Architects soon learned that tiers of galleries along the walls of the auditorium would enlarge the seating capacity. From three to seven galleries were built, supported by posts which sepa-

An Eighteenth-century Palace Theatre in rococo style at Schwetzingen, Germany; originally built in 1752 and reconstructed in 1937. Note the use of perspective in the rows of wings and in the backdrop.

Covent Garden, London, during "Old Price" Riots, 1763. Note the deep apron and the proscenium doors and boxes.

rated the galleries into boxes. Up until this time in court celebrations, members of royalty occupied seats on the floor level directly in front of the stage, but several yards back. No one could sit in front of these seats for fear of obstructing the view. Now, in the new auditorium of the Renaissance, a royal box was placed in the center of the first gallery allowing a clear view of the stage, and making it possible to increase the capacity of the auditorium by adding seats to the floor level which was sloped to improve the angle of vision.

The stagehouse became gigantic in size and complex in organization when the scene designers and playwrights required increasingly spectacular sets and effects. For example, the Salle des Machines erected in Paris in 1660 had a stage 132 feet deep. Ingenious equipment was devised for producing all manner of sensational visual displays. Mechanical systems were worked out for changing scenery which consisted mostly of two-dimensional drops and wings which could be raised and lowered, or slid in and out very rapidly. Stock sets were constructed which were used again and again, although special occasions and productions called for new scenery.

By the end of the eighteenth century, Italian-style theaters extended all over the continent, and with the architecture, the practice was established of requiring changeable, pictorial scenery as the customary background for the performers.

The audience which was attracted to these public theaters was made up of the upper and middle classes. Their taste in theater fare was not so much for spoken drama as it was for opera, ballet, and spectacular exhibitions. Moreover, the play was not always the thing, since the theater was considered a social center. Boxes became private drawing rooms for gossip and entertainment, flirtation, and ostentatious show. In attempting to insure "class," theater décor made extravagant use of ornamentation—the walls were covered with pseudo-baroque contortions of entablatures, wreaths, cornucopias, statues of nymphs and cupids, and fat rolls of swirling, gilded plaster, so that the total impression was one of a courtly love nest. An interesting parallel took place in America in the 1920's when the motion picture began to climb socially to the middle classes. Imposing "cathedrals of the silver screen" were constructed of such overwhelming design and dimensions that they became the dominant pieces of local architecture. An air of enchantment was produced through the use of soft lighting, luxurious carpeting, liveried attendants, mellow pipe-organ music, and rich surface decoration.

When the public theaters of the late eighteenth century became too crowded with the irksome hoipoloi, there was a resurgence of smaller private theaters, more suitable for tasteful performances to be given to the genteel people of quality. However, the general characteristics of the

European theater up through the nineteenth century, followed the pattern of the Italian Renaissance opera house.

The general effect of the huge Renaissance theater was to encourage spectacle and music. The dramatist was compelled to create plays in which there was ample opportunity for lavish pageantry and show. Drama was forced to be grandiose in style. As a consequence of the size of the auditorium and of the competition of the scenery, the actor faced a difficult task in making himself seen and heard. Such a theater was not conducive to the development of spoken drama. It was the smaller, private court theaters which gave the playwright a more congenial atmosphere in which to work.

From our brief description of four representative theaters it is clearly evident that the architecture imposes a strong formative pressure on the drama and its performance. Conversely, the physical theater reflects the needs and tastes of the dramatist, actor, and audience. Since this interaction is constantly at work, it is necessary to visualize a play in terms of the theater for which it was written.

MODERN THEATER ARCHITECTURE

Architects at the end of the nineteenth century were protesting against the "infected atmosphere" of traditionalism, and taking Louis Sullivan's statement that "form follows function" as a guiding premise, they began to experiment with new forms and new materials. But the theater planner found it difficult to escape from the established forms and styles. The forthright honesty of the new architecture was in sharp conflict with the concept of the theater as a "show place," obligated to carry a heavy load of pretentious décor. As a result, the modern theater continues to be dominated by the proscenium arch, its consequent pictorial representation, and the detachment of the spectator from the performer.

The architecture of the contemporary theater varies with its patronage and its function as a social institution. In Europe, where there is considerable state support of dramatic production as a cultural activity, theater buildings are often complete plants located in impressive and congenial surroundings. The theater may be augmented by the addition of restaurants, exhibition rooms, and generous lobbies and foyers. Since the repertory tradition with a permanent residential company often obtains, facilities are provided for constructing and storing scenery, properties, and costumes, and there is ample space for rehearsals which are required to keep a variety of productions available for performance. As a contrast, in New York City where the theater is entirely dependent upon box-office appeal, the buildings are crammed into parcels of expensive real estate with only the bare essentials for the production of a single play. Since the theater is rented on the basis of each individual production, it is economical to build the scenery elsewhere. There is little lobby or workshop space, and there are no facilities for dining or exhibition. A major breakthrough is now being accomplished with the construction of the Lincoln Center of Performing Arts in upper Manhattan.

Although much twentieth-century theater design shows the weight of the dead past, there has been some significant experimentation. Two Germans pioneered modern theater architecture in their efforts to provide buildings which would give the theater-goer a better chance to see and hear. Gottfried Semper, in his design for the Wagner Bayreuth Theater, devised a fan-shaped auditorium which gave many spectators a much better angle of visibility. He also eliminated the balconies and side aisles, placing all of the audience in an unbroken sweep with sufficient space between the rows of seats to allow for easy passage. Max Littman used a similar auditorium arrangement for the Künstler Theater in Munich. He devised an adjustable proscenium, and devoted himself to a careful consideration of the problems of acoustics. While the fan-shaped auditorium was widely copied, few new theaters followed the innovation of eliminating balconies. Progress in twentieth-century architecture has been confined mostly to making the audience more comfortable and to the introduction of new stage equipment.

Many of the changes made in theater architecture during the first part of the twentieth century were the result of the requirements of scene design and of the availability of electrical power. For generations, scenery consisted mostly of two-dimensional painted drops and wings which could be readily shifted. A system of ropes and pulleys enabled stagehands to raise and lower the units, most of which were lightweight in construction because the emphasis was on illusionistic painting. But when scenery became three-dimensional and solid, some other means had to be devised for moving sets quickly, noiselessly, and economically. One of the solutions was to use a revolving stage which permitted several sets to be mounted at once on a turntable. During the first quarter of a century, many European theaters were equipped with revolving stages. Another solution was the elevator stage which allowed an entire set to be moved very rapidly in or out of place. More recently, as scenery has become more suggestive and simplified, there has been a trend toward the use of wagon stages—portable platforms, large enough to mount sets. This method of shifting scenery requires a great deal of backstage space. In New York, where real-estate prices are prohibitive, wing space for wagons is not often available, but in Europe and in many American communities, public land has been used for building large stagehouses suitable for this method of handling scenery.

Electric lighting and electronic control of illumination have made marked changes in theater construction. Most recent theaters have a wide variety of positions for mounting lighting instruments. There has also been considerable interest in experimenting with projected scenery. Good stage lighting has been one of the major gains in contemporary theater design.

Another trend in modern theater construction has been to break down the barrier between actor and spectator which resulted from the proscenium arch. In some cases, designers have eliminated the arch altogether as in Copeau's formal stage at the Vieux Colombicr, Frank Lloyd Wright's Hartford plan, and Norman Bel Geddes' arena-type stage. Another tendency has been to bring the spectator as close as possible to the playing area, at least within seventy-five feet of the performer. Many new educational theaters are being constructed with fewer than 600 seats. As another means of securing a more intimate theater, the architect has made a forestage available in front of the proscenium, thrusting the actor out into the audience. A notable design in which this was successfully accomplished is the Shakespeare Festival Theatre at Stratford, Ontario, in which the main acting area is a platform projecting out into the audience, which faces the actor on three sides, reminiscent of the Elizabethan theater plans. The stage is reached by a variety of entrances from the sides, the rear, above and below. A balcony over the stage provides a useful acting area when elevation is needed. Originally a tent theater, the venture and the architecture were so successful that a permanent theater was erected preserving much of the original design. Other experiments in getting the actor closer to the audience have taken the form of movable forestages, wide aprons with entrances at the sides, ramps and steps leading up to the apron, and side alcoves. All of these efforts are made to find ways of bringing the actor forward in front of the arch and into closer communion with the audience.

A number of modern auditoriums were designed as multipurpose structures, many of them resulting in awkward and unsatisfactory compromises. Recently, however, several buildings have been erected which solve the problems more satisfactorily. For example, the auditorium in Malmö, Sweden, can be partitioned off by wooden screens so as to accommodate an audience of 400, 600, or 1200. A large forestage, mechanically operated, serves as an acting area, orchestra pit, or seating space. This very flexible theater is suitable for dance, opera, recitals and lectures as well as dramatic performances. The "small theater" at Mannheim, Germany, is a very ingenious structure providing for at least six variations of seating and performance areas. Another example of flexibility is the recently constructed Harvard Drama Center which can be adjusted for proscenium, Elizabethan, or arena staging.

In Europe, there has been a remarkable number of new theaters and

Present Shakespeare Festival Theatre at Stratford, Ontario, Canada

auditoriums built—more than a hundred in Germany since World War II! In America, theater architecture was pretty much frozen by the development of motion pictures and by the depression. No new professional theater has been built on Broadway since 1927. The number of legitimate playhouses has shrunk nearly two thirds in the last three decades. But now there is a building boom in our educational theaters. It is estimated that more than 750 new theaters will be built for high schools and colleges by 1970. It will be interesting to see how many of these new structures will reflect our changing tastes in theatrical production.

A contemporary innovation in theater form is the use of arena or center staging, in which a playing area is established in the center of the room surrounded by the audience. The environment of the action is established by the use of properties, furniture, costumes, lighting and sound effects— the emphasis being concentrated on the actor. Initially, this experiment grew out of necessity, since many producing groups did not have access to traditional theaters. As a result, many arena stages were makeshift arrangements in old classrooms and store buildings, but more recently, complete structures have been designed especially for this kind of staging. The arena theater has found considerable audience appeal because it succeeds in achieving an intimacy of production which is not only appropriate to many plays, but also provides a manner of playing with which the spectator is familiar from watching motion pictures and television. Arena staging is an effective facility for training actors, for establishing close contact with the audience, and for economical production. It is, however, a restricted form of theater because of the lack of space, and the loss of illusion is sometimes an aesthetic liability.

Questions and Exercises

1. What restrictions does illusionistic scenery impose on the production of plays? On playwriting?
2. How does the size of the theater affect play production?
3. Trace the origin and evolution of the playing area in the Greek Theater.
4. Contrast the staging of plays in the Theater of Dionysus with that of the Globe.
5. What is the effect of the proscenium arch on dramatic structure?
6. What are the problems of producing an Elizabethan play in the modern theater? Of producing a Greek play?
7. Evaluate arena or center staging. What are its advantages and disadvantages? What kinds of plays would be most effective in such productions?
8. Describe a typical modern stage.
9. Visit a theater or auditorium and evaluate its facilities for dramatic production.

Suggested Reading

ALTMAN, George, FREUD, Ralph, MACGOWAN, Kenneth, and MELNITZ, William, *Theatre Pictorial* (Los Angeles, University of California Press, 1953).

BURRIS-MEYER, Harold, and COLE, Edward C., *Theatres and Auditoriums* (New York, Reinhold Publishing Corp., 1949).

ISAACS, Edith J. R., ed., *Architecture for the New Theatre* (New York, Theatre Arts, Inc., New York, 1935).

MACGOWAN, Kenneth, and MELNITZ, William, *The Living Theatre* (Englewood Cliffs, N.J., Prentice-Hall, Inc., 1953).

KERNODLE, George, *From Art to Theatre* (Chicago, University of Chicago Press, 1944).

NICOLL, Allardyce, *The Development of the Theatre*, rev. ed. (New York, Harcourt, Brace & World, Inc., 1947).

15

The Audience

IMPORTANCE OF THE AUDIENCE

THE THEATER EXISTS for the sake of the audience. It is for the spectator that the playhouse is erected, the drama written, the players rehearsed, the sets designed, and the performance given. It is the theater-goer's response that determines the fate of the play. As Giradoux suggests, a new drama is like a piece of unfired pottery. Its true colors are not known until it has been exposed to the heat.

While the physical theater affects the way in which the playwright's play can be staged, it is the audience which dictates what kind of story he can tell, as Samuel Johnson observed:

> The drama's laws the patrons give,
> And we who live to please, must please to live.

Drama is a social and dynamic art which depends for its effect upon the collaboration of playwright, performer, and spectator. Drama must be experienced as a group response to living actors. It is not like a painting, a poem, or a piece of architecture which may be enjoyed in solitary contemplation and by gradual familiarity. The dramatic experience, like life itself, is evanescent, changing from moment to moment.

Most playwrights are like journalists who write for immediate consumption; the obvious way of measuring a play's success is at the box-office. This in turn means that the playwright must write in such a way as to elicit a ready response from a sufficient number of patrons to pay the bills and ultimately show a profit. (In these days of astronomical costs for a Broadway production, this may mean playing to packed houses for at least four months.) In an effort to attract a large audience, the playwright feels the pressure to make his work as entertaining as possible, with the result that much of our drama offers little intellectual nourishment and a slight residue of meaning. The extreme effect from the compulsion to amuse a wide audience is seen in most of our motion pictures and television programs. Oftentimes, the appeals and techniques employed are obvious and hackneyed, the material is standardized into formulas endlessly repeated, and controversial and significant subjects are shunned. The writer constantly is obliged to keep foremost in his mind the need for showmanship that will attract everybody and offend no one. Gilbert Seldes, who has made a particular study of the audiences of our mass media, levels this indictment: "The concept of the audience as boobs is satisfying to hucksters and highbrows. It is not accurate, nor is it permanently acceptable to democrats. We might as well remember that the great frauds in medicine, the most appalling superstitions about witches, the wildest social and economic panaceas, and the foulest delusions about the nature of man were all accepted by the learned and well-bred long before they reached the 'common people.'" [1] Seldes goes on to make a plea to those concerned with mass media to raise their sights, and to present popular fare that will have a more meaningful content.

In the past generation we have developed an increasingly mature and discriminating following in the legitimate theater so that the contemporary playwright is able to appeal to a substantial audience by writing plays which have more than momentary interest. It should be remembered that many great masters of drama transcended the problems of audience appeal. Shakespeare, Molière, Sheridan, Lessing, Schiller, Jonson, Sophocles —these playwrights satisfied popular taste while creating outstanding landmarks of dramatic literature. But popularity itself is no criterion of lasting value because many plays of enormous commercial success are completely devoid of literary merit. Examples from the contemporary theater are the astonishing long-runs of *Abie's Irish Rose* (2,327 performances), *Tobacco Road* (3,182 performances), and Agatha Christie's thriller, *The Mousetrap*, has played continuously for ten years on the British stage.

Many novelists who have aspired to be playwrights have failed in their attempts because they ignored, or did not grasp the importance of winning an audience response. Only the writer who chooses to limit himself to a small and select hearing may neglect the needs of the theater audience. Writers whose convictions deviate too markedly from the norm, or whose symbols are too confusing, or who have too obvious an axe to grind, may succeed on the printed page, but they will not find the stage a hospitable haven for their plays. Pioneers of contemporary drama faced con-

[1] Gilbert Seldes, *The Public Arts* (New York, Simon and Schuster, Inc., 1956).

siderable difficulty in the initial public reaction to their plays as for example the cool or hostile receptions given to Chekhov's *The Sea Gull,* Ibsen's *Ghosts,* Hauptmann's *Before Sunrise,* Shaw's *Mrs. Warren's Profession,* and Herne's *Margaret Fleming.* The point needs to be made that there are many plays which can never hope to attract a popular audience because of the nature of their subject matter or their abstruse treatment. Nevertheless, it is generally true that the dramatist must be aware of the needs of his audience so that he can engage them in a meaningful and interesting communion.

THE AUDIENCE'S CONTRIBUTION

Most drama deals with emotionally loaded situations. The action presented involves a network of strong feelings which the actor expresses in such a way as to set up a circular response with the spectator. And as the audience responds, the actor adapts and adjusts his performance. This give-and-take intensifies the effect of the play as it unfolds, until there is a relentless surge of emotion.

The audience not only enriches the play by sharing the performance with the actor, but the spectators also stimulate one another, which tends to melt away barriers of detachment. The social situation encourages the auditor to participate; it draws him into the action. The effect of a play in the theater depends upon the playwright's skill in creating it, in part it is due to the talents of the director and actors, but it is also partially due to the audience whose very presence and responsiveness add the final cumulative dimension that characterize the dramatic experience.

It is necessary to add that the response which we have been describing is the customary one sought in the theater, but there are plays not intended to elicit strong emotional involvement. An attitude of detachment is necessary sometimes, since the material of the play is calculated to appeal to our critical faculties rather than our feelings. For example, in the contemporary theater, Brecht explicitly avoided audience identification in his "epic" plays, because he wished those who saw his plays to think, rather than to feel. Thus, he constantly reminds the spectator that he is in the theater by interrupting the flow of action and by frankly presenting the play as theatrically as possible. Likewise, the plays of the "absurdists" make slight attempts to stimulate audience interest by their story line. Oftentimes, the appropriate response of the spectator to a play like Beckett's *Endgame* or Ionesco's *The Chairs* is one of annoyed confusion when he tries to find meaning in the disjointed and distorted world presented to him. But even in these plays in which the playwright rejects conventional techniques, there may emerge definite emotional reactions of frustration and horror because of the negativistic atmosphere of the

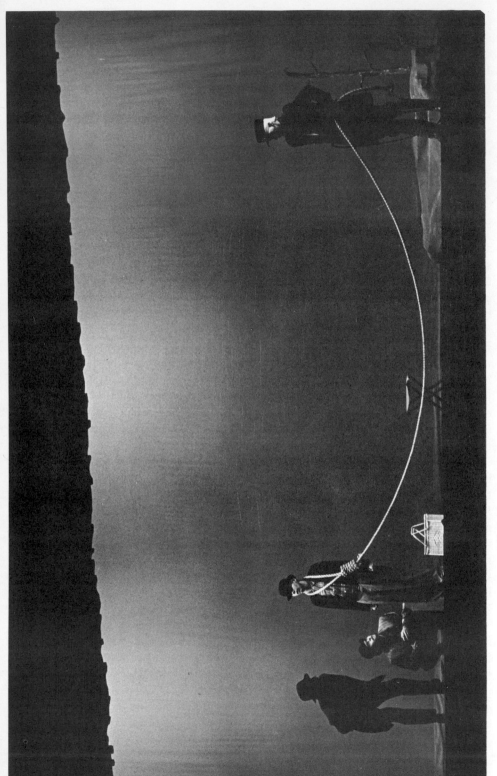

Scene from Samuel Beckett's *Waiting for Godot* as produced at the University of California, Santa Barbara, 1961, Frederick Thon, Director.

characters and action. High comedy usually requires an attitude of detachment. The appeal is intellectual instead of emotional. But these kinds of plays are the exception rather than the rule. In most instances, the dramatist seeks to engender a strong identification with his characters and plot, and to do this he must be cognizant of the nature of his audience.

THE NATURE OF ATTENTION

To create a play and a performance which will evoke an appropriate response, it is essential for the playwright and the theater-worker to know something about the nature of attention. Attention comes in short spurts. Concentration requires constant renewal, because it is impossible for us to fix our attention on a single object and hold it there as we might a spotlight. Ordinarily, a theater audience comes with the expectation of giving their attention freely to the play, but if the drama is dull and the performance monotonous, if attention is not captured and sustained, the spectator makes his escape into a world of his own imagining.

There are two kinds of attention—voluntary and involuntary. Voluntary attention implies that the spectator looks and listens by an act of the will. He makes an effort to pay attention. Involuntary attention, on the other hand, results from responding to stimuli that require no conscious effort—we hear a scream in the night, a fascinating story, or our name spoken aloud by another. The theater-worker is interested in securing our involuntary attention. Such devices are employed as bright lights and colors, movement, emotion, the use of space and elevations, sound, and visual focus. The director combats monotony by varying the groupings of his characters, by a change of pace, by making sure that actors do not imitate one another's pitch patterns, by inventing business and action—in a word, by every possible way of renewing attention. He aims to control and direct every instant of our attention throughout the course of the play. This is one of the director's most difficult tasks, since the play, by its very nature, is a stream of complex visual and auditory stimuli; attention constantly flits from one character to another and back again. The motion-picture director has far greater control of the spectator's attention because of his ability to focus the camera on one object, one person, one face at a time, eliminating all extraneous elements, and by the opportunity to edit a film after it has been shot and to order "retakes" if he thinks this desirable. But the stage director must find other means of achieving much the same effect.

A part of his problem in controlling attention is to avoid the distractions which plague a theatrical performance such as late arrivals, rustling of programs, shuffling of feet, coughs and wheezes, and the vicissitudes of production which may occur on stage—missed cues, a long wait, a poor costume, obvious make-up, scenery that shakes when the door is slammed, a crooked picture, light reflecting surfaces. Some aspects of the production itself may destroy the audience's concentration, such as some unexpected novelty that arouses surprise and comment in the audience, scene shifts that take too long or involve too much noise, special spectacular effects, or an unexpected laugh. In a well managed theater, every effort is made to focus and control the audience's interest so that their voluntary attention becomes involuntary as they become thoroughly engrossed in the action and the play.

THE AUDIENCE AS A CROWD

Although an audience comes together as individuals, the theater is a group effort. Through mutual stimulation in the release of emotions, the group may become a crowd. This has important psychological implications, because as individuals merge themselves into a crowd, marked changes may take place. The individual loses his identity, becoming more susceptible to emotional appeals, more easily swayed than the single person in isolation. He relaxes his discrimination so that he becomes more gullible. The social psychologist Emory Bogardus, states: "A heightened state of suggestibility is characteristic of a crowd. The preponderance of feelings over reason heightens suggestibility. The excitement that frequently prevails in a crowd throws persons off their guard. The force of numbers is overwhelming."

Thus, a theater audience loses some of its sense of personal responsibility. There is a temporary release from restraint with the result, that in a crowd, people may respond to stimuli which would leave them untouched as isolated individuals. For example, they may laugh in the theater at salacious humor which they might consider vulgar in their own living-room. In the crowd situation, there is always the threat that the lowest common denominator will prevail. There is the pressure to conform, the contagion to join in. These psychological phenomena of audience behavior are at least a partial explanation of how the effectiveness of a play may be transformed and augmented by a responsive audience, who willingly suspend their disbelief, and succumb to the emotions of the play.

AUDIENCES VARY

Anyone experienced in theatrical production can testify to the fact that audiences vary from performance to performance. A Saturday night crowd will almost invariably out-laugh a Monday night one. A matinee audience with a preponderance of women shoppers, reacts quite differently than one dominated by visiting businessmen from out of town. Audiences likewise differ from place to place. A performer meets a different reception in Las Vegas than he does in Boston. University campus theater-goers are quite a contrast to those in a community theater. A person may find his own response to a play varying according to the stimulation he receives from other spectators, the way he feels, the temperature of the auditorium, and the location of his seat. He will also notice that his reaction to a motion picture in a crowded theater is not the same as viewing a film in the seclusion of his own home.

Different kinds of plays attract different kinds of audiences. Compare an audience that attends an opera with that of a musical comedy, or note the difference between the spectators attending a farce and a tragedy. A striking example of audience variation may be seen in Japan where the archaic, restrained Nōh drama is met with dignified, nearly reverent attention, while the popular Kabuki audience may give the performance a noisy and enthusiastic demonstration.

As a social institution, the theater has at times served as a tribunal, a propaganda agency, a "house of the devil," a temple of worship, a meeting-place for disreputable characters, a show-case for ostentatious display, and a place for intellectual stimulation. Its status and function has depended upon the audience which patronized it. Consider, for example, three representative audiences.

THE GREEK AUDIENCE

It will be recalled the theater of Greece was a religious institution which every free male attended as a public and sacred duty at the two main festivals, in midwinter and early spring. The City of Dionysia which offered competition in tragedies, was a profoundly serious occasion. The audience did not come to be amused or titillated. They came to share in the great searching problems of mankind—problems which elevated the human spirit through suffering.

The Athenian audience was a remarkable one because of their great zest for living and thinking. Art, literature, philosophy and logic were not mere subjects of contemplation for them. They were active, inquiring men with an unquenchable thirst for learning. Their interests and tastes ranged widely, so that they could accommodate in their infrequent dramatic productions, the tragic grandeur of Aeschylus and the comic irreverence of Aristophanes, whose uninhibited shafts of unsparing ridicule are a commentary on the amazing tolerance of Greek society.

The Greeks were a knowledgeable audience, steeped in their literary heritage, with keen ears for the rhythm and texture of language, and so thoroughly familiar with the plays of their time, that they could identify specific passages of Euripidean and Aeschylean dialogue in Aristophanes' comedy, *The Frogs*. Such an audience invited dramas of great ideas and magnificent language. The religious base of the ritual challenged the playwrights to create elevated works involving profound and lofty content. The culture which produced the idea of the "golden mean"—moderation in all things—led to a drama which was clear and logically organized, free from the excesses of pathos and sentiment. Their search for truth in life, resulted in drama that was unflinchingly and relentlessly honest in confronting evil, suffering, and catastrophe. Their intellectual tolerance and sense of balance enabled them to see the sense and nonsense of Aristophanic satire which scathingly attacked the follies of the time. The fifth century B.C. Athenian was an astonishingly civilized man, and his level of culture is nowhere reflected so admirably as in the dramas which were created for his pleasure and edification.

THE ELIZABETHAN AUDIENCE

Like the Greeks, the Elizabethans had an enormous enthusiasm for life. Shakespeare's time was one of remarkable intellectual ferment. There was great interest in language, literature, music, and politics. The Elizabethan looked on man as a creature of great potentialities. The spirit of the times was positive, dynamic, tumultuous.

The theater reflected the climate of the age. It was a professional theater to which more than 30,000 customers a week flocked to see half a dozen competing companies in London offer the richest concentration of dramatic fare that the world has ever known. The theater appealed to the public's taste for pageantry and action, which elsewhere manifested itself in masques, processionals, and bear-baiting. The plays capitalized on the audience's interest in language. Marlowe, Jonson, Webster and Shakespeare wrote rich, complex dialogue such as never heard before. But the plays were more than language. The Elizabethan playwright enthusiastically followed the practice of medieval drama in putting as much vigorous and vivid action on stage as possible. Such a combination of words and action enlarged the appeal of drama so that all of the motley audience could find in the play something to suit their pleasure. For the groundlings, there was exciting and violent action. For the discriminating, there was delight in the magnificent language and food for thought in the elevated ideas. The Elizabethan audience's interests and tastes covered a wide range, and for it, the playwright wrote both serious and comic dramas which were full-bodied and exuberant, images of a turbulent and heady age.

THE RESTORATION AUDIENCE

The Restoration audience offers a sharp contrast to that of the Elizabethan. When Charles II returned to throne, the theater became the preoccupation of the court. The audience was made up of fashionable wits, fops, beaux, parasites, and women of easy virtue. So limited was the audience, that only two theaters were active in London, despite the fact that the population had doubled since Elizabethan times. For twelve years one theater was sufficient to accommodate this narrow following.

The Restoration theater-goer did not take drama seriously. It was a plaything—a toy. The theater was a meeting place for fashionable people. Such patronage resulted in drama that was artificial and deliberately unconcerned with the stern realities of life. The special achievement of the period was in high comedy which dealt with the foibles of social conduct rather than ethics. Puritan morality was satirized. When the Restoration playwright attempted to write seriously in heroic dramas, the result was exaggerated and false pseudoclassic plays "full of sound and fury, signifying nothing." Comedies dealt with the complications of intrigue and defects of manners. Craftsmanship was careless, the content coarse, the atmosphere vulgar beneath a shiny surface. The level of the playwrights' subject matter was rescued from oblivion by their brilliant use of language. They achieved a high polish in their repartee and their eloquence of style. The limited audience made it possible for the playwright to capitalize on personal invective and local and timely allusions. Thus, Restoration comedy is a particularly explicit example of the effect of an audience on the drama.

Perhaps these three historical examples are enough to make the point that people come to the theater for a variety of purposes, and that they constitute a vital force on the writing and production of plays.

THE MODERN AUDIENCE

The audience of today is colored by the status of the theater as a social institution. In Europe, there is wide distribution of professional dramatic production since nearly every city has a permanent residential company which makes drama available on a continuous basis. These theaters, usually supported in part by the state, offer a repertory of plays which include the classics as well as new plays. Thus, there is a permanent audience, sophisticated in the ways of the theater, who enable the producing group to work out a continuous program of diverse kinds of plays with some sense of security, not directly related to immediate box-office appeal.

In this country, our professional theater suffers from the fact that it has no enduring status. Plays are produced one at a time by a company assembled for a specific play performing in a theater rented for the length of the run. Our professional theater is concentrated in Manhattan so that most of the country has no access to it except for occasional road shows. As a result, 95 per cent of our population never sees professional theater but must instead depend upon amateur producing groups or else see New York hits translated into motion pictures or television plays. Much of the Broadway audience is made up of out-of-town visitors and tired businessmen seeking relaxation. They look upon the theater as primarily "show business." Their taste is reflected in theatrical production heavily weighted with musicals and bright comedies.

Serious, mature plays can succeed on Broadway, but the preponderant taste is for entertainment. There is no organization regularly devoted to the production of the classics or experimental drama except during the summer. Some of the void is filled by the off-Broadway (in New York City) community and educational theaters, many of which offer continuous and substantial programs of important plays, but in general, we do not have in America a permanent and widespread audience who regard the professional theater as a significant social and cultural institution. The effect of this lack of organization and continuity is enormous not only on playwriting but also on all aspects of production from acting to ticket-selling. It is a moot question whether or not the problems of making professional theater available to the American public will ever be solved, or whether we will settle for amateur productions, or plays revised for performance on film or television.

Questions and Exercises

1. How does the audience affect the playwright? The actor?
2. What limitations does the audience impose on the play and the theater?
3. How does the playwright hold attention?
4. What is the nature of attention?
5. What are the characteristics of a crowd?
6. After attending a play or motion picture, analyze the audience. What was the effect on the audience? What kind of an audience was it? Cold? Responsive? Was there any empathic response?

Suggested Reading

BROWN, J. M., *Art of Playgoing* (New York, W. W. Norton & Co., Inc., 1936).
CHENEY, Sheldon, *The Art Theatre* (New York, Alfred A. Knopf, Inc., 1917).

HEWITT, Barnard, *Theatre, U.S.A., 1668-1957* (New York, McGraw-Hill Book Co., 1959).

HOLLINGWORTH, H. L., *Psychology of the Audience* (New York, American Book Co., 1935).

NICOLL, Allardyce, *British Drama* (London, Harrap, 1947).

INDEX